TOWN HALL TONIGHT

Concert Hall, Beaver Dam, Wisconsin

Ed Kuekes, *Plain Dealer* cartoonist and Pulitzer Prize Winner for 1953, is the artist.

HALL TONIGHT

Harlowe R. HOYT

BRAMHALL HOUSE · NEW YORK

To JOE
Who Remembered,
Who Helped,
But Who Died All Too Soon

Contents

Town Hall Tonight

PROLOGUE

"Take in your linen. The players are coming to town."
—Old Saying

"Take in your clothes lines, too. Their managers are with them."
—Modern Version

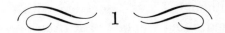

1

THIS is the story of the country theater of the eighties and nineties, and though it treats somewhat specifically with the visitors and people of a little Wisconsin town, it is the story of each of the Town Halls that spotted the nation during those twenty years.

And in the main that story is identical, whether it was the Swetland Opera House in Mayville, New York; the Old Masonic Theater in What Cheer, Iowa; Clough's Opera House in Chillicothe, Ohio; or my own Concert Hall in Beaver Dam, Wisconsin. Each of them and a thousand or more like them played the same plays, met with the same misadventures, and made their amateur productions from scripts purchased from the same play agencies. Except for the amateurs, this was equally true of the show boats that played the Mississippi River towns.

All of which was inevitable. These theaters were the outgrowth of the first Town Halls built on the same pattern and equipped with the same standard scenery. For economic reasons, few companies carried any of their own. They came for a week's stay with a nightly change of bill and matinees Wednesday and Saturday. None played on Sunday, for a goodly portion of these small town folk still looked upon play acting as the devil's own handiwork.

They were real troupers who cheerfully faced an existence of cheap boarding houses, slow trains, dirty day coaches and meals often snatched at way stations with twenty minutes for lunch. Their reward was a brief strutting across the stage of some dingy theater and, as often as not, no salary at the week's end.

Of the arts none is so ephemeral as that of the actor, be he a Broadway star or a bombastic ham such as traveled the sticks in those days. Painters and musicians, authors and playwrights, leave authentic records of their work. But once a player passes on, only tradition remains, for even recordings of his voice are but ghosts of his personality.

For the small town actor reports of his visits were scanty, photographs were missing and the history of his theater was largely a word of mouth recital handed down by those who were there and who too often garbled it in the handing. Although I was associated with the closing days of all this period and learned about the rest of it from eye-witnesses, it was not until I undertook to write about it that I realized the paucity of available material. There should have been plenty as I remembered it, but it quickly reduced itself to a few stray programs, an odd photograph here and there and a host of memories that had withstood the test of time.

Particularly was this true of the small time player of those days. The Booths and Barretts, the Irvings and Mansfields, the Forrests and Jeffersons had their historians in the daily newspapers and in the friends and admirers who turned their talents to biography. But the "rep" players left practically nothing to mark their visits or prove their worth. In some communities they were little better than the rogues and vagabonds who pioneered their dramatic trail, for religion still wore the iron corset of bigotry in many a small town.

Nor did they leave photographs of their plays since insipid theatrical lighting and wet plate cameras made it next to impossible to shoot photographs within the theater. In the early eighties, Thomas Edison had installed overhead lighting for Steele MacKaye in the Madison Square Theater, New York, but others were slow to adopt so drastic an experiment. Gas jets and kerosene lamps afforded insufficient lighting, wet plate cameras required instant processing, and none of the society photographers who made theater shots had gumption enough to devise a portable darkroom. In addition, theatrical photography was still somewhat déclassé and not to be over-emphasized.

So the Broadway stars were photographed in groups of two or three in the studios of Sarony, or Mora, or Anderson, and occasionally they crowded as many as possible into a single picture. Magazine and newspaper illustrations were sketched on chalk plates since photoengraving was being slowly perfected. Yet the small town player was denied even these advantages. Country weeklies couldn't handle illustrations, and had they been able to do so, the troopers could not have supplied them. The best they could do was to display cabinet photographs of their leading people before the theater or in some show window and for the rest to depend upon street parades, throwaways, billboards and word-of-mouth advertising.

Since the plays were standardized, dealers in billboard paper enjoyed a national patronage. They stocked their shelves with scenes from these offerings and they needed only a streamer to carry the name, date and place to make them ready. Among others they bought their paper from the Morgan Lithographing Corporation of Cleveland; Han Grieve of Milwaukee; or the Public Ledger Co. of Philadelphia, who issued stock books with reproductions of what they had on hand. The buyer indicated his choice by number.

And that is why *East Lynne, Ten Nights in a Bar Room, The Octoroon, The Ticket-of-Leave Man, Our American Cousin,* and *The Two Orphans,* among many other favorites, were played simultaneously by rep companies throughout the country. The only difference was the producing company and the playing cast. Handicapped by meager scenery and restricted stage space, each solved its individual problems in just about the same way. There was a strange uniformity in all of these shows, including make up, costuming and stage business.

Some shows were wild-catted with the company manager jumping ahead to book the next stand and arrange billing. Some laid out their routings in advance but these were the well established shows like the Fox Comedy Company, the Little Allie Spooner Dramatic Company and, in later years, the Winninger Family that traveled out of Wausau, Wisconsin, with two companies that included Frank, John, Adolph and Charley, until he left for Broadway and the films and his brothers continued alone.

But the country manager was not wholly dependent upon luck in dating new companies. There were "turkeys" every year, fly-by-nights often formed by stage-struck amateurs with more ambition than ability. They might get by for a time, but soon their bookings played out and they were writing home for railroad fare.

One medium that gave these reports wide coverage was the *Opera House Reporter,* a small confidential sheet published by James S. Cox in Estherville, Iowa. It was the last word for the small town manager in confidential criticism and it could be depended upon since it was made up largely from what they sent in themselves. Their reports ran something like this.

PECK'S BAD BOY, two nights, good company. Clever specialties. Fair first night. Sell out the second. Ought to draw for you.

UNCLE JOSH SPRUCEBY. "The Old Homestead" with the saw mill from "Blue Jeans" for good measure. It's a stinker. DON'T.

SHE—Rider Haggard's story advertised as a big scenic production. One curtain, three flats, gas effect and eight people. No business. Even books didn't help. Better not.

Reference to books was a comment on the advance publicity:

"Every person purchasing a ticket will receive a complete book of "She" free.

"The cast is an unusually strong one; the scenic effects are gorgeous; and the height of realism is realized in the wonderful Dance of the Hot Pot, showing the African savage in all his barbaric ferocity."

These were some of the conditions that surrounded the presentation of these plays in a period when, though none realized it, the small time theater was on its way out. And at the same time, the stock companies of the country were being reshaped to different ends.

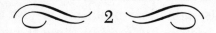

During these twenty years, stock companies were changing with the

Boston Museum, Boston, Mass.

Famous Stock Company played there for 50 years.

trend of the times. James W. Wallack and A. M. Palmer were losing their hold on New York's theater goers and Augustin Daly was finding stiff opposition from the brash young Frohman brothers, Daniel and Charles. But each was self-sufficient with their own players, a cast of fledgling stars destined to dominate the theater for years to come.

So, too, with Mrs. John Drew and her family circle at Philadelphia's Arch Street Theater. And the Boston Museum with the aging William Warren and the young George Wilson, Joseph Haworth and John Mason. These and a score of others were reinforced by visiting stars before improved railroad transportation brought traveling companies intact.

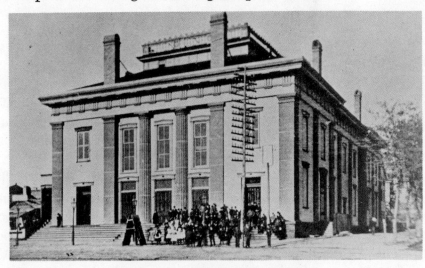

Salt Lake Theater, Utah

Brigham Young Built It and His Daughters played with the Deseret Dramatic Association.

In Utah's capital, Brigham Young had built the Salt Lake Theater, the largest in the United States west of Chicago. The Deseret Dramatic Association furnished the players, some of them from his own progeny. He followed the star system and one visiting favorite was Julia Dean, a charming young actress, who played a long engagement there. Brigham decided to make her a Mormon and add her to his Bee Hive. But Julia married James G. Cooper, who happened to be the Gentile secretary of the Utah Territory.

San Francisco had its Bush Theater with young David Belasco as its first stage manager. By the eighties, the Academy of Music came into the hands of Al Hayman, later to join the great theatrical syndicate. Robert Mantell, Joseph Haworth, W. J. Ferguson, Henry Miller, Maurice Barrymore and

Mary Shaw were on its roster. Denver had its Palace Theater and the Denver Amateur Dramatic Association.

In Cleveland, John Ellsler headed slowly toward bankruptcy with his attempts to manage stock productions at the Academy of Music, the Euclid

Palace Theater, Denver, Colorado
Pioneer Theater

Avenue Opera House and the Lyceum Theater. He had been the small time manager of Joseph Jefferson and had taught that comedian the rudiments of German dialect for his Rip Van Winkle. Actor and producer with ideals, Ellsler's artistic ambitions outran his financial judgment and he lost money, though he helped develop such players as James O'Neill, famous for *Monte Cristo;* Clara Morris, a leading emotional actress of her day; Jimmy Lewis, later leading comedian with Augustin Daly; Roland Reed, actor-manager and father of Florence Reed; Effie Ellsler, John's daughter; and Charles W. Cauldock. Steele MacKaye's *Hazel Kirke* was given its first production by him. With Miss Ellsler in the title role, and Cauldock as Dunstan Kirke, Hazel's father, it continued at the Madison Square Theater in the New York production for five hundred performances.

But these organizations were falling apart at the seams. Road shows visited the larger cities and stars brought their own supporting cast and production. And a new edition of stock followed, companies that remained season after season, each with its matinee favorites continuing on under their own impetus without benefit of a big name.

Milwaukee had one of the best at the Academy of Music, where Edwin Thanhouser presented the same cast for years. At the Davidson Theater, summer stock filled in between the regular bookings, while one of America's two German stock companies alternated between tragedy, comedy and light opera at the Pabst Theater. Head of the brewing company that bore his name, Capt. Fred Pabst was its owner and principal patron. Thanhouser's downfall came when he decided his public wanted new faces. So he dismissed his entire company at one fell swoop and brought in a new one. After a season or two, he operated a stock company in Chicago and then quit the legitimate for the Thanhouser Film Studios on Long Island, where he made a fortune in the movies. Arthur Friend, a Milwaukee attorney with a flair for the theater, took over the management of the Academy, by this time renamed the Shubert, and after a couple of seasons, left for New York

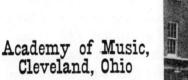

Academy of Music, Cleveland, Ohio

John Ellsler's Famous Stock Company Played Here.

Pabst Theater, Milwaukee, Wisconsin
One of the two German Stock Houses in the United States

where he was instrumental in forming the Famous Players with Sam Goldwyn, Jesse Lasky and Cecil B. DeMille.

Ellsler's in Cleveland was replaced by Vaughan Glaser, actor manager, who moved into the new Colonial Theater to become one of the great matinee idols of stock days. Fay Courtenay was his leading lady, and together they followed the new trend in abandoning standard dramas for Broadway successes as soon as they were available. Glaser was responsible for the dramatization of Augusta Evans' novel, *St. Elmo,* but he may be forgiven for that since it caught on with stock followers like wildfire. When he moved on, Robert McLaughlin, reformed newspaperman and press agent, managed summer stock at the Euclid Avenue Opera House and the Ohio Theater. He returned to the star system with Broadway actors. And he wrote two plays, *The Eternal Magdalene,* which brought Julia Arthur from retirement, and *The Pearl of Great Price,* one of the imitation morality plays that held vogue for a time. Claudette Colbert was in the cast.

In Boston, John Craig's Castle Square Players picked up when the Boston Museum ended its fifty years, while Mr. and Mrs. Charles Coburn were deep in Shakesperean productions before they found *The Yellow Jacket,* an Americanized version of the Chinese theater. William Parke's Stock Company of Pittsfield, Massachusetts, was another well established group; and William Frawley's Players entertained the twin cities of Minneapolis and St. Paul, Minnesota.

In Denver, a playhouse known from coast to coast opened in 1890. It was the Elitch Gardens Theater intended as a minor part of the garden's entertainment. But it was developed into a national theatrical center by Mary Elitch Long, who managed it for a quarter of a century. Broadway's leading actors and stars played there and any number of young actors were given their first course of sprouts upon its stage.

But of all these latter day stock companies one of the best known was the Bonstelle Players, directed by Jessie Bonstelle, who had a stock company in Rochester, New York, and brought it on each summer to play at the Garrick Theater. Miss Bonstelle hoped for a municipal theater and in 1928, she established the Detroit Civic Theater in the old Temple Beth-El, rebuilt for the purpose. Her list of celebrities was long, besides proving a training school for such future stars as Katharine Cornell, Ann Harding, Frank Morgan, William Powell and many others. She gave premières of nineteen plays, including *Seventh Heaven* and *Little Women,* whose dramatization came through her efforts. Broadway's producers sought her for tryouts and William A. Brady produced a number of these plays. His daughter, Alice, created the role of Meg in *Little Women* and played it in New York, while Katharine Cornell appeared in the part in London. When Jessie Bonstelle died in 1932, the theater closed. It had been the achievement of one woman's inspiration and devotion to the stage.

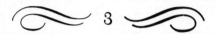

During these years the stock system changed. The star system went out, local companies opened, and a weekly change of bill came in. Some said the system was a great training school. Some said that it warped talent and killed ambition. Whatever it was, it proved hard work, exacting every ounce of effort from a conscientious player.

With a weekly change of bill it was no small task to get up a part, costume it, and open the following Monday night. The management dressed costume plays, but these were a rarity and the women of the cast were always put to it for new outfits. Stock followers came week after week and not too frequently could the same dress be worn. There were fittings and alterations with dressmakers and these took time and cost money.

From my own experience, this was the stock routine. Monday was devoted to a dress rehearsal starting at ten o'clock and continuing indefinitely. All scenes were set, properties placed, makeup and costumes donned and inspected, and a complete performance was given. You ate when you could, made it in time for your first entrance, and thanked your lucky stars when the tag was spoken.

During the day you had consulted the call board to see if you were on next week. Your contract called for a certain number of layoffs without salary when small cast plays were chosen. Given an enforced vacation, you dressed and left in record time. Otherwise you waited until the assistant stage manager brought your part for next week.

As it was well after midnight when you got out of the theater, the director was easy on you on Tuesday. You needn't report until eleven o'clock. Then he read the play, and you checked your lines and formed a general idea of what it was all about. After which you went home and studied until time to report for the night's performance. On Wednesday you checked in at ten o'clock and went through the play until twelve-thirty. Then you grabbed a bite and played a matinee and a night performance. The rest of the night you spent memorizing your lines.

Thursday and Friday were the long days. You started at from 10 to 11, depending upon what night celebrating the director was indulging in, and rehearsed until 4:30 or 5 o'clock. On Friday you were "rough perfect." You kept your part in your hand, glancing at it when you forgot. On Saturday, though, this comfort was denied you. The director prompted you from the play script and you were expected to get along with a minimum of prodding from him, for he was busy smoothing out the business and positions and making the ensemble jell. Then came matinee and night performance again.

But Sunday was the real test. You were expected to give a letter perfect performance. After that you played a matinee and night performance and went away, tired but happy, with your pay envelope in your pocket. Monday came the dress rehearsal and the rat race started all over again.

Some stock companies were even worse. They played daily matinees with weekly change of billing. Harry Davis of Pittsburgh, Pennsylvania, was one of these; and hard as was the grind, he never seemed to lack players.

It was a tough training school. Some bogged down in the routine and kept at the grind until they found release as movie extras in Hollywood. But others profited and became Broadway stars. For it depended upon the innate ability of the person and that indiscribable something called personality for want of a better name.

What follows, then, is the story of the passing of one phase of the theater for twenty years, all but blotted out by the twilight of forgetfulness and fast disappearing in the nightfall of oblivion. For it, my brother, Joe, and I spent many days comparing notes, perusing country newspapers, searching our attic for tattered programs, discussing the past with the elders of our family, and melding the whole into what we hoped would be an intelligent recital of it all.

Much, no doubt, has been overlooked. But the picture is there as we remembered it—a story of the last days of the vanished era whose rallying call was "Town Hall Tonight."

Chapter 1

THE TIME,
THE PLACE AND
THE HALL

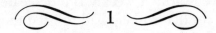

1

THEY called them the Elegant Eighties and the Naughty Nineties; and so they were in the slow transition that supplanted the Victorian redowa and schottische with the two step and cakewalk, the horsehair sofa and mahogany whatnot with golden oak monstrosities, cosy corners and Morris chairs.

Women were discarding their three-layer bustles and leg-of-mutton sleeves for ankle length skirts and peek-a-boo shirtwaists, which aroused no end of criticism. They were joining Bellamy Clubs—*Looking Backward* was a best seller—and subscribing to the extension courses of the Chautauqua Institute, the first correspondence school of its kind.

There was a decade of the horse and buggy, rutted country roads, crushed stone and dismal local trains that snailed along at twenty miles an hour, distributing hot cinders and acrid smoke. In Detroit, Michigan, a bemused artisan was monkeying around with the idea of a mechanical buggy; and down in Dayton two Ohio boys named Wright were saving their nickels, hoping someday to own a bicycle shop.

There was a decade of Nick Carter, Old King Brady, and Frank Merriwell; of Sweet Caporal Cigarettes with pictures of Lillian Russell, Della Fox, Cap Anson, Cy Young and Pink Hawley, the Duke of Pittsburgh. Every barbershop table had its *Police Gazette* and colored prints of Sullivan and Corbett decorated walls that held racks of shaving mugs while cologne mingled its sweetish odor with mustache wax used to pompadour the noodles of adolescents emulating Gentleman Jim.

There was a decade of the upright piano and parlor organ; of "The Maid of the Mill," "Little Annie Rooney" and "The Sidewalks of New York"; of mandolin, banjo and guitar clubs; of the transition from "Better Than Gold" and "After the Ball" to "My Gal's a Highborn Lady" and "Georgia Campmeeting"; from polka and quadrille to Sousa's Marches and Barney Fagan's ragtime.

Tiring of twenty-four years of Republican domination, the voters sent a Buffalo politician to the White House. Tom Edison was slowly converting the public to his new electric lights, and his talking machine was being demonstrated at county fairs. In the middle west, conservative villagers admitted that the newfangled telephone might some day come into general use. Interior plumbing was slowly supplanting the wooden backyard shanty, and baths were not necessarily a weekly rite dedicated to Saturday night.

Puritanical consciences that so long had resisted the theater were softening up and a few forthright straightlaces even conceded that some God-fearing Christians might be found among the actors. Tremendous respectability was bestowed upon Augustin Daly when Alfred Lord Tennyson graciously permitted him to adapt *The Foresters* for his new stock company with Ada Rehan, John Drew and Otis Skinner. Since Tennyson was Queen Victoria's own poet laureate, this epitome of respectability went a long way toward scouring the tarnished reputations of vagabonds and strolling players.

The larger cities supported stock companies and visiting stars came from time to time to play with them. But the stock star system was passing since the prolific Dion Boucicault, playwright, producer and actor, had introduced what he termed the combination system, sending his New York companies out on the road intact. It was a revolutionary proceedure, but the copyright laws were lax and he did it to stop the pirating of his plays.

A Southern lawyer, Marc Klaw, employed to prosecute copyright infringements, found himself pushed into management. Three sons of a Sandusky businessman became theatrical press-agents: Gus, Dan and Charles Frohman. At the latter's suggestion a syndicate was formed in 1896 that for twenty years dominated the American Theater with Klaw and Erlanger as its figurehead. By controlling the nation's theaters and shows, this Ohio combination with the Liebler Co. and others put the final quietus on the visiting star system.

But of all this the communities of the midwest knew little and cared less. The larger cities had their permanent stock companies and matinee idols. Road shows came and went with Broadway stars in New York hits. Some of them even visited the smaller towns for a one night stand to break their jumps between their week engagements. But these were the more pretentious one nighters with theaters equipped to handle a big time production. The smaller towns depended for their entertainment upon the traveling companies that played the local town hall.

For every town had its town hall. It might be the Odd Fellows Hall, Masonic Temple, Music Hall, Opera House, or just a hall with the owner's name hitched on to it. But whatever the name, it was the place wherein centered the cultural life of the community and where any variety of entertainers paid their brief visit.

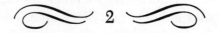

2

Ours was called Concert Hall; and since these buildings were built along identical lines, this one was typical of the country theater, or opera house, or town hall, or what have you. Their general appearance remains unchanged and as they were sturdy pioneers you can still spot them as you motor through the old towns. They are three story buildings of dingy white brick, weatherworn with the years, designed along the lines of an upended orange crate. Stores occupy the first floor, offices the second, and the third is given over to the old hall, or what is left of it. That there may be no mistaking, the building's name is engrossed on the capstone across the front.

Dr. Joseph Babcock, my grandfather, was a general practitioner, fresh from college when he set down on the Wisconsin prairie and rode saddlebags among the scattered farms. When Beaver Dam was well founded, he moved there and continued to practice until he died. Somewhere along the way he bought Concert Hall.

The family from my grandmother down was theater minded. My mother played a Somers square piano piled high with sheet music bought from visiting minstrel shows. She was a leader in amateur productions, *The Culprit Fay* among them, and was an adept with bones and castanets and on the mouth organ.

Uncle Bee—his formal name was Benjamin Franklin Butler Babcock—reading law by night preparatory to entering the University of Wisconsin, perused his weighty legal tomes in bed; and when he tired of Blackstone and Chitty, picked up his fife and shrilled "The Devil's Dream" or "Titus March" upon the still midnight air. Our house was well removed from our neighbors and since none of the family objected, he continued his musical interludes undisturbed. He played the flute, too, and to my mother's accompaniment regaled us with "Annie Lisle" and "Listen to the Mocking Bird."

Brother Joe traded his yellow clarinet for a five-string banjo and with that the two of us were off. We picked up a guitar and a mandolin, and since all of us sang we turned out to be a musical family.

Concert Hall was far from a handicap, for besides offering both of us a play place, it gave us entree to the visiting dramatic companies, dances, masquerades, patent medicine shows, athletic events and roller skating that took over the hall. In the betweens, there were amateur theatricals in which we took part, performances from *Beyond the Rockies* and home minstrels to more pretentious offerings such as *Robert Emmet* and *A Gilded Fool.* Mother would get up on the bones and black up as endman when The Lady Minstrels performed for a church benefit, and both Joe and I filled in at times with banjo solos or duets.

Grandmother contributed her bit by devising costumes from the stock of discarded clothing in the attic, refashioning old trousers into strapped, side buttoned barndoor pants for period plays, or bedecking one of grandfather's hats with an ostrich feather to complete a lady's riding habit. Uncle Bee contented himself with managing and promoting the small town offerings.

The good fathers who erected the building—Grandfather Babcock bought it long after he came from the prairie in 1847—built it against futurity. Three storied brick, it was a skyscraper in its period and remains today the tallest business block in Beaver Dam. Many of its timbers were hand hewn and the best craft of the community went into its construction.

Two stores occupied the first floor. Between them a stairway of Alpine steepness led to the hallway above. In the rear was the office of the Beaver Dam *Citizen,* where Tommy Hughes nursed the news and a bottle of "cough medicine," sometimes with astonishing results. At one side were the rooms of the Revera Club, where the young bloods of the town were wont to foregather; and across the way, an attorney's name decorated a glass door near where the ticket window opened upon the cloakroom. At front right, a dozen steps led to a landing from which a longer flight brought entrance to the rear of the hall.

The hall proper was an oblong ninety feet long with a level hardwood floor. Two rows of iron pillars supported the flat tin roof. At no time, to my knowledge, was this protection ever free from punctures which necessitated nocturnal pilgrimages at ungodly hours for the placement of pots and pans to frustrate an ignoble downfall of trickling rain.

A huge stove stood at the head of the stairs. Another opposed it in the diagonal corner. These furnished warmth none too generous on bitter Wisconsin winter nights. Straight-backed kitchen chairs, numbered on their crossbars, flanked the walls for dancing or skating, waiting to be neatly rowed when the hall was turned into a theater. Behind the stairway's entrance, long straight-backed benches were in reserve for late comers; and when these were exhausted—a common happening at political rallies—chairs at intervals were spanned by six inch planks, thoroughly patinated by the posterial buffings of many a restless auditor.

The stage was four feet high, twenty feet wide and eighteen feet deep. Its proscenium arch, towering majestically at some twelve feet, opened between two walls that set off a room at either side while the apron extended seven feet before the front curtain. That drop displayed the Bay of Naples, sans advertisements. Grandfather Babcock frowned upon the practice of circumscribing such artistic efforts with block-lettered squares extolling the virtues of Chandler's Corner Drug Store or Veling Brothers Photographic Studio.

It was a spot dedicated to the cultural phases of life, he contended, and though Uncle Bee pointed out that a skating rink was for physical rather than mental development, Grandfather remained adamant to the last. Beaver Dam's citizenry was obliged to go elsewhere to discover that Miescke and Byron dealt in Fine Fruit Confectionery or that Hiram Booth, merchant tailor, stocked a splendid line of "Wauken-hose."

At either side behind the proscenium arch stood a tormentor, a piece of scenery masking the edge of the stage and affording cover for the side entrances. These were decorated with an eight-foot vase on a square pedestal, each base spouting a tangle of what appeared to be a cross between a cabbage rose and a purple sunflower. The tormentors were permanent, as immutable as the law of gravity. Come paper snow, or Indian battle, or Kaats-kill storm, or Dartmoor prison escape, they flowered there serenely and none thought the less of it. The reason was simple. They were nailed there to stay and there they remained backing up Naple's Bay and adding their florid tribute to the scene.

For Brother Joe and myself, the mystic recesses behind the curtain line were a veritable fairyland. True there was the odor of sizing glue and vegetable paint and half-smoked cigar stubs that permeates every country theater. Yet all the ottars of Araby could not have titillated our nostrils half so tantalizingly. No painted players or "mammoth scenic production" added to the magnificence. But there was the house scenery and curtains and a stage prop or two—a discarded sword or a forgotten jacket overlooked in packing. And Concert Hall was ours for a brief hour of strutting before an imaginary audience.

The curtains were on rollers, one of them a small tree stripped of its bark, sandpapered and varnished. At either side, running the depth of the stage, a stout square timber was fastened just above the proscenium opening. At intervals along its top were mortices to receive the battens to which the curtains were nailed. Studding its lower side were pairs of wooden pegs to steady the flat side pieces. Standing on a chair, a man could remove a curtain with little difficulty; and since they were painted on both sides, a turnabout was a regular part of every performance. The bellying of the front drop, bespeaking the mechanical struggle behind stage, always aroused enthusiastic applause.

Besides the front drop, the house scenery consisted of two curtains with side flats to match. One curtain was an elaborate parlor with a prison interior on its reverse. The other was a kitchen or a bosky wood, depending upon the side displayed. So, too, with the flats. A prison wall could become a tree and a parlor "pillar and urn" a dingy kitchen wall.

As usual, Uncle Bee was there with an explanation. The hero, he pointed out, always went to prison from a dismal hovel, represented by the kitchen. He made his escape into the woods and returned to the magnificent parlor to denounce triumphantly the villain who had robbed him of his birthright and fair name. Since prison backed parlor, and woods backed kitchen, kitchen and prison faced the audience together and the turnabout to woods and parlor could be accomplished at the same time.

There was some truth in what he said, for most of the old plays followed a general theme of thwarted love, a nincompoop hero wrongfully accused, a persecuted heroine, a diabolical miscreant who pursued them violently, and vindication through the exposure of those dastardly plotters against virtue triumphant. "Boy meets girl, boy loses girl, boy gets girl" was doubled under the weight of years while Hollywood was still a howling wilderness.

Scanty and threadbare though it was, the scenery met a multitude of needs. It could pass for a thieves' hideaway; the damp cellar retreat of the poor newsboy who generously shared his lodgings with the lachrymose heroine; Monte Cristo's dungeon in the Château D'If; the cell where Friar Lawrence gave Juliet her sleeping potion; the prison where Marguerite died in the arms of Faust; and even the den of the notorious Frochards of *The Two Orphans*.

No matter how frequently they met it, the spectators received it with the delight of greeting an old friend. Imaginative audiences at the crossroads of the eighties accepted those mildly suggestive scenic offerings as avidly as did their Elizabethan progenitors in the old Globe Theater.

The lighting was primitive, for the new electric lights were looked upon as something to experiment with and gas had not supplanted kerosene in the hall. Square glass lanterns such as underlit the town's streets were spotted at the head and turns of the stairs. The hall was lighted by iron chandeliers, each one holding four kerosene lamps, painted green. For footlights, a green tin pipe, three inches in diameter, ran the width of the stage and contained the kerosene. Lamp sockets were screwed into its top, and the chimneys were backed by green reflectors with highly silvered fronts. The contraption was set in a shallow trough from which the reflectors' circular tops peeped timidly like some deadbeat who had dodged the ticket taker and was witnessing the performance scotfree.

There was neither water nor toilet facilities. Beaver Dam was still in the plank sidewalk stage, and while the city fathers talked about a water and sewerage system, it got that far and no farther. A town pump and watering trough relieved visiting farm teams, and when the firebell sounded the volunteers hauled out Old Ready and Willing and pumped their water from the nearest cistern. Or if the fire was downtown, they dropped the feed hose into the sickly river that ran half-heartedly behind the buildings on Front Street.

Actors had their choice of hauling in their water supply or of removing their makeup in the privacy of their boarding house. Many preferred the latter, and it was not uncommon to see the soubrette and the leading man hobnobbing it out of the hall, still bedaubed with the grease paint of their profession.

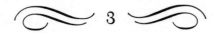

As in similar auditoriums of its day, theatrical etiquette in Concert Hall depended entirely upon the type of entertainment.

If it was a political rally—too often a knock-down-and-drag-out affair—benches and planks were set up with shallow wooden boxes of sawdust for the habitual tobacco chewers. These were strictly precautionary measures since chairs became lethal weapons if wielded in the heat of argument and it was next to impossible to remove tobacco stains from the waxed floor.

Loud and vehement were the execrations of Grandfather and Uncle Bee as they viewed the damage after each campaign gathering. But it was root-hog-or-die while supporting a Cleveland or Bryan candidacy, so the old hall endured much desecration in those battles against Wall Street's hated octopus.

Lectures and concerts were tea-and-ladyfinger affairs and chairs were arranged neatly for the elite from Yankee Hill. Benches were seldom needed for rarely was there a capacity audience. But when *The Danites,* or *The Dep'ty Sheriff,* or *Desperate Chances,* promised an overflow crowd, chairs and benches and emergency planks failed to measure up and always there were standees at the back of the hall.

For such shows, the perpetual quid was spat upon the ground before entering while its habitues endured the pangs of deprivation until the final curtain, since these performances commenced at eight, lasted until eleven, and were practically continuous. There were "specialties" between the acts —a bit of magic, a song-and-dance by the comedian, a solo on cornet or violin. If the action permitted, the heroine might warble "The Pardon Came Too Late" while she filed the handcuffs from her imprisoned lover, and the soubrette was bound to burst into song upon the slightest provocation, if any.

Most of the programs were single sheets with the play's cast and the title of the following bill boldfaced across the bottom. More ambitious managers might splurge with a four page program affording space for such enlightening announcements as these:

A FEW SIMPLE REQUESTS
Do not use your feet to applaud.
Do not spit tobacco on the floor.
Do not eat peanuts in the hall.
Do not whistle or shout in applauding.
Do not stand on the chairs.
Do not rush for the doors before the curtain drops.

And to reassure patrons of their two-bits worth of value received, the following promise:

> It will be the aim of the Companies to stage all pieces in the most realistic manner so as to render all productions as perfect as possible. A number of Companies will have "Specialties" between the acts and all should keep their seats. Any grievances should be reported at once to the Manager of the Hall.

Realism may have been promised, but bitter realization too often emphasized the necessity of imagination. Some poor players arrived with only a trunk or two, fortunate to possess even these. If their hard luck tale was convincing—and usually it was, since Grandfather's love of the drama was equalled only by his kindness of heart—hall rent was held in abeyance until after the show. And then, as invariably happened, if they promised to "send it back from the next town," the ten dollar hall rent was remitted and the company faded away, to vanish until another season, when their importunities again fell upon sympathetic ears.

Many of these thought they were putting one over on "Old Doc Babcock," but I am sure Grandfather reckoned his personal enjoyment well worth the cost of the kerosene and janitor service. It was, after all, a command performance of sorts when for one night he became a pseudo-producer in his own right.

With its low stage, flat floor and temporary seating, Concert Hall was designed to be all things on all occasions. It was in turn a theater and a ballroom; a lecture hall and a skating rink; an arena for athletic events and a concert auditorium; the chambers of the city council, a voting place on election day, a campaign headquarters and a drillroom for the National Guard.

The expansive apron of the stage could accommodate a piano recital, a violinist, a lecturer, or a row of political bigwigs ranged before the front drop. Hugely impressive was it to hark to "Hear me, Norma," or "Angel's Serenade," or "The Rise and Fall of the Mustache," "The Carnival of Venice" or a thundering denunciation of "Rum, Romanism and Rebellion" against that background where a red-sailed lugger skimmed Naples' cobalt-blue waters, all oblivious to the threat of smoke crowned Vesuvius.

When the building was completed in 1858, the village aldermen adopted the hall for their council chambers. From it the Burchard Guards marched

Postcard-size colored prints were another favorite medium of advertising practiced by the more prosperous managers. *A Trip to Africa* was one of these, and the prints were distributed at performances. Many of these found a permanent place in the scrapbooks of the matinee girls, along with pictures of stage and sporting characters included in the packages of Sweet Caporal Cigarettes, and the historic prints, such as the Battle of the Monitor and the Merrimac, distributed with McLaughlin's XXXX Coffee.

away determined to put the upstart southrons in their place in ninety days.
There the townswomen met to scrape lint, roll bandages and hold their
beneficent Sanitary Fairs. And there, after Appomattox, came the veterans
—or what was left of them—bronzed and bearded men of the world who, a
few brief years before, had marched away as peach–cheeked youths headed
upon the great adventure whose significance they comprehended only too
little.

To its safety Grandfather dragged his brother, Matt Babcock, outspoken
Copperhead, when a mob threatened to string him to the nearest lamp post;
and to its sanctuary a few days later fled Judge A. Scott Sloan when a mob,
rope in hand, pursued him for helping a runaway slave on his way. On its
stage, Frederick Douglas was rotten egged and set upon for pleading the
cause of his people. Grandfather rescued him from the crowd, took him
home, entertained him and convoyed him safely on his way the next morning. Douglas, that night, occupied the room in which, years later, I was

Tom Thumb

(*left to right*) Major Nutt, Tom Thumb, Mrs. Tom Thumb (Minnie Warren),
Lavinia Warren

born. Far removed from the Mason-Dixon line though it was, Beaver Dam split over the Civil War as bitterly as did any Wisconsin community.

From the rostrum P. T. Barnum lectured on "Temperance," for a fee, and exhibited Tom Thumb and his wife, who had been Lavinia Warren, and her sister, Minnie, and Commodore G. W. M. Nutt. Artemus Ward delivered his talk on "Babes in the Wood," and Mark Twain fresh from his triumphant "Innocents Abroad," drawled his sarcastic periods. Ole Bull played his fiddle, the Black Patti (who was Sissaretta Jones) filled the hall with her golden voice, and poor Blind Tom, Negro moron and musical genius, astounded his listeners with his piano virtuosity.

John T. Kelly, "The Rolling Mill Man," came from time to time—when sober. Bill Nye and James Whitcomb Riley appeared together under the management of James B. Pond. Augustus F. Hartz displayed his magic, little reckoning that some day he would start Abe Erlanger on his way to control the nation's theaters. And the minstels came—Emerson and Hooley's Megatherian Minstrels'; Emerson and the Big Four Minstrels; Barlow and Wilson; Primrose and West; Hi Henry; Beach and Bowers; and repertory companies without number in kaleidoscopic review.

When Music Hall was built, much of the show business moved up to the other end of Front Street. Planned to double as a dance floor, the new theater offered many advantages. It was only one flight up, there were a half dozen dressing rooms and, suspended from steel rods at the rear of the auditorium, was a tiny gallery fit to accommodate a hundred lovers and numerous small boys who, from the back row, offered ribald comments in grating overtones. Besides all that, they reserved your seat at Charley Miller's Book Store. Charley took over as manager of the new enterprise and continued as such until the new Davison, modern in every respect, moved up in the line of patronage.

About the time Music Hall opened, someone started the report that Concert Hall was unsafe. The building was ready to collapse at any time, to hear them tell it, and it was particularly unsafe for dancing. But since it could handle much larger crowds than its young opposition, Concert Hall continued to draw the dance crowds. Still the rumors persisted and many a youth waxed to middle age and waned to senility and finally moved along to share the green windrows in Oakwood or the Old Cemetery, bitterly disappointed that the prophecy was unfulfilled.

So the old building struggled along, sans drama and minstrel shows, existing on medicine shows, and a skating rink, and dances, and political rallies. But its day was past and like the pioneers of its youth, it dropped

and faded and finally gave up the ghost as movies and radio put an end to
touring rep companies. And it was the first home of the Dodge County
Historical Society of Wisconsin.

And the grandchildren of the oldsters who saw the building and razing
of Music Hall, still prattle hopefully on, waiting for Concert Hall to fall
down as did Jericho's walls before the shophar blasts of Joshua's fighting
men.

Chapter 2
ELOCUTION TAKES A LOT OF DOING

Y FIRST formal introduction to the drama came with the visit of Belle Rawson. Her arrival at our house rated more than neighborhood importance for Belle was a finished reader. Parlor reading was a favorite indoor sport, and Belle was a graduate from Chicago's best schools of elocution and Delsarte. Winner of a half dozen declamation contests she had cheap silver medals to prove it.

Grandmother and Aunt Sue decided that I was to profit by Belle's coming by taking instruction from her during her two week's stay. I was only eight but I could recite "Kentucky Belle" and "The Countersign Was Mary," a Civil War effusion in which I was supported by an old forage cap and my toy gun; and I never failed with "Sheridan's Ride" to bring horse and rider safely through the twenty miles from Winchester to rest securely in the American soldier's temple of fame under the dome of the Union sky.

Grandmother rated me a child prodigy and had there been a Hollywood I am sure she would have hauled me off there to join the other brats in wearing down casting directors.

It was readily arranged. Belle agreed to instruct me in the art of parlor recitation but with two stipulations: the lessons were to be private, and I was to make no appearance before she went home.

"I'm no professional," she explained. "And I couldn't face it if I failed to improve Harlowe. And besides I'm entered in another contest in Chicago and I don't want to jeopardize my amateur standing."

Since this seemed reasonable enough, her conditions were accepted and Belle promised to devote her last week to my education. This was not an arbitrary arrangment on her part, for news of her coming brought a steady flow of nightly visitors that kept Grandmother busy all day making cookies and doughnuts, to say nothing of coconut and banana cake.

For her part, Belle was unremitting in her recitations. Like others of her clan she responded to the slightest invitation and when none was forthcoming, she went right ahead and gave a program anyway. Her repertory was varied and it must have been arranged by one of her instructors for it was nicely balanced and gave her plenty of chance to show off.

She always started with a couple of light verses such as "The Children's Hour" or "The First Snowfall," something not too heavy for a preliminary workout, much as a baseball pitcher warms up before taking the mound. With these under her belt she was ready for stronger stuff. "Curfew Must Not Ring Tonight" was not too heavy and gave opportunity for characterization. There was the tearful Bessie, tragic in her fear for her lover's safety; the Old Sexton, hand cupped to ear, cackling his determination to ring the bell or break a leg; and, for the finish, Bessie flopping down with uplifted hands in supplication and then bouncing up again as Cromwell, with outstretched arm, declared:

"Go! Your lover, lives! Curfew shall not ring tonight!"

By this time, her audiences were ready for their first encounter with doughnuts and cider while Belle sipped a glass of water—"Never eat when you are reciting; it may cause you to belch"—and preened herself in the compliments showered upon her.

After a brief intermission, the scene was set for "Ostler Joe."

The Dagonet Ballads gained their popularity with "The Lights o' London" and "The Old Actor's Story," but Cora Urquhart Potter set the pace for parlor reciters when she banned herself from New York's Four Hundred by declaiming this story of a humble stablehand and his faithless wife. Certainly it was nothing but corny pathos, but polite society of that era pretended that women had no legs, or ankles either, for that matter, and that fallen women were "soiled doves," entirely ignoring the quite obvious fact that most of them probably preferred cashing in on the oldest profession to hanging over a hot woodstove for three dollars a week.

So they gave the cold shoulder to Mrs. Brown-Potter, who promptly set out to a more or less successful stage career. But New York's red meat was caviar to the middle west. "Ostler Joe" was anticipated as something a little more than risque and a little less than obscene. There was much promise in the beginning, and Belle was assured breathless attention when she squared off and started in.

"I stood at eve, as the sun went down, by the grave where a woman lies,
  Who lured men's souls to the shores of sin with the light of her wanton eyes,
  Who sang the song that the Siren sang on the treacherous Lurley Height,
  Whose face was as fair as a summer's day, and whose heart was as black
    as night."

And waiting hopefully to be shocked, they held on wistfully to the finish, though it ended on a note disappointingly flat.

"There's a blossom I fain would pluck today from the garden above her dust,
  Not the languorous lily of soulless sin nor the blood-red rose of lust;
  But a sweet white blossom of holy love that grew in the one green spot,
  In the arid desert of Phryne's life when all else was parched and hot."

So the promise was unfulfilled, especially for those who anticipated something red hot and were paid off with a run-of-the-mine poem. But it gave rise to speculation. Why did New York think it so wicked? *East Lynne* had the identical story and nobody thought of that as off-color. They even played it at the Saturday matinee for children. George Sims always had a moral and certainly there was one here.

Belle meantime did a bit of promotion by explaining that she had chosen "Ostler Joe" to replace "Lasca," far more thrilling and dramatic, which she'd do next time. Then to close the evening she really went to town. She let down her back hair and gave them "The Sands o' Dee"; and after Mary had gone to call the cattle home, she would end up with:

> "Would ye come back to me, Douglas, Douglas,
>   In the old likeness that I knew,
>   I would be so loving, Douglas,
>   Douglas, Douglas, tender and true."

For this Mother was impressed to furnish the musical background on our Somers square piano. The impact I can truthfully say was nothing short of sensational.

On the Monday of her last week with us, Belle took me into the front parlor and shut the folding doors.

"Now remember," she cautioned. "You're not to breathe a word to anyone —Joe, or Mother, or Grandmother—not a single word! And you're not to recite a thing while I am here. Now, promise me."

"Cross my heart and hope to die if I do," I replied stoutly.

"All right then. We're ready to start." She looked at me thoughtfully. "We haven't time to go into the gestures and besides you wouldn't know how to use them."

The gestures were a set of principles pounded into the heads of aspiring speakers to give them "platform presence." "1-Hand out right"; "2-Hand elevated"; "3-Hand to the Head": each had its key number that was spotted through the text to make memorizing as painless as possible.

"Go over across the room from me," she ordered. "Stand up straight. Feet together. Hands by your sides. Take a deep breath. Let it out. Take another. Breathe naturally. Good enough.

"Now this is a recitation about a little girl and a little boy. Just imagine you're the little boy. The easiest way for you to learn it is to repeat each line after me and do exactly as I do. Repeat this line and put out your right hand, like this.

> "Said Ethel to Dick,
>   (*Right hand out from shoulder*)
> 'Come hurry—come quick',
>   (*Lean forward and beckon with your finger*)
> And we'll do and we'll do and we'll do."

Here Belle placed a hand on either hip, arms akimbo, and with each "do" indulged in an undulating gesture that would shame a stripper at Minsky's; and I, in my placid innocence, following her every move, imitated her with added emphasis.

> "Our mothers away
>   (*Point to the right*)
> And they're gone for the day,
> So we'll kick (*kick here*) up, a hullabaloo,
> While we do—and we do—and we do."

There was no doubt as to my sincerity. I gave the recitation everything I had. We went through it twice from start to finish before she called it quits and dismissed me, again cautioning me about spouting off prematurely. And again I renewed my promise. Belle was a luscious miss of eighteen, trim-waisted and merry-eyed, to be admired from afar and, in my childish estimation, she could do no wrong.

By the week's end I was letter perfect in word and deed in the recital of the doings of Ethel and Dick. Belle left for Chicago on the Monday night train and when she kissed me goodbye I was transported to the seventh heaven of infantile rapture.

"I want this to be a public recitation," she told Grandmother. "I've worked hard with Harlowe and I'm sure he'll show it. But," she added, apparently as an after thought, "don't let on that I had anything to do with it. It might jeopardize my amateur standing, you know. Let them think he worked it out all by his little lone self. It will be so much cuter if you do."

Grandmother assented eagerly. She knew she nurtured a budding dramatic genius and anything that redounded to my prowess was grist for her mill. So she saved me for the next meeting of the Universalist Society.

The Universalist Society might once have held some commerce with Hosea Ballou, but when I was old enough to take notice it had dwindled to a group of elderly women who met once a month to gossip, knit and sew, and play at maintaining an organization by reading minutes, electing officers and reporting on a modest treasury. The rest of the time they moved serenely along, their husbands joining them in the afternoon when a bumptious country dinner rounded out the day. The two-bits a head contributed by their guests went into the treasury for what purpose nobody seemed quite certain. But it was all very cosy and maintained a contact for the old timers, most of them York State folks who had pioneered Beaver Dam together.

The afternoon was well along with a lull in the conversation that preceded the call to dinner when Grandmother intruded me into the conversation.

"Harlowe has a new recitation for you," she announced. And to the polite buzz of casual interest: "He worked it out all by himself. Harlowe, stand over there by the door and speak your new piece."

I remembered to take my position, to keep my feet together and to gesture as I had been told to do.

"Said Ethel to Dick:
'Come hurry—come quick—
And we'll do—and we'll do—and we'll do.' "

By the third "do," a murmur of surprise rippled about the circle while a look of puzzled and agonized surprise spread across Grandmother's face. Confident that I was creating an impression—though what kind I little realized—I continued:

"Our mothers away,
And they're gone for the day,
So we'll kick up a hullabaloo,
While we do—and we do—and we do."

At this point, Mother, white with anger, yanked me into the kitchen where Uncle Bee was watching the performance with undisguised enthusiasm. Mother was all for going over me with the rough side of a hair brush, but Uncle Bee interfered.

"Why blame him?" he said. "It was all Belle's idea of a practical joke. And at that she did only a half a job. She should have given him an encore."

"Just what do you mean?" Mother asked suspiciously.

"Why, that thing of Blake's for instance.
'Little lad, who made thee? Dos't thou—' "

But before Uncle Bee could commit further mayhem on Blake's verse, Mother hustled me upstairs and put me to bed without any supper—an unjust punishment that Uncle Bee rectified by the time the second table was under way.

Though she gained some recognition as an actress in later years, Belle Ransom never visited us again. But it was a long time before I found out that it was really Willie and not Ethel who proposed an afternoon of riotous fun in the absence of maternal supervision.

Grandfather (*seated*) and Peter Beule

Uncle Bee

Harlowe

Joe

Grandmother (*standing at extreme right*) and some of the Universalist Society

Mother

The Family Album

Inauguration

Even the Universalist Society got into the political activities from time to time; and when U. S. Grant was inaugurated on March 4, 1869, not only the ladies themselves but the entire community joined in the celebration.

Schuyler Colfax was Grant's running mate; the opposition was Horatio Seymour and Francis P. Blair. Grant wrote "Let us have peace" in his letter of acceptance, and this became the campaign slogan. The campaign was a hot one, and the Republican ticket won out by only a 300,000 popular majority.

So Beaver Dam turned out to celebrate. Vocal and instrumental selections were given by the talent of the town backed by the Beaver Dam Cornet Band. Tables groaned under an "old fashioned New England dinner", featuring oysters and ice cream. And all this was offered for only twenty-five cents a couple. No disposition was announced of the profits, if any; but the good ladies were lucky if they broke even.

INAUGURATION
Festival.

The Ladies of the

UNIVERSALIST SOCIETY,

Of BEAVER DAM and vicinity will give one of their

GRAND FESTIVALS,
AT

CONCERT HALL,

In the city of

BEAVER DAM, WIS.

On next

THURSDAY, MARCH 4TH, 1869

The day of the Inauguration of the

PRESIDENT AND VICE PRESIDENT.

Tables will be spread with an OLD FASHIONED

New England Dinner.

OYSTERS,

ICE CREAM,

And other delicacies will be served. The usual entertainments of such occasions will be presented, and various usual and fancy articles for sale.

VOCAL AND INSTRUMENTAL MUSIC

Will enliven the occasion.

ADMISSION TO HALL, - - 25 CTS. PER COUPLE.
SINGLE TICKETS, - - - 15 CTS.

By order of Commmittee of Arrangements.
BEAVER DAM, Feb. 27th.

Chapter 3

"TOMORROW NIGHT, EAST LYNNE"

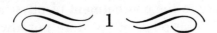

1

NEW YORK of the eighties and nineties was far removed from the outposts of the drama presented in Concert Hall.

Broadway came to Milwaukee, but that was sixty-five miles away and it was doubtful to most of us if the satisfaction of viewing a play compensated for the effort entailed in getting there. From time to time, theater parties did endure the rigors of a rickety daycoach to witness a performance at the Davidson Theater. Excursion rates were available to parties of ten or more, but even at that only a select few could afford to sacrifice a five dollar bill before the altar of Thespis.

Attending the Davidson Theater partook of the nature of a major operation. Plans were laid weeks before and reservations made against the sortie

Davidson Theater, Milwaukee, Wis.

Summer Stock played here season after season.

upon this citadel of art. It was an adventure fecund with physical discomfort. Following an early supper, you were herded aboard the five o'clock train for three hours of torturous travel and disheartening delay that threatened the success of your trip.

You crept into the Milwaukee station at last, dashed wildly up the half block to the theater and, fortune favoring, got into your seat in time to see the rising curtain disclose an unctuous butler in amorous repartee with a saucy housemaid. With the final speech, you dashed back to the depot, boarded a midnight train and got back home between three and four o'clock in the morning.

Unless you had the foresight to provision yourself, you entered the family domicile overflowing with mental manna but sadly deficient in the mundane provender so necessary to the contentment of physical well being.

I must admit that these pilgrimages were not always inspired by a desire to view the best in dramatic fare. Once in a while the more affluent of us could raise the two-fifty demanded for an Irving-Terry performance though we usually chose Mathias in *The Bells* to Hamlet or Shylock. There was a real kick in the trial scene, and the burgomaster's death left you with something to chew upon for weeks to come.

Numbers and not dramatic sapidity controlled these excursions since no party of ten, no cut rate. Of course you could make the trip alone by promoting a surreptitious financial transaction with Conductor Bill Russell. There were no checkers on the division and Bill was not averse to turning a soft dollar for himself. But on your return you probably would be stuck with a strange conductor to view you with bilious eye and demand surcharge because you had no ticket. That these surcharges went into his own pocket was none of your business. So the majority ruled and we went to see Modjeska in *Camille,* and Robert Mantell in *Monbars,* Frederick Warde in *Virginius,* and Robert Downing in *The Gladiator,* while a visit with Joe Jefferson and Rip Van Winkle was an annual event.

One misguided group, casting convention to the winds, put out with no other ambition than to see Lottie Collins sing "Ta-ra-ra Boom-de Aye." Fresh from the London music halls, Lottie had refurbished the shabbiness of the can-can with a flowing gown, Gainsborough hat and a doggerel chanson to an accompaniment dominated by the bass drum. A dapper figure, she minced onto the stage and into the spotlight. Naughtily she declared:

> A smart and stylish girl you see,
> Belle of swell society,
> Not too bold but rather free,
> Yet I'm nice as nice can be.
> Ta-ra-ra Boom-de-Aye!
> Ta-ra-ra Boom-de-Aye!
> Ta-ra-ra Boom-de-Aye!
> Ta-ra-ra Boom-de-Aye!

While Lottie's foot flew higher than her head, each "boom" was emphasized by a resounding wallop of the bass drum. Lottie was not content with the conventional quarter-to-six when she kicked. She made it a real bull'seye at high noon.

These venturesome souls returned, poorer but wiser, complaining bit-

The Bells

After Henry Irving produced *The Bells* in London in the seventies, it wasn't long before other versions of the hair-raiser were to be had. The melodrama was an adaptation of a French play, *Le Juif Polonais*, by Erckmann-Chatrian, and it was a simple matter to alter it a bit and claim that another version had been made from the original script which had no American copyright.

The play tells of an innkeeper, Mathias, who some years before has murdered a Polish Jew, a peddler who stopped at his hostelry. On the marriage day of his daughter, which coincides with the anniversary of his crime, Mathias dreams that he falls under the power of a hypnotist and confesses his crime in open court. It was a fat part for any actor, with a bedroom at the front of the stage and a gauze backdrop which, when illuminated, disclosed the court and the hypnotist.

This scene, much more elaborate than any reproduction in small time, was from advertising material used by Irving during the original production at the Lyceum Theater in London.

Photo from "Introducing the Theater" by Ernst Short
(Erye and Spottiswoode, London, 1949)

terly that though Lottie's kicks were highly arched, the elevation was all too brief to satisfy their curiosity.

"Darn it all," Matt Peacock confided to the boys in Lambeck's barber shop, "she lived up to her advance notices all right. She kicked high just as it said but she was so gol-darned fast you couldn't see a blamed thing."

Proving, if anything, that the leg, like the hand, is quicker than the eye.

During this time, the American stage was parturitioning amid mountainous labor that too often brought forth something resembling a spinning mouse since it came from nowhere and ended up exactly where it started. But slowly and laboriously a renaissance was being effected in New York.

From San Francisco's stock and the itinerant companies of the west, David Belasco came east to team up with H. C. DeMille, who quit teaching school to try his hand at playwriting. Together they set a new style in dramatic fare with *The Wife, Men and Women*, and *The Charity Ball*. Dan and Charlie Frohman built a famous stock company at the Lyceum Theater, while Brother Gus faded from the picture.

Augustin Daly found the brothers smart opposition as he turned from the tawdry histrionics of *Under the Gaslight* to make Ada Crehan into Rehan, dramatic star of *Divorce* and *A Night Off*; and with *The Merry Wives of Windsor, As You Like It* and *A Mid-Summer Night's Dream* to prove Shakespeare something really human and not dependent upon oratorical mouthings to be acceptable to the groundlings.

Clyde Fitch had just graduated from Amherst and with his first sprightly comedies was putting a lightsome froth on the rising tide. He wrote *Beau Brummel* and a song-and-dance man realized the dream of every comedian by remolding himself into a great actor. The Beau, and Baron Chevral in *A Parisian Romance*, were roles with which Richard Mansfield hoisted himself by his stage bootstraps above the hilarious nonsense of John Wellington Wells in Gilbert and Sullivan's *The Sorcerer*.

Steele MacKaye changed a play's title from "Cast Adrift" to "An Iron Will" and finally settled upon *Hazel Kirke*. Marc Klaw, lawyer turned producer, picked up Effie Ellsler in Cleveland and took her to New York in the title role. At her father's Euclid Avenue Opera House, Gus Hartz, manager, made the acquaintance of a sharp young box office man, named Abe Erlanger, who followed eastward to help organize the powerful syndicate of Klaw and Erlanger.

MacKaye has been accredited with many theatrical innovations but little notice has been paid the bit he played in establishing this most dictatorial of all theatrical dynasties. He built the Lyceum Theater, which the Frohmans inherited, and in it opened the American Academy of Dramatic Art, the first in this country. He appreciated the possibilities of electricity and was the first to use it in the theater. He may not have devised the box set that supplanted curtains and wings but he did demonstrate the effectiveness of stage illuminations. Belasco profited by it and built his reputation upon Belasco lighting long after MacKaye, practically bankrupt and all too young, died of overwork.

Still this renaissance in the east scarcely touched the players who came to Concert Hall. Of it they knew little and cared less. Except for expropriating an occasional Broadway success and disguising it with an alias, they continued to wildcat their bookings and present the standard repertory of the road.

Rip Van Winkle

Before Joseph Jefferson made *Rip Van Winkle* his own, there were at least five different companies playing five different versions of Washington Irving's story and each with a different star. Thomas Flynn's dramatization played in Albany, N. Y., in 1828. The next year James H. Hackett brought a version to the Park Theater in New York. F. S. Chanfrau was seen in another version at the Old Bowery Theater a year later.

Jefferson's version was a combination of all of these worked over by himself and Dion Boucicault. Charles Burke, Jefferson's half brother, had his own version in 1850, and young Jefferson had to content himself with the minor role of School-master Knickerbocker.

When the rep companies took over, they fell back upon these earlier versions, and throughout the eighties and the nineties that of Charles Burke was presented most frequently since it was in printed form and easily procured. It was a standby for John Kelly when he headed the Kelly and Angell Co. or came alone as an independent producer.

This was a truly old fashioned melodrama—a combination of singing and acting with music cues for every entrance and incidental background besides. It opened in the square before the tavern with villagers drinking air from empty tin cups and disporting themselves by nudging each other in the midribs.

CHORUS

In our native land, where flows the Rhine,
In infancy we culled the vine;
Although we toiled with patient care
But poor and scanty was our fare.

SCHOOLMASTER KNICKERBOCKER

Till tempting waves with anxious toil,
We landed on Columbia's soil,
Now plenty all our cares repay,
So laugh and dance the hours away.

Rip makes his entrance and after a drink or two, takes his turn at song.

List, my friends, to caution's voice
Ere de marriage knot you tie;
It is de devil mit shrews to splice,
Dat nobody can deny, deny,
Dat nobody can deny.
When a wife to rule once wishes,
Mit poor spouse 'tis all my eye,
I'm damned if she don't vear the breeches,
Which nobody can deny.
Yet dere is a charm about dem
Do dere voices are so high,
We can't do mit dem,
We can't do mit out dem,
Which nobody can deny.

Rip's entrance to the mountain retreat of Hendrick Hudson's ghostly crew is accompanied by the "rolling of cannon balls" which the spectres evidently pre-ferred for their game of bowls. Rip meets Swaggrino, one of the crew, toiling un-der a cask of liquor. Rip takes the load and they exit as the scene shifts to the place of merrymaking.

There is song and laughter, for the merry villagers of the first act have donned brown Mother Hubbards and tow whiskers to become the ghostly ensemble. Some are bowling; some are drinking; some are "playing at battledore and shuttlecock" —at least they were in the original Burke version though the rep companies that came through contented themselves with a quartette of singers who rolled an anemic ball or two, borrowed from the town's bowling alley. Their song gave the plot another nudge.

GAUDERKIN

Since on earth this only day
In fifty years we're given to stay,
We'll keep it as a holiday!
So, brothers, let's be jolly and gay.

ICKEN

But question: where's the lazy wight,
Who, soon a sun withdrew its light,
Was for the earth's rich beverage sent,
And has such time in absence spent?

GAUDERKIN

Perhaps with some misfortune he's been doomed to meet,
Crossed, no doubt, on the road by mortal feet.

ICKEN

But what's the punishment that you decree
On him who on our mysteries makes free.

GAUDERKIN

Twenty years in slumber's chain
Is the fate that we ordain;
Yet if merry wight he prove,
Pleasing dreams his sleep shall move.

ICKEN

Our brother comes, and up the rugged steep
A mortal, see, Swaggrino's presence keep.

OMNES

Twenty years in slumber's chain
Is the fate that we ordain,
He comes! He comes! Let silence reign!
Let silence reign! Let silence reign!

So Rip drank with them and joined in a grotesque dance, when he dropped down asleep to a final chorus of the song and a rousing "ho-ho-ho!" as the curtain fell.

In time all but the final chorus of the song was eliminated, and the play was shaped into four acts, whereas Burke had written it as a loosely constructed effort in two acts and some nine scenes. And Jefferson's toast replaced that used by Burke. Jefferson's toast was:

"Here's to your goot health, und your family's, und may you live long und prosper."

Quite an improvement on the original of: "Here is your go-to-hell, unt your family's go-to-hell, unt may you all live long unt prosper."

Rip Van Kelly borrowed the family shotgun for his fowling piece and had to be content to remove the bolt so that it fell apart at the twenty years' awakening and he could use the barrel for a cane. There was no attempt to give it a rusty appearance and its sheen was as glossy as when Rip lay down on the ground cloth twenty years before and went to sleep with his head on a set rock. After all, it was Uncle Bee's favorite double-barreled twelve-gauge shotgun and he proscribed all monkeying with it.

Harvard University Theater Collection

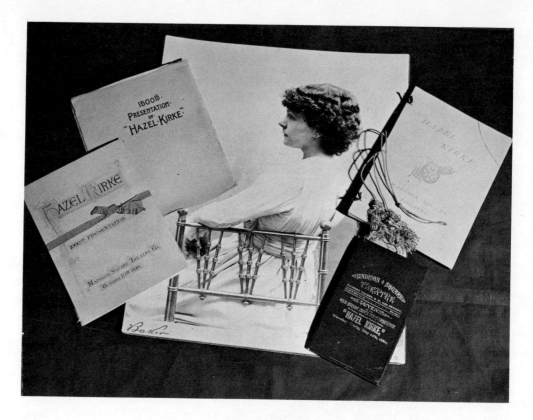

Hazel Kirke

Steele MacKaye wrote many plays, but the one upon which his reputation was based and for which he is remembered is *Hazel Kirke*. It ran for 500 performances when it was produced at the new Madison Square Theater in New York in 1880. A dozen companies took it on the road, and it became a stock favorite.

But more than that, it was played by the small time rep companies. There had been versions of it as *The Green Fields of England* and *An Iron Will*, and the latter name was chosen by most of the country troupers who pirated it.

The story concerns Dunstan Kirke, an English miller, who ran in debt to a middle-aged neighbor and would have married his daughter Hazel to him to clear it up. But Hazel weds a young man saved by her father from drowning near his mill. Disowned by the angry man—a fine denunciation of "never darken my door again"—Hazel finds that her husband is importuned by his mother to marry a rich girl to save their property from being taken. Add to this the fact that her husband is a nobleman and she but a humble miller's daughter, and there was reason for the wife's running away to clear up the situation.

Dunstan goes blind. His mill is foreclosed. Hazel attempts suicide. But after all this, everything ends happily and everyone is forgiven. The play was popular since it followed the established melodramatic pattern. It was said to have been played with restraint in New York, but the small time ranters certainly gave it everything they had, and their audiences ate it up. Effie Ellsler was the original Hazel, and more than 1500 performances were given by her in the part.

Photo from Cleveland Plain Dealer
Advertising bill from New York Public
Library

East Lynne

Of the plays that came back year after year, never to lose their appeal, *East Lynne* topped them all. Ellen Price Wood wrote her novel of English high life in 1861. It was dramatized on the dot, and continued on and on as long as rep shows played the small towns.

With the subtitle "The Elopement," this "great moral sensational play" dealt with Lady Isabel married to Archibald Carlyle, a credulous soul who believes his wife unfaithful while she, in turn, suspects him. So she elopes with Sir Francis Levison, leaving her infant Willie to the care of the husband. Carlyle remarries; Levison deserts. the trusting Isabel, who after some eight years returns to the old home; and since she wears blue goggles, none recognize her.

Little Willie is stricken to death, and as he nears the end, Madame Vine—that's Lady Isabel with goggles—leans over his crib and discloses her identity.

"Willie!" she cries. "Don't you know me, Willie! I am your mother!"

And Willie, viewing the familiar face sans goggles, sits up, cries: "Mama," and promptly dies.

Then Sir Francis Levison is unmasked as a murderer and led away in handcuffs—"gyves" was the proper word in those days—and Lady Isabel, returned to her true estate, solves the matrimonial triangle by dying herself.

All of this is to the strains of "Then You'll Remember Me." *East Lynne* was a favorite mid-week matinee offering, and you could identify the play without entering the hall. The combination of feminine sniffles to an accmpaniment of Balfe's music proclaimed *East Lynne* beyond a doubt.

Program from the Townsend Walsh
Collection
New York Public Library

Colonial Theater, Cleveland, Ohio

Vaughan Glaser Stock Company played here for many years.

Rep companies that came for a week's stand tagged themselves with titles to emphasize their entertainment value and to impress upon us that while their presentations were primarily for amusement they possessed a rich educational and moral substrata and were guaranteed to offend no one, whatever might be his religious denomination.

Stage people were by no means approved of by New York's purity brigades and in the smaller communities, churchgoers had to be convinced. There was no indication that one day a Gould, whose father turned a fortune by rigging the stock market, would condescend to marry an actress, even a gifted one of unimpeachable character, or that a Belmont could transform a star of the stage into a star of society.

Vaudeville was a dubious amusement, and burlesque was never mentioned above a whisper. The customers wanted something wholesome like *Robert Emmet,* or *Our American Cousin,* or *The Old Homestead;* or what they fondly imagined portrayed British high life, such as *Lady Audley's Secret;* or any of the melodramas and comedies that time had made respectable for the road. So the players came as the Fox Comedy Company, and the Hattie Irving Comedy Company, and the Sweitzer Comedy Company, since patently there was nothing heretical in wholesome laughter. They sounded so festive and harmless that we quite overlooked the fact that their plays differed little from those of the Little Allie Spooner Dramatic Company, of the Fifth Avenue Theater Company, or the Henry F. Adams Dramatic Company, or the Noble Dramatic Company, or one that was listed honestly enough as the Wilson Theater Company.

To further reassure the churchly and the timid who feared their wrath, the word "melodrama" never was mentioned, while "drama" was rarely employed. With little variation, all of these plays were "comedy-dramas" and this went for such ripsnorters as *Michael Strogoff* and *Dr. Jekyll and Mr. Hyde.* *The Octoroon* might be termed "A Story of the Old South," *Rip Van Winkle* was "A Legend of the Catskills," and *Ten Nights in a Bar-Room,* "A Vivid Temperance Lesson." But these were welcome meat for the denominations who whooped it up in straw and canvas at seasonal camp-meetings and who went through life happy in the misapprehension that *Ben Hur* was something akin to the Passion Play of Oberammergau.

Michael Strogoff

Before electricity and improved methods made it a simple task, photographing scenes of a play in the theater and on the stage was an impossibility. All that could be done was to round up the actors in a photographer's studio and make the best of it.

Both of these scenes were made in the early eighties when the stock company of the Boston Theater was functioning in that city. The first shows the raft scene from *Michael Strogoff.* The company was augmented for this production, and a large ballet participated. It was voted a huge success but nothing in this crudely posed picture hints of such a happy result.

The other scene is from *The Soudan,* a drama by Henry Pettitt and Augustus Harris that had played the great Drury Lane in London, under the title of *Human Nature.* To give everybody an even chance, the photographer combined a number of situations into a hodge-podge without rhyme or reason.

Photographs from "History of the Boston Theatre," by Eugene Tompkins and Quincy Kilby (Houghton Mifflin Co.)

The Soudan

It was considered smart business to keep the play a secret until the eve of the performance. A letter to Grandfather would ask for a week's time, or an advance man might breeze in, casually announcing that his show was in Watertown and figured on playing Concert Hall next. This hit-and-miss system of booking was known as wildcatting and a good many companies favored it since its flexibility often enabled them to beat their rivals to the better stands. The average town was good for a week of rep shows about once a month. Lectures and minstrel shows and amateur performances might worry along during the other three weeks but rep bookings closer than four to six weeks were bound to finish in the red.

The booking made, the company's coming was announced. Advertising was mostly by window cards and small window bills, known as half-sheets. A half-dozen three-sheets might be plastered up in vacant store windows and on convenient fences. Billboards were unknown and a barndoor or the side of Bill Wade's Livery Stable were choice spots, particularly the latter as it stood opposite the Milwaukee depot and was on display for all the townsters who flocked down to see the morning and afternoon trains come in.

This advertising announced the name of the company, the date of engagement and the title of the first play, illustrated with a prison escape, a buzz-saw rescue, a duel with knives, or some other situation adapted to litho-

East Lynne

Of the plays that came back year after year, never to lose their appeal, *East Lynne* topped them all. Ellen Price Wood wrote her novel of English high life in 1861. It was dramatized on the dot, and continued on and on as long as rep shows played the small towns.

With the subtitle "The Elopement," this "great moral sensational play" dealt with Lady Isabel married to Archibald Carlyle, a credulous soul who believes his wife unfaithful while she, in turn, suspects him. So she elopes with Sir Francis Levison, leaving her infant Willie to the care of the husband. Carlyle remarries; Levison deserts the trusting Isabel, who after some eight years returns to the old home; and since she wears blue goggles, none recognize her.

Little Willie is stricken to death, and as he nears the end, Madame Vine—that's Lady Isabel with goggles—leans over his crib and discloses her identity.

"Willie!" she cries. "Don't you know me, Willie! I am your mother!"

And Willie, viewing the familiar face sans goggles, sits up, cries: "Mama," and promptly dies.

Then Sir Francis Levison is unmasked as a murderer and led away in handcuffs—"gyves" was the proper word in those days—and Lady Isabel, returned to her true estate, solves the matrimonial triangle by dying herself.

All of this is to the strains of "Then You'll Remember Me." *East Lynne* was a favorite mid-week matinee offering, and you could identify the play without entering the hall. The combination of feminine sniffles to an accmpaniment of Balfe's music proclaimed *East Lynne* beyond a doubt.

Program from the Townsend Walsh Collection
New York Public Library

graphic reproduction. Further than that it did not go. To have offered a detailed bill-of-fare and permit the thrifty villager to pick and choose from the entire table d'hote would have padlocked their wallets except for one or two favorites. As it was, they were high pressured with fast sales talk and lured along from day to day.

The next day's bill was announced each night by the manager or one of the actors after the third act. He pushed his way before the front drop to tell his audience how delighted they all were to be back again among their old friends and how the management was prepared to give bigger and better productions than ever before. There was intimate confidence in this footlight chat and though on the first night he sometimes mentioned the last stand instead of Beaver Dam, this was laughed off as a joke and by the

East Lynne

Little theaters and collegiate dramatic groups revive *East Lynne* from time to time as did these Rollins College Players. This is the homecoming of Lady Isabel to the not overwelcome domicile of Archibald Carlyle. Played with restraint, it was not greatly overexaggerated and gave an approximate presentation of the acting of other days.

New York Public Library Collection

third day he would be running like a well-oiled phonograph, convincing his auditors that this particular company lived the year around awaiting the one week that brought them to Concert Hall.

And then, in conclusion, came the announcement:

"And now, ladies and gentlemen—no, not ladies and gentlemen but friends—our friends, for I know you all are, each and every one of you—and now, in conclusion, it is my proud privilege to announce for your amusement and entertainment—tomorrow night—*East Lynne——*" or *The Black Flag* or *Queen's Evidence,* or whatever might be on the schedule.

The publicity campaign opened up about ten o'clock the next morning when the manager got out his paper trunk to check up his supply. He saw to it that some handbills were printed at each stand so the Dodge County *Citizen* and the Beaver Dam *Argus* caught an odd job or two on each visit while the extras were stacked away for the next town. These bills read something like this:

TONIGHT
The Little Allie Spooner
Dramatic Company
Presents
"THE OCTOROON"
A Story of the Old South
SEE
The Murder of Weenie Paul
The Burning of the Steamer Magnolia
The Duel in the Swamp
The Death of Zoe, The Octoroon
Admission 30 — 20 cents
Children under ten — 10 cents
Tonight — Concert Hall — Tonight

The last line was printed in blue ink with a rubber hand-stamp.

By the time the rest of the company came dragging into the hall a half hour later, there was no lack of small boys at the foot of the main stairway to distribute the throwaways. It meant a free admission for them if they satisfied the manager that the bills went into mailboxes or around doorknobs and not down some convenient culvert. At that, the manager took no chances. He went along himself to see that the job was properly done.

Most of the male players doubled in brass as a band for the noon street parade and the evening concert before the theater, and those who could

The Octoroon

Since the big scene of *The Octoroon* was the burning of the Mississippi river packet *Magnolia* it was the standard display for the billboards of the presenting company. But any resemblance between the billing and the actual presentation was purely coincidental. For the *Magnolia* became a bit of the bow of the steamer protruding from an upstage wing, and the conflagration meant that red fire was burned on a shovel offstage instead of on a pie tin.

Harvard University Theater Collection

be spared furnished incidental music with piano, violin and perhaps a cornet. These makeshift orchestras were ever in a state of continuous flux, and a big cast of characters kept the musicians ducking back and forth and substituting to catch up on their cues. Necessarily there was no time to remove makeup so we thought nothing of it to hear the villain denounced and then, five minutes later, to find him rendering "Hearts and Flowers" on the piano while the luckless heroine, victim of his miscreancy, wandered the stage, forlorn and friendless.

With the parade formed and the small boys whipped into a semblance of order, there was just sufficient time for an opening march before the noon whistle emptied stores and factories and started the youngsters home from school. This noon parade was timed to catch the small fry, who were certain to lug a handbill home and add their importunities to the delights emblazoned on it.

Little reliance was placed in newspaper advertising. The two weeklies announced that the company was coming, that it was there, and that it had departed. Even *The Daily*, a short lived anemic tabloid of four pages, failed to do any better. After all, the editors argued, everybody knew the show was in town, so why talk about it? Besides, these people were strangers. What their readers wanted to be told was who had gone to Portage for the day or what legal business had summoned Attorney Michael E. Burke to the county seat at Juneau.

Besides the throwaways and word-of-mouth advertising, the most effective appeal was two three-sheets in front of the hall. Most everyone in Beaver Dam passed there during the day, and those who did not were too incapacitated by illness or age to be reckoned potential customers.

Chapter 4

HE INVENTED
THE DIAMOND DYE
SHOW

WHILE Steele MacKaye was reconditioning production methods in the east, small time produced a genius, who, in a minor way, was just as important. Clarence Bennett, of Anderson, Indiana, wrote *A Royal Slave* and because it had locations far removed from the standard house scenery of the country theater, he faced the probability of going broke lugging his production around the country.

All of these theaters had the same house scenery as Concert Hall. The ceiling was represented by unattractive strips of some neutral shade that masked the top of the stage. Later they hid the overhead lights but at that time illumination was furnished by the footlights and three bracket lamps at either side offstage. If a light on stage were called for, a kerosene lamp was used.

You might also find a property stump, a painted rock or two, a garden gate, a bit of fence, and a set of steps for a rundown from the front of the stage. There was a trap door stage center through which some unfortunate actor could disappear and battle suffocation until his cue released him. The ground cloths, one green and one brown, served all conditions, though the former was down most of the year.

Drops and set pieces painted on canvas required careful handling, were awkward to ship and ran up transportation. They went by express if the manager couldn't bribe a station agent to check them as baggage. Bulky and unwieldy, more often than not they showed up the worse for wear. The canvas, treated with a foundation of glue sizing, was painted with colors that were none too lasting and under wet weather and rough handling scenes were constantly peeling off. Curtains had to be carried on rollers to prevent cracking, and flats, though crated, were continually punched full of holes and had to be patched and repatched to last out the season.

Besides acting and playwriting, Bennett had a knack with the paint brush. He hit upon the idea of taking scrim and painting it with diamond dyes. These curtains could be folded and a half dozen trunks would carry enough settings for a week's engagement with a nightly change of bill and two matinees. Since a brilliant coloring stood out vividly under the weak kerosene lighting, the results were far more pleasing than the battered painted settings. Bennett's diamond dye scenery was as revolutionary in the small towns as Steele MacKaye's electric lighting was to Broadway, but Bennett obtained his effects of lighting without lights. Diamond dye stuff caught on quickly and before long the road companies blossomed out with elaborate productions. More than that, they added many plays that could not be attempted under the old system. "Productions in the realistic manner" marked the company as a diamond dye show.

Clarence Bennett came to the small time circuit with an apprenticeship labeled "He played with Booth." That an actor had "played with Booth" even then was a decrepit wheeze almost flatulently bereft of hot air. *Puck* and *Judge,* dominating the humorous magazines, devoted as much space to the ham actor as they did to the "Bah Jove" Dundrearyed English fop and the "By Gosh!" Yankee hayseed. Plug hatted, fur collared, broken shoed and rag tag, this cartoon down-and-outer, a caricature of Booth, counted the railroad ties through the magazines' pages, recounting past glories and trying to resemble the great tragedian.

Many a down-and-outer was a faker of the first rank, but many of them had really played with Booth. The stock company was universal when

Booth became a star, and each theater maintained players well up in the standard plays and possessing wardrobes for the parts they enacted. The visiting star brought only his own personal property and a manager to keep watch of the box office. A single rehearsal was considered sufficient to set up the performance and iron out any particular pet notions of the distinguished visitor. Any actor employed by one of the houses that Booth visited could honestly announce that he had "played with Booth," though his part may have consisted of a single line.

Bennett had earned substantial theatrical rating before he started out as a small time star. He had traveled the country with Booth and then branched out as Hamlet, Svengali, Monte Cristo and Mephistopheles in his own version of *Faust,* patterned after that of Lewis Morrison's who, in turn, had patterned his after that of Sir Henry Irving. Mrs. Bennett and her two daughters, Edna and Lydia Marshall, played with him. He became the producer of a half dozen different shows and "The Bennett Journal," a four page folder of personals and theatrical gossip, was mailed out to members of his companies. Joe and I got hold of one of these occasionally, but since the contents hugely extolled the virtues of the Bennett enterprises and of the people who worked for him, they were of little value to us. We were more interested in the plays than in those who played them.

Besides being the first diamond dye show, *A Royal Slave* certainly went to town in scenes and sensationalism. The slave was El Aguila, "Child of the Sun," of royal Aztec blood who, for some indefinite reason, was a faithful servitor in the family of the Countess de Oro, whose county seat overlooked the City of Mexico and Popocatepetl, which itself was no small feat, considering the size of the stage. Her daughter, Isadora, was pursued by Count Pedro Martinez, who fronted for a robber band as the mysterious "El Capitan." She was loved by Carlos Castillo, a lieutenant in the Mexican Army, and rescued from start to finish by the opportune El Aguila. All of this necessitated:

A—A whip and machete encounter between El Aguila and El Capitan.

B—A knife duel between El Capitan (a very busy man indeed) and Carlos, in which Carlos is treacherously stabbed.

C—A kidnaping of Isadora by El Capitan and the First and Second Murderers and the seizure of El Aguila (if anything, more busy than El Capitan).

D—The imprisonment of El Aguila who, despite fetters and leg irons, makes his escape after a hand-to-hand battle with his jailors; and

E—Swims through shark infested waters—killing one on the way to reach the island cave where Isadora is held; and

F—Cuts her free from the tree to which she is bound, kills the First Murderer, and throws his body to the sharks.

After which, "The Child of the Sun" rested until the final curtain, probably to ensure enough wind to pronounce a blessing upon the happy couple and to supervise the death of the villainess, who became lost in the shuffle early in the excitement but who succeeded in getting back in time to commit suicide at the final curtain.

Another popular diamond dye show was managed by William McConnell, who hailed from Chicago. He, too, was a graduate from the Booth ranks. His stock in trade was William Owen, a handsome young matinee idol, whose father of the same name was famous for his Falstaff and King Lear. McConnell was ever finding a new angel and blossoming out with a new show, carrying on hopefully until the funds were exhausted and the company headed back home.

McConnell went in for the classics, and his production of *Romeo and Juliet* was an eye opener to us youngsters who rated Shakespeare as something to be studied in school and laboriously committed to memory. That there was action and life to the story never entered our heads or if it did it failed to register enough to leave an iota of scar tissue. Joe and I were brought up on Sir John Gilbert's Shakespeare with woodcuts sowed through every page of the huge red volume. These went a long way toward infusing reality into the characters, but even at that, McConnell brought us a welcome surprise.

Romeo and Juliet came in the late spring close upon the start of summer vacation time. Cherry and apple trees were in bloom and the wooded river banks below Beaver Dam hung heavy with their fragrance. The day of the performance was spent in bringing in these pink-white laden boughs and building a leafy edging about the proscenium opening. In this framework of outdoor orchardry, the story of the two lovers of Verona never was told more effectively under such cramped circumstances.

The diamond dye backgrounds appeared more gorgeous to Joe and me than did the settings of Sothern and Marlowe and Mansfield at a later day. Camilla Reynolds was a Juliet to be worshipped from afar, William Owen a Romeo of dash and vigor, and McConnell contributed dignity as Friar Lawrence. Our disappointment came when we left the theater that night and hastened to our red-covered Gilbert only to find ourselves wrecked in a sea of words and quotations of the complete play. It was our first lesson in the necessity of tailoring a drama to meet the fashion of the day. Next season, when they returned with *The Three Guardsmen,* McConnell proved his ability as Cardinal Richelieu. Their theater trunks showed that the costumes were those used in the E. H. Sothern production, which smacked of big time stuff.

These rep companies were a great training for young actors. Jeanne Eagels came from Dubinsky Brothers' tent show. In fact, she married Morris Dubinsky, who played the heavy roles, and had a son by him. Long after, she came from Texas to upset Broadway in *Rain.* Charley Winninger was a mainstay of the Winninger Brothers Players. John Kelly quit his own little show to tie up with Harry Clay Blaney in shotgun melodramas, and

Uncle Tom's Cabin

When Eliza jumped from soap box to soap box fleeing her pursuers and the Great Danes masquerading as bloodhounds, *Uncle Tom's Cabin* got under way with a bang. And it ended with an explosion quite as tremendous when Simon Legree beat the living daylights out of poor old Uncle Tom and told them to "drag him out and throw him to the hogs."

New York Public Library Collection

Lenore Ulrich played Wisconsin small time before she made a hit in *The Bird of Paradise.*

In Bennett's companies, James Kirkwood mastered the fundamentals that carried him to *The Great Divide* and to Hollywood as a film star. Willard Mack picked up the trick of playwriting from Bennett and proved it with *Kick In, Tiger Rose* and a score of other plays. In one of the *Royal Slave* companies, Lulu McConnell learned enough to qualify for big time and radio.

McConnell had his fledglings, too. Guy Bates Post left him to become a star in *Omar the Tentmaker,* in which his leading lady was Louise Cook, another Winninger product. Lee Baker moved up to stock and to Broadway in *On Trial* and *Mourning Becomes Electra,* and Arthur Johnson went into Stair and Havlin melodrama and became the first recognized film star under David Wark Griffith with the old Biograph concern.

The list is endless. Some actors left the big time to produce rep shows. Some left rep shows for the big time. In each instance, the medium served its purpose well.

Chapter 5

"POOR OLD UNCLE TOM HE'S GONE"

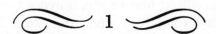

1

OF MY recollections of *Uncle Tom's Cabin* most vivid of all is the mule ridden by Lawyer Marks, since its image is etched upon my memory as indelibly as though planted there by the off hind foot of that ubiquitous animal.

This is not because mules were a rarity in my childhood, for there were many upon the farms that fringed the village; nor is it because the shyster and his patient jackass made a comedy duo in the street parade as did the circus clown and his infractious January. The reason is that any mule sufficiently gifted in histrionic arts to appear before the footlights had to be able to climb three flights of steep stairs unassisted. Somehow that ascent quite overshadowed the apotheosis of Little Eva.

Luring Marks' mule into the upper recesses of Concert Hall was the bright spot of Uncle Tom Day. The hour was seven-thirty when the band gave its open air concert before the evening's performance. Awaiting the event was a small mob of enthusiastic youngsters who cheered the progress of the beast and its caretaker—usually Marks himself—from Wade's Livery Stable around the corner where it had been undergoing a thorough de-hydrization against any untoward accident to mar the even tenor of the play.

Sometimes the unpredictable animal would barge into sight dragging its exasperated keeper like a land-going sea anchor. More often, though, Marks hove into view hauling his recalcitrant charge by main strength. In either instance, the event became the occasion for loud cheering and the ribald comment that only small boys can devise.

In one way or another, the main entrance was reached and the pair faced the first long flight, looking the steeper because of the narrow treads of the stairs. There it remained for Marks to take a strategic position in the rear, retaining a firm grip on the halter rope. Doubling into an accordian pleating, the mule would rest its rump affectionately upon Marks' shoulder while it viewed the fearsome prospect with terror whitened eyes.

Encouraged by enthusiastic suggestions from his ardent spectators, one or two of whom might lend a hand upon occasion, Marks would brace his legs and throw himself forward in one gigantic push. The effect upon the mule was comparable only to that of the discharge of a jet bomb. Up the stairs in full flight the animal would spring, Marks skimming after with agile bounding that permitted him to touch every fourth step.

Man and beast reached the top in utter exhaustion. There was a pause to regain wind and strength. A short flight at the right led to a turn in the stairway. Here was a simpler procedure. Hanging on to the rope's end, Marks climbed to the landing. Leaving the sanctity of the box-office, the company manager would sneak up from behind, plant a stupendous kick upon the mule's rear; and on the instant, the surprised animal would find the space negotiated.

The final lap was a repetition of the first, sans small boys, but with the ticket taker, Grandfather and Uncle Bee to assist. And once the hall was reached, the triumphant pair meandered among the early comers down the center aisle to rest from their labors in the privacy of the dressing room.

Often though I saw the ascent of Marks' mule to the upper regions, I was never blessed with a view of its descent to terra firma. Uncle Bee confided to me that Legree had to carry it down on his back for being so mean to poor old Uncle Tom. As to that I wouldn't know, for by the time I was old enough to hang about after the final curtain, *Uncle Tom's Cabin* had become a tent show, and the mule browsed contentedly in the backyard until summoned to the stage.

2

There are no Uncle Tom shows now. From time to time, sporadic attempts are made to resuscitate the old play and infuse new life into its moribund carcass. But that strange race of actors known as "Uncle Tommers" like old soldiers have faded away, and their few survivors are lost in the ranks of Hollywood's extras.

The last of the dyed-in-the-wool Uncle Tom troupes closed down in a little Pennsylvania town in the summer of 1931. Its passing was quite in accord with the best traditions of a tent show.

It rained. In fact, it deluged to such an extent that the lighting system failed to function. Then the mongrel enacting the pack of ferocious bloodhounds became peeved at one thing or another, bit a chunk out of Phineas Fletcher and vanished rapidly into outer darkness, never again to be seen. Lawyer Marks developed a bad case of quinsy and George Harris was obliged to double for him. Legree lost his whip, Uncle Tom lost his wig, and when it was found that there were more people on the stage than in the audience, the sheriff plastered a summons on the show and took the gate receipts.

It is sad to note that Uncle Tom, in such sad fashion, went the way of all dramatic flesh. For of all entertainment typically American, but two smack of the soil: one is the black face minstrel show; the other is *Uncle Tom's Cabin.*

For the "Tommers," as they were known, were a race of actors apart. Like members of the circus profession, they were born into a charmed circle, lived within it and died within it. They were not actors in the general sense of the word. They knew nothing and cared less for the finer phrases of Shakespeare, the scintillating wit of Solon Shingle, or the melodramas of Dion Boucicault or George R. Sims. Occasionally a repertory company might include "Uncle Tom" in its week's change of bill but those performances fell flat. You had to be a Tommer to play *Uncle Tom's Cabin.*

A "Tommer" never played anything but a Tom show. A girl started as Little Eva. If it was a boy, they clapped a blond wig on him and nobody was the wiser. A feminine Little Eva graduated into Topsy. When the demands of this part became too exacting, she might become Eliza, or Mrs. St. Clair, or Aunt Ophelia, depending upon physique and countenance. Or if she was very bad, they made her play Cassy.

With the stronger sex, it was different. Each man must be up in several parts and double in brass. Brought up with the bloodhounds and the pony which Little Eva drove in the street parade and right across the stage upon her first entrance, they learned their parts along with their A-B-C's. So when they came to young manhood, they were promoted to the dignity of a half-dozen roles and became dyed-in-the-wool Tommers.

Legree, of course, was a fixture. So were Uncle Tom and Lawyer Marks. But the remainder differed according to the exigencies of time and place. A player might be George Harris one night and at the next stand chase Eliza across the ice or stand in the wings and help the bloodhounds bay.

As time went on, various versions outcropped, and in the years which passed after Harriet Beecher Stowe's tearjerker was put into dramatized form, scripts were forgotten. You can buy printed copies from play publishing companies, and these are in demand for amateur performances. But I wonder if any company of "Tommers" ever rehearsed in any fashion other than by going into a huddle. Each player knew one or more of the differing versions; so when the company assembled for the first time, a compromise was made of the various parts and a new version of *Uncle Tom's Cabin* became a reality.

Just as an example, one of these followed the book. When Uncle Tom was found succumbing to the lashings of Simon Legree, his young master retaliated by knocking the brutal overseer to the floor. In time, however, this became too commonplace. Virtue must be rewarded and sin must pay the extreme penalty. So, at the crucial moment, in walked Lawyer Marks.

"What shall we do with the body?" was his question.

"Take him out and throw him to the hawgs," was Legree's sneering reply.

Whereupon Lawyer Marks produced an ancient horse-pistol, examined it carefully, shot Legree neatly and thoroughly, and watched him writhe in agony.

"Take him out and throw him to the hawgs," the little shyster returned.

And as the kind young master knelt by the dying Tom, the curtain fell amid frenzied cheers.

When this time-honored method was disregarded an entirely new ending originated. William A. Brady made an all-star revival of the show in New York City in 1901. Wilton Lackaye and John E. Kellerd alternated as Uncle Tom, and Theodore Roberts was Legree. Roberts, one of the truly great actors of the American stage, decided to die by being hit over the head with a whiskey bottle. A bottle made of a tar composition was filled with blood mixture and the villainous old reprobate was felled realistically, his brains oozing over his face.

Uncle Tom's Cabin

Probably the most elaborate production ever made of Harriet Beecher Stowe's anti-slavery story was the one staged on Broadway in the Academy of Music by William A. Brady in 1901. Though there were a dozen or more Uncle Tom shows traipsing around the country, the astute Brady decided that New York's sophisticates and visiting firemen would like to see the old tear jerker with an all star cast and a super-colossal production.

For Simon Legree, Brady picked Theodore Roberts, one of America's truly great character actors. Roberts made up Legree as a red-headed, broken-nosed, scarfaced thug in direct contrast to the established stage character with the black goatee and flowing hair. He socked poor Tom over the noggin with his whip handle at the conclusion of the flogging, and met his own death when Mark hit him over the head with a whiskey bottle.

Poor Old Tom alternated between Wilton Lackaye and John E. Kellerd. Lackaye was an established star who created Svengali in the American production of Trilby. Kellerd was a standout as the drunken sergeant in *The Heart of Maryland,* in which Mrs. Leslie Carter gained her first real recognition under David Belasco's banner. Later Kellerd was to go on to establish an all time Broadway run in *Hamlet.* He played the part for 102 consecutive performances, topping John Barrymore's 101 as Barrymore had topped Edwin Booth's 100 presentations. And the Ghost in Kellerd's company was Theodore Roberts who made it his last Broadway role before journeying to Hollywood and film fame.

Maud Raymond was Topsy, Annie Yeamans was Ophelia, and Agnes Ethel was Little Eva. There were 200 singers and dancers to add the necessary plantation atmosphere, and after a successful run at the Academy of Music, the show went on to Chicago, where it was just as successful.

The flogging scene shows Roberts giving the works to Lackaye while an unnamed slave watches the proceedings. Probably she was Chloe.

Theodore Roberts as Simon Legree

Roberts confided to me in after years that he was sorry he ever thought up the stunt. He trusted no one to make the bottles, so during the run most of his spare time was devoted to fashioning these properties to attain the best theatrical results with the least personal danger and discomfort.

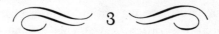

Whether they came to Concert Hall or worked under canvas, the Uncle Tommers could be depended upon to give a totally different version of the play upon each occasion. No two productions ever were identical, nor were the lines of the actors ever the same.

Naturally there were certain trade-marks that never varied such as Topsy's "Golly, I'se so wicked!"; Miss Ophelia's "How shiftless!" and Marks' repetitious "I'm a lawyer and my name is Marks! Have a card!" And certainly none would ever dare to improve upon Legree's "Tom, I've made up my mind to kill you," though Joe and I agreed that it was an expensive gesture for one so to vent his spite upon an obdurate parcel of human property. But perhaps we fell short in our estimate of the theatrical niceties or maybe our innate Yankee thriftiness overbalanced our otherwise calm judgment of the drama. For there the speech was and there it stayed so long as Legree continued a menace to all blacks, be they slave or freed men.

Finally there was Uncle Tom's declaration of principles: "My soul ain't yours, massa! It's been bought and paid for by one that is able to keep it and you can't have it!"

But for these exceptions, anything was likely to happen and generally did. One Gumption Cute decked himself in a Happy Hooligan disguise, tin can, splay feet and all. But we learned that he was only a refugee from a vaudeville chain gang who lasted less than a week. Uncle Tommers were a clanny lot and their circle was as hard to break as that of any labor union. This made more remarkable the achievement of Charles Brickwood. For years Brickwood played Marks on the Wetherell and Dowd Show. His real name was Charles Brickett and he hailed from Haverhill, Mass. From his youth, he was interested in amateur dramatics and he renounced the law to follow bloodhounds and mule. The remarkable part of it all is that Brickett was a Harvard graduate—the only one to be entered in the records of his alma mater as an exponent of Uncle Tomming.

The best remembered versions of the play opened with Eliza pounding on the door of Uncle Tom's cabin, her boy, Harry, in her arms. Shelby had sold Harry and Tom to Haley, the slave trader, but Tom refused to run away. In a river tavern, Phineas Fletcher stalled her pursuers while she climbed through a window. And then Eliza crossed the ice, leaping from soap box to soap box against the wood backdrop while a pair of uninterested Great Danes loped after her dispiritedly. Great Danes always doubled for bloodhounds since their presence was far more convincing than those flop-eared pooches who looked about as savage as a friendly beagle.

This cutting of the play possessed three advantages: the cabin was introduced at the first curtain; Eliza's escape started things off with a bang; and since little Harry had no speeches, a child actor was eliminated and Eliza lugged an overstuffed doll in her arms.

The next high spot came with the escape of George Harris and his family. It gave Phineas Fletcher his big opportunity, too. By this time his love for a Quaker lass had bedecked him in pigeon gray and by some occult means had refashioned his speech into something never spoken anywhere beneath this sun. Yet his expression of pacificism and threats always evoked unstinted applause.

"I don't want to involve anyone," George told him. "If you will lend me your vehicle and direct me, I will drive alone to the next stand."

"I cannot say if thee can get a vehicle," Phineas would reply. "Or any other kind of ve-ho-cle. But I will be glad to carry you thither in a carriage. Yea-a-a! Veri-lee! Veri-li! Veri-low! Veri-lum! Veri-low!"

And when Eliza, the child in her arms, perched atop a kitchen table disguised as a boulder, George hurled his defiance at Loker and Marks.

"We have arms to defend ourselves and we mean to do it. The first one that comes within range of our bullets is a dead man."

"Pistols and bullets and firearms have I none," Phineas contributed. "And fighting is unbecoming a regenerated man. But if worst comes to worst, this right hand is sudden death and this left hand is six weeks in the hospital. Yea! Veri-lee! Veri-li! Veri-low! Veri-lum! Veri-low!"

The applause was deafening when Marks cowered behind his open umbrella on the O.P. side while the redoubtable Phineas threw Haley bodily into the wings with the explanation:

"Friend, thee is not wanted here! Yea! Veri-lee! Veri-li! Veri-low! Veri—"

(Curtain)

Tom's scenes with Little Eva, we both passed over lightly as we did others without Ophelia, Topsy or Marks. These went by the boards while we

Word and Music by G. C. HOWARD.

"Oh! I'se So Wicked!"

When George Aiken dramatized *Uncle Tom's Cabin* for the G. C. Howard players at the Troy (N. Y.) Museum, the part of Topsy was played by Mrs. Howard. For his wife, Howard wrote this song retailing the story of the "little black imp." It was sung not only by Mrs. Howard but by many another Topsy who followed after her.

waited for the whipping scene. Marks' declaration and Tom's reply brought the blacksnake into action. Tom held his hands high above his head while Legree belabored him about the waist where the padding was thickest—once—twice—three times. Never more and never less. From this abuse, Tom collapsed on the stage and Legree socked him over the head with his whip-handle. Thus poor old Uncle Tom was ready to assist in the grand transformation scene.

Repeated viewings of the play convinced Joe and me that ante-bellum society, high or low, held an international record for hasty demises. Its members announced that they were about to die and then made good their promise with a minimum of delay and bother. Little Eva's death, long one of the high spots, was a mere flash in the pan once you broke it down. Little Eva lay upon a sofa brought for the occasion from McKinstry's Furniture Store. Uncle Tom knelt at the foot. Ophelia stood at the head. St. Clare was behind it. Entered Cousin Marie.

MARIE
St. Clare! Cousin! Oh, What is the matter now?

ST. CLARE *(hoarsely)*
Hush! She is dying!

MARIE *(sinking on her knees beside Tom)*
Dying!

ST. CLARE *(bending over her)*
Oh, if she would only wake up and speak once more. Eva!
(Eva uncloses her eyes, raises her head and tries to speak.)
Do you know me, Eva?

EVA *(throwing her arms feebly about his neck)*
Dear papa!

(Her arms drop and she sinks back)

ST. CLARE
Oh, heaven! This is dreadful! Oh, Tom, my boy, it is killing me!

TOM *(points to Eva)*
Look at her, massa.

ST. CLARE
Eva! She does not hear! Oh, Eva! Tell us what you see? What is it?

EVA (*feebly smiling*)

Oh! Love! Joy! Peace!

(*She dies*)

TOM

Oh, bless the Lord! It's over, dear massa, it's over!

ST. CLARE (*sinking on his knees*)

Farewell, beloved child! The bright eternal doors have closed after thee! We shall see thy sweet face no more! Oh! Woe for them who watched thy entrance into heaven when they shall awake and find only the cold, gray sky of daily life and thou gone forever.

(*Solemn music. Curtain*)

St. Clare's end was still more abrupt. Ophelia, Topsy, and, of course, the ubiquitous Tom clustered about him as he sat on the McKinstry sofa. Legree had stabbed him in a barroom brawl.

ST. CLARE

Tom—poor fellow!

TOM

Well, massa?

ST. CLARE

I have received my death wound.

TOM

Oh, no, no, massa!

ST. CLARE

I feel that I am dying. Tom—pray!

TOM (*sinking on his knees*)

I do pray, massa! I do pray!

ST. CLARE

Tom, one thing preys upon my mind. I have forgotten to sign your freedom papers. What will become of you?

TOM

Don't think of that, massa.

ST. CLARE

I was wrong, Tom, very wrong to neglect it. I may be the cause of much suffering to you hereafter. Marie—my wife—she—oh—

OPHELIA

His mind is wandering.

ST. CLARE

No! It is coming home at last! At last! At last! Eva! I come!

(*Dies to slow music. Curtain*)

Tom rounded out the death toll, since by this time Marks had disposed of Legree, and his was the most extravagant death scene of all. George Harris, who had changed his hat and clapped on a mustache to become George Shelby, showed up prepared to take the poor old slave back home.

TOM (*on the floor*)

Massa George! Bless de Lord! It's all I wanted! They haven't forgot me! It warms my soul! It does my old heart good! Now I shall die content!

GEORGE (*kneeling beside him*)

You shan't die! You mustn't die! Nor think of it! I have come to buy you and take you home!

TOM

Oh, Massa George, you're too late. The Lord has bought me and is going to take me home.

GEORGE

Oh, don't die! It will kill me! It will break my heart! To think what you have suffered, poor fellow!

TOM

Don't call me poor fellow. I have been poor fellow but that's all past and gone now. I'm right in the door, going into glory! Oh, Massa George, Heaven has come! I've got the victory! The Lord has given it to me! Glory be to his name!

(*Dies*)

GEORGE

Poor old Uncle Tom—he's gone!

(*Curtain*)

No matter how tawdry the production, every Tom show carried an allegory. Its cheapest form was a backdrop with its center painted upon scrim that faded out when lighted from behind. More often than not, Little Eva climbed a stepladder, spread her angelic robes to cover it and extended her arms in benediction toward Tom and George. Red fire was burned on a shovel beside her while offstage the company raised its voices in:

The poor old slave has gone to rest,
We know that he is free;
Disturb him not but let him rest
Way down in Tennessee.

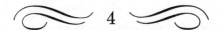

4

In the days when I wept with the St. Clares at the bedside of Little Eva and exulted when the unspeakable Legree got his lumps, it never entered my head that someday I might meet the collaborator of the play and learn of its writing from one of the authors. Though the Civil War still was a reality—aged veterans wobbled into Grandfather's office for pension examinations—and though Grandmother spoke familiarly of Harriet Beecher Stowe, who had lectured at Concert Hall, the play itself remained a thing quite apart from the humdrum of every day. It possessed the unreality of makebelieve as did any fairy story that, like Topsy, just grew through repetition.

Arch Street Theater, Philadelphia

Where Mrs. John Drew and Her Family Played for Years.

When I did meet him I found a gentleman of the old school who treated me with a courtliness worthy of St. Clare himself—an actor rounding out his career in a production which I heralded as a bumptious press agent. He was Frank E. Aiken, who, as a stripling, collaborated with his brother George in the first real dramatization of the Stowe book. Cast as John Marshall Glenarm in *The House of A Thousand Candles* in support of E. M. Holland, Aiken appeared briefly in the last act. So he found plenty of time to tell of the days before he was playing leads with the Boston Stock Company and at Mrs. John Drew's Arch Street Theater in Philadelphia, or starred in *Peep o' Day*, or played the Earl with Elsie Leslie in the original production of *Little Lord Fauntleroy*.

A distinct literary tinge colored the boys of the Aiken family. One brother, A. W. Aiken, wrote dime novels for Erastus Beadle. Another, George L., was a member of the George C. Howard players at the Troy (New York) Museum. His contract with Howard was similar to the arrangement entered into by and between Mr. Vincent Crummles and Nicholas Nickleby. George did juvenile business and adapted plays to suit the company, as, when and where the management demanded. And as luck would have it, seventeen-year-old Frank visited Brother George in Troy in the summer of 1852.

The Howard company was largely a family affair: Howard, his wife, and his daughter Cordelia; Mrs. Emily Fox and her son George; Mrs. Howard's mother and brother; and George Aiken, Mrs. Fox's nephew. Howard was looking for an opportunity to feature his precocious four-year-old, quite as Vincent Crummles tooted the horn for the Infant Phenemenom. *Uncle Tom's Cabin* was the talk of the nation and Eva, the angel child, offered a perfect part for little Cordelia. Aiken was commissioned to fashion a vehicle with the child interest played to the limit. There were no restrictions in dramatizing the book since no copyright protection had been arranged. The cost was the two volumes in which it first appeared between covers, its only illustration a woodcut of a Negro cabin as a frontispiece.

George and Frank took the two volumes to their boarding house and set to work. It was a tremendous undertaking, for the plot was discursive and the characters were multitudinous. A reading convinced them that there would be plenty of action if they ended the drama with the death of Little Eva. This would build up to the stellar climax Howard desired for his daughter. There was need for doubling also since the characters of the book far outnumbered the members of the company. Together the Aiken boys ground it out and Howard called the company for a first reading. And then the trouble began.

In those ante-bellum days, the play was a radical experiment. The previous month Charles W. Taylor had produced his version of the book at Purdy's National Theater in New York. But to do this, he had eliminated Topsy and Eva and had rewritten the story beyond recognition. It lasted eleven nights. Now the proposition of idealizing a Negro on the stage became a bone of contention.

Green C. Germon, the leading man, naturally was cast as Uncle Tom, while to Mrs. Germon was assigned the role of Topsy. They argued that the Negro never had been portrayed upon the stage except in minstrel form and that the appearance of a "cork-face" would be a signal for laughter. Howard argued and begged, entreated and pleaded. He pointed out the inadvisability of casting a Negro for the role. The part demanded sympathetic acting and must be put across to score. Germon reluctantly consented to try it. Until his death, he appeared in no other character.

Mrs. Germon on the other hand was obdurate. Entreaties proved unavailing and in desperation, Howard turned to his wife.

"Will you play the part?" he asked.

"I will," she unhesitatingly said, to the surprise of all.

She did more, for, padded and gray bewigged, she doubled as Old Chloe in the first act. So great was her success that she played the part until she retired from the stage thirty-five years later. Mrs. Germon settled for Eliza and Cassy and soon passed from the picture.

Quite by chance Frank Aiken was called upon to play Marks. The little shyster is only a minor character in the book and in this first version of the play he appeared more as a feeder for the fat parts than for any other purpose. Though still in his teens, Frank's bent for stagecraft was evidenced in his collaboration, and when George suggested him to Howard, the manager handed him the part, overjoyed to make an end to his nightmare of casting.

The play was produced in the Troy Museum on Sept. 27, 1852, and to George L. Aiken was attributed the sole authorship. It was a success but all agreed that something was lacking. Particularly critical was John Davis, cast as Simon Legree and Haley. Fresh from reading the book, Davis argued that the conflict was between Tom and Legree and the plot should continue to the death of both. Howard saw the light. The Aiken brothers set to work again and turned out two acts more to complete the script as it finally was presented at Purdy's National Theater, in New York City, on July 8, 1853.

Aiken took advantage of his family connections to build up the part of

Marks with every performance. By the time the play moved to New York, the role was well shaped for an actor named Herbert to take over. But it was long before a mule became an intrinsic part of Marks' act, nor did baying Great Danes pursue Eliza in her frantic flight until 1879, when some forgotten genius was inspired to outfit the production with livestock.

Frank dropped out at the end of the summer to pursue his later stage career elsewhere. So, too, did C. Leslie Allen, father of Viola Allen, who created Shelby; and W. J. Lemoyne, long a Broadway favorite, who originated Mr. Wilson and Deacon Perry. But the Howards and Green Germon went on to Broadway, where George Fox was added to the cast. He was to be remembered not as Gumption Cute but as the Humpty Dumpty of all time.

Cordelia Howard outgrew the part of Little Eva in eight years and gave up the stage for good. But her mother continued as Topsy, and her father took to the role of St. Clare so realistically that he played him, on stage and off, for the rest of his life. His entrance into a hotel with cane, tall hat and fancy vest, immaculate stock and bestrapped pantaloons, was the best advertisement the old show ever could ask.

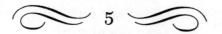

5

When the singing Hutchinson Family was traipsing the country dispensing abolition and temperance through their harmonizing, Brother John Hutchinson wrote to Mrs. Stowe for permission to dramatize her book. Her reply is a classic.

"I have considered your application and asked advice of my different friends," she wrote. "The general sentiment of those whom I have consulted so far agrees with my own, that it would not be advisable to make that use of my work that you propose. It is thought, with the present state of theatrical performances in this country, that any attempt on the part of Christians to identify themselves with them will be productive of danger to the individual character and to the general cause.

"If the barrier which now keeps young people of Christian families from theatrical entertainments is once broken down by the introduction of respectable and moral plays, they will then be open to all the temptations of those which are not sure, and there will be, as the world now is, five bad plays to one good.

"However specious may be the idea of reforming dramatic amusements, I fear it is wholly impracticable, and, as a friend to you, should hope that you would not run the risk of so dangerous an experiment. The world is not good enough yet for it to succeed.

"I preserve a very pleasant recollection of your family and of the gratification I have derived from the exercise of your talents, and it gives me great pleasure to number you among my friends."

Mrs. Stowe never received a penny for her dramatic rights to *Uncle Tom's Cabin*. Howard gave George Aiken a gold watch for his work of

The Colleen Bawn

Beset upon but forgiving was poor Eily O'Connor, the Colleen Bawn of Dion Boucicault's dramatization of Gerald Griffin's story, *The Collegians*. Written for Laura Keane, it was soon picked up by small time troupers who offered it under a number of names, the most popular of which was *Kathleen Mavourneen*.

Hardress Cregan has married the Colleen Bawn in a secret ceremony, since Eily is a poor uneducated peasant girl whose attractions are her overwhelming beauty and indomitable virtue. Mrs. Cregan is on the verge of bankruptcy and Mr. Corrigan, a pettyfogging attorney, is ready to take over Torc Cregan on the banks of Killarney unless the old lady is prepared to marry him. But Mrs. Cregan has other ideas. She'll marry Hardress to Anne Chute, the Colleen Ruaidh, who has lots of money and isn't hard to look at.

Hardress is attended by Danny Mann, a hunchbacked servant, who is ready to do anything to help Hardress. Eily has promised good Father Tom, the parish priest of Garryowen, that she will never surrender her marriage certificate which Hardress decides he must have. Under stage law destruction of a marriage certificate apparently nullifies the ceremony. So Eily fights tooth and nail to prove herself an honest wife and not a maid betrayed.

There's the comic relief in Myles-Na-Coppaleen, a poacher and moonshiner, who keeps the countryside supplied with fish and potheen. All else failing, Danny lures Eily to a rocky cave at the lakeside and when she refuses to give up her marriage papers, throws her into the water to drown. But Myles has a hideout in a cave above, and mistaking Danny for an otter, he shoots him. Then he rescues Eily, and Danny dies, and Hardress tells the truth, and everything ends happily except it's not quite evident why the scoundrelly Corrigan didn't foreclose his mortgage on good old Torc Cregan on the banks of the Killarney.

"Save me. Don't kill me. Don't, Danny. I'll do anything only let me live."

Harvard University Theater Collection

dramatizing it. Frank Aiken received no credit for his part in the writing, but the experience started him on a stage career. Nor could any of them anticipate that for seventy-eight years, *Uncle Tom's Cabin, or Life Among the Lowly* would be played in every nook and corner of this country, advertised as "Moral, Instructive and Educational" by a company of seven people, cleverly doubling in the parts, and a "Troupe of Genuine Siberian Bloodhounds."

Joe and I raised the question as to how Mrs. Stowe ever came about attributing the philosophy and characteristics of Uncle Tom to an uneducated plantation hand. But as usual Uncle Bee had a ready explanation.

"She just took her brother, Henry Ward Beecher, blacked him up and put a white wig on him," he said.

And perhaps Uncle Bee was right after all.

Chapter 6

"A SET OF PARLOR FURNITURE GIVEN AWAY SATURDAY NIGHT"

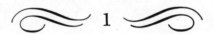

1

T IS a simple matter today to look back upon those old plays and dismiss them with a patronizing smile as something stilted and unreal, conceived in puerility and born in inanity. Yet each decade has its accepted drama form. Construction and interpretation quickly become adolescent and outdated much as a man of thirty wonders how he could have been such an unmitigated ass fifteen years before.

These plays reflected the time's tempo. They followed a set form since, for the greater part, they were written for a touring star supported by a permanent stock company or for one of the stock companies such as was maintained by Augustin Daly or A. M. Palmer or the upstart Frohmans in New York. Dion Boucicault had started the first touring company in 1860 when he sent *Colleen Bawn* on the road. But the stock-star system hung doggedly on until the eighties and quit then only because players of the stature of Booth and Barrett took to the road with shows of their own.

It was a period of emotions rather than reason. Problem plays were few and far between, at least in our territory; and even such mild themes as *The Wife, Men and Women* and *The Charity Ball* were safe from molestation by rep managers. Their audiences demanded something of the strong, simple school. The hero must win against all chances. The villain must get his bumps and the heroine must protect her virtue against all comers, though equipped with no more spirit than a mouse with a cold.

The plays that came to us were shaped in this mould and picked to entertain such a clientele. Beaver Dam was founded in 1842 and the heads of its substantial families cleared the ground and made their modest fortunes there. Many had lived no adventure other than the comparatively simple task of breaking in a new soil and dickering with half-civilized Indians bereft of their legendary traits in the pursuit of idleness and fire-water.

Dodge City and Tombstone were familiar to many of these old timers. Most of them had fought through one or two wars, and a few had survived Andersonville and Libby prisons. Lately laid in his grave, Jesse James was a current celebrity some had taken by the hand, and the Dalton gang still rode the railroad right-of-way and held up the midnight limited. On a sortie to the west, Grandfather Babcock, by a slim chance, escaped death at the Benders' notorious axe, while Grandfather Hoyt headed a caravan of a hundred Conestoga wagons from St. Joe to the California gold fields in forty-nine.

With only two daily trains on a spur line, and with the telephone more or less discredited, our mores changed slowly and painfully. Children and grandchildren were tailored to the family pattern. A play's motivation is conflict, be it spiritual, or mental or physical, and these good people demanded something with which they were familiar and which carried a wallop as well. So they enjoyed violent action with the best man winning honestly and without subterfuge. That he always was the hero was purely coincidental. Fisticuffs or gunplay it might be if only on the up-and-up. Underhanded tactics invariably must bounce back upon the perpetrator; and in strategy, right always must outmaneuver the wicked.

Few of these plays were taken seriously. Far from it, they were enjoyed as the development of an exciting narrative just as one takes up a modern whodunit or as we youngsters were wont to dip surreptitiously into "Old

Sleuth" or "Nick Carter." They furnished relaxation and an escape from realities when magazines were few and costly, and they were a welcome change from the standardized wordy novels of Dickens and Scott, which we knew by heart from repeated perusal.

Nor do I mean that all of these plays depended upon mayhem and murder. Some in a gentler vein were *Rip Van Winkle* and *Fanchon the Cricket; East Lynne* and *Hazel Kirke; Little Lord Fauntleroy* and *The Hidden Hand;* and *The Dep'ty Sheriff* and *Our American Cousin;* or *Our Boys, Still Waters Run Deep, The Phoenix* and *The Silver King. The Phoenix* had its catch line "And the villain still pursued her," and *The Silver King* had Wilfred Denver's agonized prayer: "Oh, God! Put back Thy universe and give me yesterday."

To Oblige Benson was another, and *The Lancashire Lass,* and *The Daughter of the Regiment.* One of the goriest was *The Artful Dodger,* a dramatization of *Oliver Twist,* where Nancy Sikes, beaten to death by her paramour, crept to the footlights the better to display her battered countenance and to expire amid gasps and sobs. That it was Dickens and therefore approved literature was all that saved it from churchly condemnation.

There were any number of Irish plays, Boucicault's *The Shaughraun* and *Robert Emmet* among them. There was history in the latter and the good Irish folk packed the house to hear the famous death speech:

> My Lords, as to why judgment of death and execution should not be passed upon me according to the law, I have nothing to say. But as to why my character should not be relieved from the imputations and calumnies thrown out against it, I have much to say. I should bow in silence to the fate that awaits me. But the sentence of the law which delivers my body over to the executioner consigns my character to obloquy.
>
> Let no man write my epitaph. For as no man who knows my motives now dares vindicate them, let not prejudice or ignorance asperse them. Let them rest in obscurity and peace. Let my memory be left in oblivion, and my tomb remain uninscribed, until other times and other men can do justice to my character.
>
> When my country takes her place among the nations of the earth, then, and not till then, let my epitaph be written.

Each company stuck pretty closely to its own repertory season after season. The Hattie Irving Comedy Company starred the soubrette in *A Mountain Pink, Fanchon the Cricket, Fun in a Boarding School, Life Among the Mountains, Dot the Waif, Peck's Bad Boy* and *That Boy of*

Dan's. The Switzer Comedy Company, with Nina Richie and Jule F. Switzer, offered *The Danites, My Partner, Kathleen Mavourneen, The Silver King, Black Diamonds, East Lynne, Peril, Divorce, Hazel Kirke, Over the Hills to the Poor House* (Will Carleton's poem was being sobbed even then by amateur elocutionists), and *Ten Nights in a Bar-Room.*

The Harry F. Adams Dramatic Co., headed by Harry A. Ellis and Mrs. Freddie Bookman, gave us *Paradise Lost, The Daughter of the Regiment, The Artful Dodger, Monte Cristo, Lost in London* and *The Phoenix.* The Noble Dramatic Co. purveyed *Mixed Pickles, Storm Beaten, Lucky Ranch, Robert Emmet* and *Passion's Slave.* The Buchanan Comedy Co. saw to it that we were made intimate with *The Shaughraun, Our Bachelors, Lost in London,* and *Cross Roads;* while the Wilson Theater Co., boldly proclaiming its dramatic intent, staged *A Great Wrong, Deeds and Dollars, A Celebrated Case, The Two Orphans, Queen's Evidence* and *A Galley Slave.*

These plays were typical of the sort brought to us. In the east Belasco and DeMille, and James A. Herne were blazing a new trail in American drama.

During most of his career, Belasco continued a melodramatist. His early training included service as Dion Boucicault's secretary and he never quite divorced himself from the influence of that prolific Irishman. He worked with Herne to transform *The Mariner's Compass* into *Hearts of Oak.* It was a success but it ended their professional partnership.

Herne started the naturalistic trend with *Shore Acres,* and a real dinner served on the stage, which set the pace for a flock of rural drama from *Way Down East* and *The Old Homestead* to Langdon McCormack's *Out of the Fold.* Belasco lifted melodrama to new heights with *The Girl I Left Behind Me;* and by transmuting "Curfew Shall Not Ring Tonight" into *The Heart of Maryland,* crowning his series with *The Girl of the Golden West* and *The Son Daughter,* big time stuff but still old school melodrama, Belasco made money. Herne, a serious and an abler playwright by far, withered on the dramatic vine, never attaining full maturity with the theater going public.

And after them came Augustus Thomas, who started with *Alabama* and progressed to *The Witching Hour;* and Bronson Howard, with *Shenandoah* and *Saratoga;* and William Gillette, and Clyde Fitch, and all those other young Americans who made our stage their own.

Gradually our bills changed in Beaver Dam and plays took a metropolitan tinge. Rep managers brought Broadway productions when they were handed over for stock use, advertised them under their true names, and even paid royalties for the right to produce them.

But Concert Hall had long since passed by then, and Music Hall was a movie house, and Charley Davison, who was to become an honored and dignified judge, had promoted a theater devoted to the drama and measuring up more than adequately to the demands made upon it.

Oliver Twist

Some of the old melodramas were steeped in enough blood to satisfy even the most enthusiastic disciple of Mickey Spillane. But none was more gory than the popular dramatization of Charles Dickens' *Oliver Twist*. The good country folk might insist that they went because the book was a classic and because the story of poor Oliver was something to weep over. But the truth was they were there to witness the enactment of as cold-blooded and brutal a murder as was ever staged.

The misadventures of ill-starred Oliver were emphasized at the start of the play, but before long Bill Sikes and his woman Nancy shared the spotlight with despicable Fagin. Nancy contacted Mr. Brownlow with information concerning Oliver, and Noah Claypole, spying upon her, promptly reported back to Sikes and Fagin. Sikes comes to the ill-kept room where he and Nancy live. Nancy is in bed and Sikes wakes her.

SIKES

Nance! Nance! Every word was heard.

NANCY

I never said a word against you. (*He drags her from the bed*)
I never said a word agin you, Bill. I swear it. (*They struggle*)
Before the Lord I swear it! (*He seizes her*)
What are you trying to do to me? (*She rushes to the window*)
Help! Watch! Murder! Police! Help! (*Sikes grabs her by the hair, drags her to the center of the stage, throws her down and beats her head upon the floor. Screams and curses. Nancy wrenches herself free and rushes off stage to the next room. Sikes follows.*)

NANCY

Don't do it, Bill! Please don't do it! I never said a thing! Please! Please! (*A blow. A loud scream. Another blow. Another scream. Another blow. A groan. A heavy fall. A faint moan. Silence.*)
(*Sikes backs into the room, glaring back. His hands are red with blood. He stares at them in a daze, backing toward the footlights. Nancy creeps into the room on her hands and knees. Her face is covered with blood. She falls full length, reaching toward Sikes, and creeps up to him, inching along until she touches his feet.*)

NANCY

Bill! It's dark here! Light me a candle and then run for your life! I love you, Bill, I love you. If only I knew how to pray! I didn't say a—(*She drops forward on her hands. Blood gushes from her mouth. She falls flat, and Sikes rushes from the room.*)

There were great gouts of blood and acts of extreme cruelty in many of the old plays but none surpassed this scene. Perhaps that was why *Oliver Twist* was given so infrequently. In many houses it was the practice to put down a square of oil cloth where Nancy died. Grandfather favored this, for it saved the ground cloth from the stains of blood mixture.

Harvard University Theater Collection

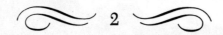 2

Before rep producers took to paying royalties, there was good reason why so many of their plays were of doubtful lineage and unidentified authorship. The play pirate was the reason.

Play pirating flourished royally throughout the nineteenth century and lapsed over into the present one for twenty years or more. Chicago and New York were the principal headquarters, and not only did rep managers depend upon them but reputable stock companies were not above patronizing them, especially when there was a reasonable excuse for trafficking.

There was no international copyright law, and anything from England was considered fair game with the season never closed. Particularly true was this of such books as Rider Haggard's *She*, Mrs. Henry Wood's *East Lynne*, Charles Reade's *Foul Play*, and George R. Sims' dramatized poem,

The Lights of London. From across the channel Dumas' *Monte Cristo* and George Sand's *Fanchon the Cricket* were dramatized in any number of versions. The Kiralfys made a gigantic spectacle of *Michael Strogoff* and Jule Verne's story drifted on to us, sans chorus and spectacles, but with its melodrama intact.

Michael Strogoff, the Courier of the Czar, even in its simpler form, was a thing to lift the youthful auditor right out of his wooden chair. We knew the story by heart and could follow it from the time the indomitable Michael set out on his errand with the Tsar's (so they spelled it then) message ringing in his ears:

"Go, then, Michael Strogoff! Go for God! Go for Russia! Go for my brother and for myself!"

Our idea of Russia was based upon steel engravings of snowy steppes where desperate travelers tossed their children from speeding droshkys to pacify the pursuing wolf pack. So we naturally accepted the situation when Michael was subjected to the blinding treatment from a white-hot sword flashed across his eyes, nor were we supposed to know that he escaped unharmed until the final encounter when he overtook the traitorous Ivan Ogareff, who was impersonating him, with the gleeful announcement:

"Yes, I see! I see the place where I am about to strike you! Defend your life! It is a duel I deign to offer you! My knife against your sword!"

Being of heroic stature, Mike naturally would willingly handicap himself in a death struggle, and being a dutiful son, filial affection would be responsible for his escape from blindness. He thought of his dear old mother as the white steel approached his eyeballs and the blinding tears counteracted the insidious torture.

Defense that a pirated version was not identical with the one from which it was stolen was entirely true since the very method of obtaining scripts insured that.

The play pirate did his stuff hidden away in some dark gallery corner where he took shorthand notes. His immediate discovery was always imminent and his certain knowledge of what would follow was conducive neither to peace of mind nor accurate recording. Not only were ushers alerted but managers and box office men prowled around spotting suspicious characters. So these records might be extremely sketchy. Entire scenes might be deleted or only partially set down, or bridged with mere suggestions of action to fill the gap.

Descriptions of sets might be summed up in "Cottage Interior," "Wood Drop," or "Center Door, Fancy" and the purchaser must picture his surroundings from the action of the play. And with little business noted beyond entrances and exits, an almost entirely new and original show might be the result.

There were all sorts of loopholes to make pirating simple. Perhaps the most ridiculous interpretation of the law was one through which the most flagrant violator could plead innocence. If a person could prove to the satisfaction of the court that he had witnessed a performance of the play and had memorized it, he had the right to present it as he saw fit.

Absurd as it was, the defense proved adequate on more than one occasion. Teddy Byron, with a photographic memory which far outshone his ability as an actor, was reputed able to memorize a play at a single sitting, which probably was not true. But he could do so after several visits and by various subterfuges he managed to make himself obnoxious to every New York producer. That he spent much of his time in arnica and court plaster was accepted by him as just an occupational hazard.

Oddly enough, the most persistent borrower, right and left, was the leading champion for the copyright provision of 1856 which gave dramatists the exclusive right of presenting their own plays or allowing them to be presented. Dion Boucicault lifted, adapted, stole and wrote some one hundred and fifty plays, with and without credit.

Even then, so resourceful were the pirates that Boucicault refused to take advantage of this protection. It is not generally recognized that an uncopyrighted article remains an author's personal property so long as it is not published. This is a matter of common law, for whoever procures a copy of such material has committed a criminal offense and is liable to prosecution. A copyrighted article resolves itself into a civil suit for damages and since most of the rep companies had little financial backing, judgments were worthless.

Marc Klaw prosecuted play pirating for the Mallory Brothers before teaming up with Abe Erlanger and did much to turn the offenders into the ways of righteousness. But the stock star had almost positive protection for a play written for him. When the script was sent ahead for rehearsal, his lines were indicated only by cues. Since this was the major part of the play, and since he carried it in his head, lifting it was well nigh impossible.

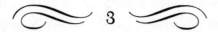

3

Giveaway programs, from the set of dishes once offered by movie houses to the mink coats and Cadillacs dished out ad nauseum on TV, were old hat when rep shows flourished. Gift shows were an established custom of many of them, but topping them all was Gus Hartz, the magician.

It was a great day when a magician came to Beaver Dam. They were all too few and too many of them were small calibre even for small time. Some of them drove their own outfits, usually a reconditioned livery wagon big enough to house the performer, his apparatus and scrawny live stock. Some magicians entertained for a patent medicine pitch. But Gus Hartz ranked as a rival of Hermann the Great and Robert Heller, and his coming was long remembered.

Hartz worked with glass-topped tables, the further to mystify his audience, and was famous for two effects. He vanished a woman from a chair placed on newspapers in the center of the stage, and he filled that stage with articles produced from a borrowed hat.

He played several nights in these smaller stands, and his last performance was to standing room only. For that was Gift Night. You were given a numbered slip with each ticket and these were picked from a hat by a committee selected from the audience. The more numbers you held, the better your chance of winning, which made for good business during the run. Since Hartz varied his program considerably, it was not too monotonous if viewed for three successive nights.

His gifts were numerous and varied. Vegetables and groceries; Yankee notions and cheap jewelry; toys and candy for the youngsters; smoking tobacco, cigars, chewing tobacco and snuff; needles and thread, darning eggs and pincushions; and pamphlets advertising the Great Hartz for everyone, were included in his largess. They were cheap goods, but so were his prices and he must have played his last performance to little more than the expense entailed by his generosity.

I missed the Great Hartz, for by the time I was old enough to care, he was in Cleveland at the Euclid Avenue Opera House, which he managed for many years. He had taken over the Park Theater intending to resume his magical career, but the house burned with all of his equipment. So he remained to become a considerable factor in theatrical history.

His daughter, Fanny Hartz, married Arthur Friend, a Milwaukee lawyer with theatrical aspirations, who talked Cecil B. DeMille and Jesse Lasky into forming the Jesse F. Lasky Feature Play Company that pioneered Dustin Farnum in *The Squaw Man* on the corner of Vine Street in Hollywood.

My acquaintance with the Hartzes began in Milwaukee when Friend was managing a stock company in which Fannie Hartz was the leading lady. I was called upon to play Jake Wallace, the black face minstrel, in *The Girl of the Golden West,* in which I impressed the family banjo. I had played it before with Mary Hall as The Girl and Theodore Roberts as the sheriff.

With his brother, Hartz had opened the first magic shop in New York later to become the legendary Martinka Shop. He remembered Robert Houdin, pioneer of modern magicians, whose performance inspired the brothers to magic. And his part in the theater was long and honorable. He planned a biography as his contribution to magic history and asked me to collaborate with him, but beyond a few vagrant notes nothing much developed before his death.

Gus Hartz' imprint on Concert Hall remained long after his departure. A three-sheet pasted on the dressing room wall showed him in stage makeup set off by circular vignettes of his mysteries, including the vanishing lady. This effect puzzled me no end until Uncle Bee pointed out that the news-

Schubert Theater, Milwaukee, Wis.

Formerly the Academy of Music. Home of the Edwin Thanhouser Stock Co. Also the Arthur Friend Stock Co.

papers beneath the chair were directly over the stage trap and that they, too, were probably prepared so the lady could descend to those unhappy regions below stage.

Rep show gift nights were of a different sort. There were, as well, consolation matinees for youngsters. For a time a five dollar bill was given the child producing the largest number of words from the company's name. This custom fell into disgrace when one manager, in a moment of mental abstraction, gave the prize to a youth who had copied most of Webster's Unabridged Dictionary. Other contestants became convinced that the list was accepted without checking and started making theirs up a year in advance. The result was positively gruesome, and thereafter these intellectual tests were dodged as persistently as a sheriff with a lien on the box office.

There were many gift matinees where each child was given a paper bag with a half dozen pieces of candy. Grocery stores sold the stuff by the pail and the sacks were filled back stage while the manager doled them out through the audience keeping a wary outlook for repeaters. But the big blow-off was:

"A Set of Parlor Furniture Given Away Saturday Night."

The campaign started with the announcement at Monday's opening. It continued each day with a reminder hand stamped on the throwaway, and fuel was added by displaying the prize suite in the show window of McKinstrey's Furniture Store in the middle of Front Street, all properly placarded. This buildup ensured attendance during the week, especially on stormy nights, since coupons accompanied each ticket of admission.

During the Saturday night band concert the display was carted to the theater and lugged upstairs. John Kelly was a furniture giver and since *Ten Nights in a Bar Room* concluded his week, the sofa and two chairs dressed the last act parlor curtain when John Morgan, reformed drunkard, came into his own again.

The drawing may have been honest enough. There was no way of telling. But more often than not, one of the ushers was the lucky winner and the outfit was back in the show window the following Monday morning. This coincident was brushed aside with the statement that the winner had accepted a cash settlement in lieu of the furniture. For some reason or other, this explanation always was accepted without question.

POOR OLD SLAVE.

Arr. by E. M. F.

Poor Old Slave

Lachrymose lyrics of the old minstrel days had to do with the faithful old slave whose love for his master increased in ratio to the abuse he endured. "Poor Old Slave" recorded the demise of the titular character and, for good measure, of his daughter as well. Composed by G. W. H. Griffin, it was featured by Stephen B. Ball, famous contra-tenor in the early fifties. Ball appeared with Ordway's Aeolian Vocalists, a minstrel organization founded by Dr. John P. Ordway, who gave their first performance in Harmony Hall, Boston, Mass., and played in that city from 1849 to 1859. Dr. Ordway then returned to the practice of medicine and served in the Massachusetts legislature. Steve Ball quit blackface after five years to direct Boston's Old School Street Church and to become a vocal teacher. Besides being a minstrel favorite, "Poor Old Slave" was often used as incidental music at the death of Uncle Tom.

Chapter 7

"FATHER, DEAR FATHER, COME HOME WITH ME NOW"

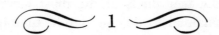

1

MOST of the companies that played Concert Hall came either for a week or for a single night. There were few split weeks and these usually went to shows limping homeward at the end of a bad season.

One thing was certain about the one nighters. They were either very good or very bad. There was no half-way about it. William McConnell played one nighters and gave you your money's worth. Plays like *Uncle Josh Spruceby* tarried long enough to collect at the box office and then got out of town before the enraged populace could commit wholesale mayhem upon the alleged players. But it didn't take long for the imposters to be marked down and given short shrift if they returned, which was seldom, as most of them failed to last a season out.

Companies playing a week's stand year after year became old favorites whose arrival was anticipated and who established personal friendships with many of the townspeople. Outside the theater, Joe and I found them quite ordinary folk, living sedate lives and enduring the trials and troubles of our common lot entirely apart from the glamorous adventures of the stage world.

Besides our contact with them in Concert Hall, we viewed them in their domestic habitat at odd times, for Powers' Boarding House adjoined our family lot and those who did not patronize the Clark House put up with the two sisters who ran it. So we could observe that the character man usually beat the juvenile at croquet; that the soubrette was the wife of the manager and mother of the two-year-old baby often carried on; and that the heroine was married to the villain who might threaten her on stage but who submitted to wholesale henpecking after hours.

Many of these organizations were family affairs and remained intact season after season. One or two new members might be added annually but the principals stayed on. They brought a new show or two with each visit, but certain standbys were demanded and always in the listing. A week's engagement included six night performances and a Saturday matinee, though some threw in a Wednesday matinee for good measure. These mid-week sessions aimed at the feminine trade, offered *Lady Audley's Secret,* or *East Lynne,* or some other drama of English high life with sorrow sufficient to exhaust the tear ducts of the most lachrymose females who came to weep and remained to devour untold quantities of slippery elm bark and peppermint drops.

Early in the season it seemed to us as though the companies were always rehearsing, for all their spare time was spent in the hall going over the night's bill and sharpening its rough edges. Shaping up a season's repertory was a task to challenge even a veteran stock player accustomed to a weekly change of bill. Stock actors perfected a play in one week's time while appearing in another for seven nights and three matinees, which, indeed, was nothing to sneer at.

But because it was a custom to rehearse for two weeks without salary, rep players starting from scratch had to get up in seven or eight parts and be ready to play them in that time. At the end of a fortnight, they put on the road willy-nilly, trusting to luck that everything would come out all right.

At the first rehearsal, a play was read and parts given out. Two days later they were stumbling through it with prompting and studying the second play. A third followed in another two days, and then a fourth, and so on until the week's list was being committed in a mad fashion that seemed without rhyme or reason. Seasoned players unaccustomed to such high pressure would have thrown up their parts and quit in disgust. But somehow or other these hardened troupers accepted it as a matter of routine, sorting out their lines as they went along, originating business on the spur of the moment, rehearsing from eight to ten hours a day, studying their parts continuously, except for sleeping, and in some mysterious fashion, coming up at the end none the worse for it all.

It wasn't that they had only to memorize their lines and work out their stage business. There was the matter of costumes, for each furnished his own, though this was not as tricky a problem as might appear. Costumes for *East Lynne* served equally well for *The Octoroon, The Ticket-of-Leave Man* and *Our American Cousin.* The women wore them, too, in *Monte Cristo, Robert Emmet* and *The Two Orphans,* while one outfit of knee breeches and their accessories set up the male players for all of these. A slouch hat and a flannel shirt were enough for westerns including, of course, the ubiquitous boots. Boots were a must for every man in the company. Of patent leather, with no bottom but a footstrap, they could be slipped on with any pair of shoes and closed along the leg with snap fasteners. Modern plays were a cinch. An extra suit and frock coat covered a multitude of needs, while one top hat was always included in the company props.

As to music, some plays were themed with a single song. Early in *East Lynn,* unfortunate Lady Isabel warbled "Then You'll Remember Me" from *The Bohemian Girl* and the piece was played again and again as the lady sank deeper and deeper into the mire which, according to mid-Victorian standards, could end only with her death.

> Kathleen Mavoureen, the gray dawn is breaking,
> The horn of the hunter is heard on the hill,

was a natural for the play of that name; while poor blind Louise, begging along the Paris quais in *The Two Orphans,* invariably bemoaned her lot with:

> Hungry, neglected, and unprotected,
> Homeless and friendless, sad to behold;
> Eyes red with crying, careworn and sighing,
> Shivering and shaking out in the cold.

More than that, little was required. Extemporized *mysterioso* accompanied the plotting of the villain, a chord in G emphasized a climax or a tableau, while Czibulka's "Winter Tales" and "The Flower Song" were everlastingly played when the heroine said farewell to the old homestead or the stern father regretted: "One year ago I drove her from my door—my only child!"

To our way of thinking, the character man was the most important member of the company. Leading men and women were all right in their place, but many of these plays had been written for stars where the leading role was inherited by the character man. John Morgan dominated *Ten Nights in a Bar-Room* and Salem Scudder was a principal factor in *The Octoroon*. Dunstan Kirke certainly loomed hugely over his daughter—they did *Hazel Kirke* as *An Iron Will*, though the version partook hugely of *The Green Lanes of England*, its source material. Hawkshaw, the detective, in *The Ticket-of-Leave Man; Rip Van Winkle* and any number of other plays were fat fare for the character man, while not infrequently, Monte Cristo fell to his lot. He played bedeviled unfortunates or philanthropic individuals, but whatever they were you could count upon his winning out in the end.

The leading man was either a victim of circumstance or else nitwit enough to be in hot water from the first act to the last. In westerns he was suspected of murder, theft, highway robbery or all three. In Irish dramas, he was a broth of a boy fighting to free dear Old Ireland, captured by the King's Own and saved from the gallows by the character man or the comedian. In native plays he was wrongfully accused by the end of the first act so that the remaining three might be devoted to establishing his innocence.

With the leading lady it was always a question as to whether she would live out the show with her virtue intact. All the brothers might have been valiant but this poor bit of femininity was an orphan, or a poor working girl, or a betrayed wife, or a rural miss with only her stern parents to stand between her and disgrace. If she had a brother, he was a worthless oaf she had to protect and in so doing usually managed to incriminate not only herself but the leading man as well.

Next to the character man, the heavy held a warm place in our hearts. Every play had at least two, but the second was so underdone in evil that he did general utility and doubled in other parts after he had been killed off, as he usually was in the second or third act. But the heavy himself could be counted upon to keep things moving, and the character man was ever at his wits' end to circumvent his deviltry. Sometimes the leading man tried it but he always fell short. Then the character man took over and saved the day.

In westerns the heavy was a bearded roughneck, quick on the draw but not quick enough to dodge a dose of lead in the end. In other plays he turned up invariably with cigarette, boots and riding whip. Sometimes he wore a high hat, but this was not compulsory; it could be Stetson, pulled low over the brow. There was no particular reason why he should arrive fresh from a canter along Rotten Row or through Central Park, but this was a traditional characterization and he clung to it.

There was a time when all villains were roughnecks. That was before Henry Arthur Jones wrote *The Silver King* for Wilson Barrett. The man who made life miserable for Wilfred Denver, enacted by Barrett, was the Spider, who was abetted by the customary first and second assistant murderers. A rising young actor named E. S. Willard, who was assigned the role, decided that the roughneck was outmoded. So he created the Desperate Desmond that heavies copied for years—a cigarette smoking, whip-carrying, silk hatted miscreant whose polished exterior and hypocritical smile disarmed everyone except the audience.

Willard became a star who for many years was a bright light on the British and American stage and whose annual visits were a delight to lovers of *The Middleman, Colonel Newcome, Tom Pinch* and *The Man Who Was*. Perfectionist and master actor himself, he inspired his supporting cast to accomplishments that few of them realized after they left him. Joe and I believed him the greatest actor it was our privilege to see. Many others have since agreed with our estimate.

There was the soubrette. Though some companies carried both, you could get along without an ingenue if you had a capable soubrette. She played all sorts of parts from *Fanchon the Cricket* to Billy Piper in *The Danites* and the Boy in *Peck's Bad Boy*. If sufficiently versatile, she was Louise in *The Two Orphans* and that despicable angel child Cedric, in *Little Lord Fauntleroy*. And she introduced specialties in the play and before the curtain during intermission. She shared top honors with us along with the character man and heavy, and some companies thought enough of her to give her star billing.

With the soubrette was the comedian. He usually paired off with her, and between them they sang and danced and stabbed furtively at romance.

Loie Fuller in the Skirt Dance
(Her original conception)

If the soubrette rated the attentions of the leading man, the comedian played opposite the character woman; but whichever of the two it was, you could anticipate their being set up for marriage at the end of the show.

For us, the others didn't count for much. The second woman played heavies and odd parts; and there were two or three men and an extra woman who did bits and general business, helped out in the orchestra, took tickets at the door, rustled properties, attended to setting the stage and held a prompt book when one was considered necessary, which wasn't often.

No self-respecting rep show would think of starting a season unless bolstered by specialties. These varied from songs during the action of the play to more elaborate entertainment with special effects. One of these was the skirt dance.

Originated by Loie Fuller, the skirt dance was quickly imitated by every fly-by-night entertainer in search of a novelty. La Fuller wore a voluminous skirt of sheer material reinforced with a wire contraption by which it could be raised and fluttered in butterfly fashion. Since she stood stock still and moved only her arms, the dance partook of a routine with Indian clubs. As she went through her calisthenics, the skirts waved in undulating formations while colored lights were thrown upon them from a stereopticon. On a darkened stage it was a spectacular effect for so simple a medium.

The soubrette might engage in a Spanish dance with mantilla and castanets, or the comedian might break out with "The Man on the Flying Trapeze," "Over the Garden Wall" or "The Fellow Who Played the Drum." The latter recounted a blasted romance with an alluring charmer who had eyes only for the drummer in a theater orchestra.

> She wouldn't go into the balcony, or into a circle stall;
> She wouldn't go into the gallery for fear that she would fall.
> She wouldn't go into the boxes—it made her feel so glum;
> She wanted to sit in the front of the pit with the fellow who
> > played the drum.

The comedian was a jolly fellow, but for some reason most of his songs concerned love affairs that failed to jell and from which he emerged the loser while another swain ran away with the object of his devotion. An exception was a flirtatious duet with the soubrette in which her heart went pitty-pat and his head went whirly-gig and each agreed that the other was the cause of these delightful symptoms.

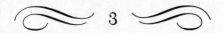

3

Playwriting and play production were largely a catch-as-catch-can affair with the winner collecting the purse when and where he was able. The nation was an expanse of towns and villages sparsely covered by transportation or news sources, and touring companies could travel season after season wildcatting standard drama under different names with none the wiser. Little wonder, then, that plays never heard of before or since were common fare at Beaver Dam's two theaters. It was years before we discovered that *The Dep'ty Sheriff* was *The Messenger from Jarvis Section;* that *Desperate Chances* was an alias for *Under the Gaslight;* and that *In Old New England* really was *Way Down East.*

At one period, two Broadway productions projected an influence into small time territory none the less real because their progenitors knew nothing whatsoever about it. They were *The Old Homestead* and *Blue Jeans,* and due to them Joe and I developed an allergy to all "Uncle" shows. These "Uncle" shows had nothing in common with the "Papa" shows of a later era when gentlemen protectors of the chorus backed a production for some impecunious producer with more nerve than ready cash. Invariably, these

"Uncle" shows finally turned out to be *The Old Homestead* in disguise.

Denman Thompson was playing a rowdy skit, *The Female Bathers*, when James W. Hill, a Chicago storekeeper with managerial aspirations, spotted its potentialities and had it revamped into *Joshua Whitcomb*. It progressed to *The Old Homestead*, and Thompson, who had started as a comedian with material of a decided indigo tinge, became the embodiment of an honest rural philosopher whose generosity was exceeded only by his gullibility. By the modern playstick it was a pretty sad affair, but it suited the temper of the day and was accepted as a true picture of the people it pretended to portray. In a rough way *The Old Homestead* was shaped after *The Messenger from Jarvis Section*.

Scene from "The Old Homestead." Denman Thompson as Joshua Whitcomb finds
his son, Reuben, before Grace Church.
'Why, it's my boy, Reuben! Rube! Rube! My boy! My boy!"

Uncle Si Shows

During the heyday of the rep shows, country theaters were obsessed with companies presenting "Uncle Si" shows. They were variations of *The Old Homestead* and *Blue Jeans*. Sometimes they combined the two in a fashion that stretched the imagination to the breaking point.

The Old Homestead served Denman Thompson year after year just as *Rip Van Winkle* did Joseph Jefferson. It was the story of the Prodigal Son modernized in a rural setting at Swanzey, New Hampshire; and for contrast in a banker's mansion and on the streets of New York. Joshua Whitcomb, typical rural stage character of that era, goes to the big city in search of his son Reuben, who set out to make his fortune and forgot the good folks back home. He finds the young man drunk in the gutter before Grace Church, rescues him from his dilemma and brings him back to the old homestead to take up where he left off.

Blue Jeans, another rural melodrama by Joseph Arthur, was laid in Rising Sun, Indiana; and the plot was pointed to the big scene when the hero was thrown across the carriage of a circular saw while the heroine smashed down the mill-room door to rescue him in the nick of time. The effect was palpably suggested by the railroad rescue of Augustin Daly's After Dark.

The Old Homestead was given in pirated editions and gradually it was rewritten to introduce the saw mill scene from Blue Jeans. Then came the plague of "Uncle Si" shows until the novelty wore off and other bucolic dramas replaced them.

So while Thompson played the big time, road shows brought us "Uncle Si Slocum," or "Uncle Jud Hawkins," or "Uncle Seth Bascomb," all of which proved to be another version of The Old Homestead with Uncle What's-His-Name chasing across the stage in his nightshirt at a false alarm of fire, or goggling at a crudely bedaubed Venus de Milo that we were presumed to consider a fine statue of Parian marble.

Along with this came the repercussion from Blue Jeans. Joseph Arthur's rural melodrama left its imprint on the dramatic sands for two reasons: an old man turned the portrait of his erring daughter to the wall, and the heroine rescued the hero from bisection by the whirling blade of a buzzsaw. The situation was a barefaced steal from Augustin Daly's Under the Gaslight, where the heroine chopped her way out of a railroad shack to release a cripple from the railroad tracks as the midnight limited sped by. Patrons of Blue Jeans were familiar with the older melodrama, but the similarity passed by unnoted. There was an added thrill in watching the hero inch closer to death while the heroine battled valiantly to break down the door.

After Blue Jeans, there was an inundation of buzzsaws combining the two plays and the ultimate in "Uncle" shows was realized in The Old Homestead embellished with buzzsaw trimmings. They were some of those one nighters that moved on as quickly as possible and by far the worst of them was Uncle Josh Spruceby. The play came to town under the sponsorship of Harry Frazee, later a Broadway producer and owner of the Boston Red Sox. In the street parade, Harry puffed away on a tuba as one of the band and at night he presided at the box office, admonishing small boys with no small degree of authority. He wore a beard fashioned after U. S. Grant and assumed a dignity befitting a small time manager.

Throughout the day and until the play started, the buzzsaw was on exhibition in front of the theater. A knock down affair propelled by hand with an iron counterweight as a safety device, it never failed to attract the curious, and a crowd of idlers were always gathered about it. None of them seemed to realize that they passed John Herr's lumber mill every day without even a glance at several practical saws buzzing away inside.

The company was as bad as the play. But, as Uncle Bee pointed out, that was because the buzzsaw occupied the stellar spot and since the people came to see the saw, the rest really didn't matter.

Because of the daily change of bill and since the prompt book was seldom in evidence, the play sometimes failed to end as anticipated by the author. Not infrequently whole scenes were cut when an actor missed his entrance, resulting in considerable befuddlement for those trying to follow the plot. On one memorable night, the actors started out bravely enough with *The Hidden Hand* but by some inexplicable transmutation along about the middle of the play found themselves involved in the farcical trial scene from *Irish Justice*. They compromised by winding up with the last act of *Our Boys*.

This prolonged session of double talk left the audience in a bemused uncertainty as to whether they or the players had suddenly become entirely addled. That it was the last performance of the season probably explained their dereliction from the customary progression to vice confuted and virtue rewarded.

Uncle Bee took this opportunity to emphasize the necessity of following the synopsis printed on the program below the cast of characters. It was there for just such emergencies, he pointed out, and no matter what bent the actors might pursue, you had the satisfaction of knowing that everything ended as it should. More than that, you could anticipate what was in store and be prepared to deal out cheers and hisses to best advantage.

One of the better "Uncle" plays with sufficient originality to set it apart from the run of the mine was *Uncle Hiram*. Its synopsis was terse and illuminating.

SYNOPSIS OF SCENES

Act I—Scene 1. The Banker's country mansion. Making preparation for Uncle Hiram's arrival. The false friend. Scene 2—Watts Street, New York. The police at work. Scene 3—James Redland's Residence. "There stands the murderer!" Tableaux.

Act II—Twelfth District Court of New York. The Trial. The verdict, "Not Guilty." Uncle Hiram on the war-path. Villainy in a tight corner. Uncle Hiram's evidence. "Officer, arrest that man!" Tableaux.

Act III—The fashionable gambling room of Arthur Murdock. Uncle Hiram sees a gold fish for the first time. Uncle Hiram changes clothes. Belle gets the forgeries. Foiled. Discovered. Uncle Hiram to the rescue. Tableaux.

Act IV—Picnic woods on Staten Island with view of Bartholdi Statue. The murderer once more at large. Uncle Hiram's first attempt at riding a bicycle. The fatal door. Uncle Hiram to the rescue. Virtue triumphant. Hunted down. Curtain.

Under the Gaslight

Under the Gaslight was written by Augustin Daly in 1867. At the same time, Dion Boucicault appeared with *After Dark*. The plays had two identical scenes: a rescue from drowning, and a victim tied to the railroad track before an approaching express train. Daly stopped Boucicault's production by injunction, but William A. Brady bought it and produced it with James J. Corbett as the star.

The two plays in time were played individually and together by rep companies, often part of one being transferred to the other. Such titles as *Desperate Chances* were given them to escape prosecution for using them.

In the Daly play, Laura Cortland, a society belle, turns out to be an adopted child and former ragged pickpocket. Byke, a thorough good-for-nothing who keeps out of the clutches of the blundering law, claims her as his child and starts with her to a hiding place across the North River. In a general melée, Laura is pushed into the river and is rescued by Ray Trafford, a former suitor still in love with her.

Taken to the Cortland home, Laura learns that she is the legitimate daughter and that Pearl, her sister, is the adopted youngster. Rather than cause Pearl suffering and disgrace, Laura runs away, ending up at a lonely railroad station. The Limited Express is due in twenty minutes; there are no other trains that night. Since Laura has no place to go, she importunes the station master, who locks

her in his shanty and goes away. Through the window, Laura sees Snorkey, a
Civil War veteran minus one arm, coming down the railroad track. He is followed by Byke, maddened because Snorkey has upset his plans by disclosing the
secret of Laura's birth. Byke overcomes the cripple and ties him to the railroad
track. Snorkey, it seems, is out to prevent Byke from committing a murder, and
Byke is out to stop Snorkey. Otherwise there is no good reason why the pair
should turn up at the same place at such an ungodly hour. But the plot demands
it, and there they are. Byke hurries away and Laura, a helpless witness, knows
that the train is due in ten minutes.

LAURA

O, Heavens! He will be murdered before my eyes! How can I aid
him?

SNORKEY

Who's that?

LAURA

It is I? Do you know my voice?

SNORKEY

That I do, but I almost thought I was dead and it was an angel.
Where are you?

LAURA

In the station.

SNORKEY

I can't see you but I can hear you. Listen to me, Miss, for I've got
only a few minutes to live.

LAURA

(shaking door)
God help me! And I can not aid you!

SNORKEY

Never mind me, Miss. I might as well die here and now as at any
other time. I'm not afraid. I've seen death in almost every shape and
none of them scare me. But for the sake of those I love I would live.
Do you hear me?

LAURA

Yes, yes!

SNORKEY

They are on the way to your cottage—Byke and Judas—to rob and
murder.

LAURA

Oh, I must get out! (Shakes window bars) What shall I do?

SNORKEY

Can't you burst the door?

LAURA

It is locked fast.

SNORKEY

Is there nothing in there? No hammer? No crowbar?

LAURA

Nothing! (Faint whistle in the distance) Oh, heavens! The train!
(Paralysed for an instant) The axe!

SNORKEY

Cut the woodwork! Don't mind the lock—cut around it! How my neck tingles! (*A blow at the door*) Courage! (*Another blow*) Courage!

> (*The steam whistle is heard again nearer and a rumble on the tracks. Another blow.*)

There's a true woman for you! Courage!

> (*Noise of locomotive with whistle. The door swings open, mutilated, lock hanging, and Laura emerges, axe in hand.*)

Here! Quick!

> (*Laura runs and unfastens Snorkey. Headlights glare illuminate the stage.*)

Victory! Saved! Hooray!

> (*Laura leans exhausted against the switch.*)

And these are the women who aint to have a vote!

> (*As Laura takes his head from the track, the train rushes past with roar and whistle from left to right.*)

CURTAIN

At least that's the way it was played on Broadway. But the rep companies contented themselves with offstage effects, pushing a cut-out locomotive front and cowcatcher from the wings, and illuminating the track—two battens laid across the stage—with an extra-powerful dark lantern.

Harvard University Theater Collection

Saved from the Storm

Whether Augustin Daly or Dion Boucicault devised it, the rescue-from-the-oncoming-train became a standard melodramatic effect and carried on into the days of Mack Sennett and his Keystone comedians. But Gray and Stephens attained the acme of something or other in their production of *Saved from the Storm.* This time it was the heroine who was tied to the railroad tracks, the victim instead of the rescuer. And the pair who saved her from the oncoming locomotive were a couple of pooches, forerunners of RinTin-Tin and his histrionic progeny— a far cry and quite the reverse from *Uncle Tom's Cabin,* where baying Great Danes pursued Eliza across the Ohio River ice floes.

New York Public Library Collection

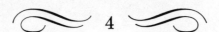

4

This land behind the footlights was quite apart from the world of every-day. It was a land of romance and adventure inhabited by people who talked as you would have talked had you been one of them. It was a land of unqualified justice, though often laggardly enforced; of joy and sorrow, and though villainy might triumph for a time, virtue always came through and vice, if lucky enough to escape a bullet in the noggin, rounded up in handcuffs and headed for the nearest hoosegow.

Of the more rabid melodrama that came each season *The Ticket-of-Leave Man* left an ineradicable mark not alone upon us but on dramatic history besides. It gave us Hawkshaw, the detective, and Jim—not Jack—Dalton. It was a perfect example of the dimwitted hero and the distressed heroine. It had a versatile soubrette, a comic man and his offset, and there was the never ending conflict between character man and heavy.

War between Hawkshaw and Dalton waged unendingly. Master detective and master crook, they endlessly fooled each other with the most transparent disguises. Dalton had only to change his hat and slap on a mustache to outwit Hawkshaw, while palpably false whiskers were sufficient to set Dalton a-twitter as to Hawkshaw's identity. Above all, the dialogue was something never to be forgotten.

Tom Taylor wrote *The Ticket-of-Leave Man* in the early sixties, but as it was timed "The Present" it remained popular for years. Tom believed in action and plenty of it. He lost no time in introducing Melter Moss, a London crook, meeting with Dalton, alias Downey, alias The Tiger. They spent their time plotting in a public beer garden in tones loud enough to be heard by everybody but those upon the stage. This was not by accident but design. It was a custom of melodrama to plot in public places in a loud voice, and the more villainous the plot, the larger the public place and the more stentorian the plotting.

The Ticket-of-Leave Man

Hawkshaw, the detective, is about to present a check for Bob Brierly to cash while genial Mr. Gibson smiles approval. Hawkshaw knows that Brierly is a ticket-of-leave man but keeps mum, believing the young man deserves a new deal. Brierly is all dressed up for his wedding but it fails to materialize when Moss, a scheming crook, discloses the young man's record to Mr. Gibson. The bill broker drops his genial attitude and fires the unfortunate clerk forthwith. This prolongs the final denouement for another act. Hawkshaw is shown here in one of his more sober moments in a costume less outlandish than most of his disguises.

New York Public Library Collection

Dalton wore a drab coat, check trousers and a hat pulled over his eyes, and this disguise not only fooled Moss but Hawkshaw as well; and as Hawkshaw wore a modest get-up of a tweed summer suit, wideawake hat and boots, the plotters failed to recognize him. The plan was to pass forged notes, for which they picked Bob Brierly, the hero, who hung around the resort spending his patrimony in a determined effort to acquire delirium tremens. Bob made friends with the heroine, a strolling guitar player, passed the notes and was hustled away to prison, but not until he had voiced a denunciation unsurpassed for asininity in the annals of melodrama. It was:

"Thou cur!"

Paroled on a ticket-of-leave and an ardent teetotaler, Brierly returned to his guitar player, now transformed into a dressmaker. There he found Sam Willoughby, who was really the soubrette, and Green Jones, the comedian, and Mrs. Jones, who called herself Emily Evremond, and who sang with her husband in the public gardens. Sam displayed the mischievousness of his bi-sexual spirit by leaping over chairs and sassing his elders and by dancing the sailor's hornpipe, while he sang "Nancy Lee." Green Jones, in the fashion of all comic men, rendered a doleful ditty about his lost love, who was:

A great big tall girl,
In her chin she's got a dimple.
Great big fat girl,
On her nose she's got a pimple.
Ever since she left me
My head's been in a whirl,
And so I ask—please tell me now
Have you seen my girl?

Being a nitwit with a prison record, Brierly promptly got a job with Mr. Gibson, a bill broker and a dithering old ass who engaged the parolee, unsight, unseen. Because he was least fitted for the job, Sam tagged along as office boy. This confirmed the imbecility of the aforesaid Mr. Gibson so far as Joe and I were concerned.

On the day of Bob's wedding to the reformed guitar player, Moss and Dalton showed up at Gibson's along with Hawkshaw. Dalton wore a blue frock coat, gray trousers and black hat, and Hawkshaw was dressed in what was described as "an eccentric suit of black"; so neither recognized the other. But all spotted Brierly, whom Moss denounced as an ex-convict. Whereupon he was given the old heave-ho, which threw him back into the web of the villainous pair.

Because this was to be their *coup de maître,* the couple sought the Bridge-water Arms, a resort frequented by most of the principals and half of Beaver Dam's stage struck youth. That this volunteer atmosphere was greeted with shouts of "Hi, Bill!" and "Hey, Wilbur! Where did you get that hat?" by enthusiastic confrères in front, in no way hampered the lusty plotting of Moss and Dalton. Before this mob of bar-room loafers, they loudly planned to rob the Gibson place with the help of Brierly.

Naturally, Hawkshaw was there, but not even Dalton suspected it, for the detective was unassumingly arrayed in a modest ensemble of corduroy breeches, waistcoat with red sleeves, and a fur cap. Besides, he sported the finest set of false whiskers ever seen in Concert Hall. As part of their own plot and that of the play, Moss, Dalton and the landlord disappeared through the stage trap to sweat in silence while Brierly penned a message: "To Mr. Gibson, Peckham. The office will be entered tonight. I'm in it to save the property and secure the robbers. Brierly."

This written, he faced the audience, holding the paper aloft at an angle of forty-five degrees for all to behold.

"And now that I have written the message," he cried, "who will take it?"
From rear stage lunged a figure to grab it, crying: "I will!"
"And who are you?"
"Hawkshaw, the detective!"

Off with the false whiskers. Tableaux! And Hawkshaw dashed away on his self-appointed task.

There must have been some further business to release the foul trio below stage before they succumbed to suffocation, but to us youngsters, the act ended there. So we sat in a happy state of bewilderment while the robbery was perpetrated through a graveyard that conveniently adjoined Gibson's place of business, and Brierly was knocked silly while crying:

"Curse you, Jim Dalton!"

Then Hawkshaw arrived in time to arrest his arch-enemy and declare Brierly only slightly damaged, which delighted the Joneses and young Sam, apparently accustomed to a midnight stroll through the cemetery, and who probably would have burst into a trio of song-and-dance but for the final curtain.

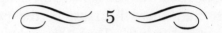

Dear to the hearts of the Blue Ribbon Band was *Ten Nights in a Bar-Room*. It was a regular each year and like *Rip Van Winkle* was a favorite of John Kelly's repertory. William W. Pratt had dramatized T. S. Arthur's morality pamphlet and the teetotalers devoured it whole.

Mr. Romain, a philanthropist, wandered in and out as a volunteer chorus, emphasizing the curse of the Demon Rum, an unnecessary procedure since it was evident at every turn. John Morgan drank himself out of his mill. Simon Slade took it over, made a neat pile and with the help of Squire Hammond bought The Sickle and Sheaf, the village tavern. Morgan spent his time sousing in the bar with Sample Swichel, the comedian, really the most persistent tippler of all. And as usual the program printed the:

SYNOPSIS OF SCENES

Act I—Scene 1—Exterior The Sickle and Sheaf. Arrival of Romaine. Swichel gives him the gossip of the village. Miller Slade turned innkeeper. Scene 2—Interior The Sickle and Sheaf. The squire's son and the gambler. Morgan gives Slade a piece of his mind. "Father, dear Father, come home with me now." The fight and the rescue.

Act II—Scene 1—Exterior The Sickle and Sheaf. Mehitable's love letter. Swichel's few remarks about it. Romaine's second visit. Scene 2—Interior the Sickle and Sheaf. Rum beginning its work. Morgan, the slave of drink. His expulsion from the bar-room. The catastrophe. "Father! They have killed me!"

Act III—Scene 1—Exterior The Sickle and Sheaf. Swichel warns Green. Scene 2—John Morgan's home. Morgan at home. "Father, don't leave little Mary tonight." Morgan's promise. Mrs. Slade visits Mary. Morgan's fearful delirium.

Act IV—Scene 1—Interior The Sickle and Sheaf. Slade in trouble. Rum's progress. Reconciliation of Willie and Green. The game of cards. The murder. Scene 2—The Woodland. Arrest of the assassin. Scene 3—John Morgan's home. Death of little Mary. Morgan's reformation.

Act V—Exterior The Sickle and Sheaf. Ten years later. Final results of the power of drink. Swichel abandons drink. Fate of Green. Swichel's successful courtship. Scene 2—Interior The Sickle and Sheaf. Slade's bar-room a ruin. Frank's attack on Romaine frustrated by Swichel. The murder. "Frank Slade, you have killed your own father!" Scene 3—Exterior The Sickle and Sheaf. Romaine points a lesson. Scene 4—John Morgan's home. Reformation.

Uncle Bee noted that the play (and its reception) was a mass of inconsistencies from start to finish. Sample Swichel, the worst souse of all, was heartily applauded because he was the comedian. He always scored when he entered from the bar-room, wiping his lips, with:

"I just had a brandy toddy. Golly, I wish my throat was as long as the Mississippi and twice as crooked."

"Why?" fed Mr. Romaine in his capacity as chorus.

"Because it felt so good going around the bend."

During the ten years of the play, Swichel boozed continuously. Morgan, financially obliged to cut down on his liquor, went from bad to worse and ended up with delirium tremens, while Swichel, happy as a grasshopper, continued well soused with no appreciable deterioration, morally or physically.

Morgan quit drinking only after a terrific battle. Swichel stopped out-of-hand when he should have been in a drunkard's grave.

Slade was forever dishing it across the bar for cash. Yet he went bankrupt. Hammond, his banker, went bankrupt. Morgan was a pauper until he reformed.

Slade pitched a wild whiskey glass at Morgan and hit little Mary. She died. Nothing was done about it.

Now Beaver Dam had a goodly German population and many beer saloons where whole families indulged together with *Gemütlichkeit* and seemed to wax fat and happy upon it. Grandfather treated whiskey as a medicine, and with us it rated with paregoric and castor oil. So we agreed with Uncle Bee that the play was pretty much a waste of time and effort.

Ten Nights in a Bar-Room was given its last serious revival by Robert

1 **The Miller Opens a Tavern.** When Simon Slade sells his mill and opens the Sickle and Sheaf tavern, he puts his protesting wife and daughter in the kitchen and his son behind the bar. Slade is genial, and the tavern, inviting.

2 **Drunkard Is Not Welcome.** Joe Morgan, Slade's former partner in the mill, is the only unwelcome guest at the tavern . . . Morgan doesn't know when to stop drinking and his daughter, Mary, calls for him nightly.

3 **"Good Heavens! He's Killed Her!"** A year later, Slade has become a hateful money grasper. In a rage he throws a glass at Morgan. The glass misses Morgan and strikes little Mary, fatally injuring her.

4 **Death of Little Mary Morgan.** Morgan, athirst for liquor, has delirium tremens at his daughter's deathbed. The mother rushes for a doctor . . . Calmed, Morgan promises the dying Mary that he will never touch liquor again.

5 **Willy Becomes a Drunkard.** Five more years pass by. Willy Hammond, once promising lawyer, has gone from bad to worse . . . His bosom friend is a gambler. Drunk, they hitch Willy's fine race horse to a buggy.

6 **"You're a Cheating Scoundrel."** The gambler, in cahoots with Slade, gets Willy in a card game. Willy calls the gambler a crook and is in turn killed . . . Willy's mother falls dead when she sees her slain son.

7 **A Deplorable Situation.** Two years later. The Sickle and Sheaf is dirty and falling into decay. Guests are coarse and vulgar. Slade has become brutal; his son a loafer. Both have become drunkards and quarrel continuously.

8 **"Frank Slade, You Have Killed Your Father."** One night the son hits his father with a bottle. Slade dies. The son is placed in jail. Mrs. Slade goes insane . . . The daughter, left all alone, is broken hearted.

9 **Citizens Vote to Close Tavern.** Joe Morgan, now reformed, leads a movement to close the Sickle and Sheaf. Citizens hold a mass meeting . . . The tavern sign is cut down. Thus ends the tavern which led so many to destruction.

Ten Nights in a Barroom

Downing when the country went dry. Long a star in heroic roles, Downing drank himself into obscurity, and turned to "Ten Nights" in his later years.

Appearing in California's Passion Play, he purchased the production and shipped it to New York. The train was wrecked, the production destroyed and Downing, penniless in New York, went on a two weeks' bender. He awoke in the Doyers Street Mission.

"I was impelled to speak," he explained. "I mounted the platform and spoke as I never had before. And from that day, I have not touched a drop of liquor."

He became a temperance reformer. With his own company, he played John Morgan in the larger cities, devoting his earnings to reclaiming drunkards. To my knowledge, he refused an opportunity to teach dramatics in Marquette University in Milwaukee because, as he said: "I can do more good this way."

Robert Downing continued his crusade and with his death in 1944, *Ten Nights in a Bar-Room* passed into the limbo of forgotten plays.

Chapter 8

"RAGS ARE ROYAL RAIMENT WHEN WORN FOR VIRTUE'S SAKE"

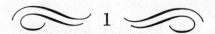

1

OF ALL the plays that came to Beaver Dam, Joe and I cast our votes for "The Octoroon." Since this melodrama was favored by its patrons, the Allie Spooner Dramatic Company always included it in its week's fare, nor did we ever fail to witness it with undiminished enthusiasm. And for good reason: there was a murder, the burning of a Mississippi river packet, a duel to the death—"with knives"—and a climacteric apotheosis which, in our critical estimation, outrivalled the time-dulled ascension of Little Eva into the stunted reaches of Concert Hall.

The Allie Spooner Dramatic Company was an annual visitor to Beaver Dam. The players arrived with the vernal equinox as regularly as the sap sugared the maple sentinels that flanked the street before our house. There were Pa Spooner, and Ma Spooner, and Baby Spooner; a character man with a silky blonde mustache; a heavy who tipped two-hundred-odd and could have doubled for John L. Sullivan, without the mustache; and J. Ashley Rush, who did everything from juveniles to old men and characters, along with others sufficient, by resourceful doubling, to round out a nightly change of bill and Saturday matinee.

The Banker's Daughter

The Banker's Daughter, Bronson Howard's melodrama of high society in America and Paris, played first in the Union Square Theater, opening on November 30, 1878, and continuing for 137 performances. After that it went on the road, was played by the small time companies, and was particularly popular with amateur groups.

The plot concerns Lilian Westbrook who marries John Strebelow to save her banker father from ruin when the bottom falls out of his financial world. Lilian loves Harold Routledge, artist, and is also sought by Count de Carojac, "prince of swordsmen." Lawrence Westbrook, Lillian's father, declares himself the best fencer in America too. All of them meet in the American Embassy in Paris, where the Count insults Routledge, who knocks him down out of hand. A duel follows, Routledge is mortally wounded, and Strebelow learns that his wife was forced into marriage and that she loves the wounded man.

Following the inevitable separation, Lillian and Strebelow are reunited, and life resumes its even course. The duel was the attraction that drew audiences to performance—any duel was sure fire in the small towns—and the scene was displayed on the billboards wherever the show played.

New York Public Library Collection

Featured was Little Allie herself. She may have been sixteen or twenty-five but she played child roles. She was Capitola White in *The Hidden Hand;* the blind Louise in *The Two Orphans;* Weenee Paul in *The Octoroon;* and that unspeakably sanctimonious brat who haunted our existence in *Little Lord Fauntleroy.*

SCENES IN THE PLAY OF "THE TWO ORPHANS," NOW RUNNING AT THE UNION SQUARE THEATRE

The Two Orphans

Before *The Two Orphans* became a rep show and when it was running at the Union Square Theater in New York with the original cast, this reproduction of the billboard posters advertising the show was printed in the daily papers.

The abduction of Henriette and abandonment of the blind Louise is shown at the upper right hand; and in the opposite corner gallant Chevalier de Vaudrey engages in a duel to save the kidnaped girl from a fate worse than death.

The center oval is the street scene where blind Louise sings doleful melodies while crippled Pierre covers her with his thin jacket to protect her from the falling snow.

Lower right shows Louise attempting to escape from her confinement in the Frochard's den only to find Sister Henriette has been brought there in another abduction.

At the bottom center is the hand-to-hand knife engagement between the Frochard brothers—Jacques and Pierre—which brings the melodrama to its conclusion. The other vignettes show (*left*) the Count de Linières with de Vaudrey in an official session, and (*right*) the count with his wife. Lower left is the meeting between the Countess and Henriette.

Harvard University Theater Collection

For our money, *The Two Orphans* ran a close second to *The Octoroon*. It offered *two* duels—one "with knives"—and a mob wholesaling villainy so lavish that it must have taxed their imaginations to invent something new. One duel brightened the opening scenes when a sympathetic cavalier snatched the bedraggled Henrietta—played by Ma Spooner—"from the lecherous embraces of her wishful abductor." An all-too-brief encounter with swords, still it was a mild aperitif for things to come.

Begging for sous along the Seine reduced Little Allie to so pitiful a condition that she willingly interpolated one of her traditional vocal specialties, "Shivering and Shaking Out in the Cold," eminently appropriate for the snow scene.

As Picard, the efficacious servant, Pa Spooner did his bit to relieve the tension. Visiting La Frochard's den on reconnaissance preparatory to rushing up a rescue party with the esprit of a Marine landing corps, he listed Pierre's knife-grinding outfit as "one threshing machine," then wandered to the footlights to render "Ma, Ma, Where is Papa?"

> Ma, ma, where is papa?
> Gone to the White House, darling.
> Making the laws, serving the cause,
> Gone to the White House, dear.

Only recently had Grover Cleveland admitted paternity of an illegitimate son, and Tin Pan Alley's pioneers, not caring who made the nation's laws, had molded it into a song.

So while J. Ashley Rush limped about as crippled Pierre, we impatiently awaited the supreme moment—"The Duel of the Two Brothers," as blazoned across the throwaways of "Tonight's Bill." So little was thought of them that the opening encounter and Henriette's rescue weren't even mentioned.

Whatever the production's shortcomings, they were forgotten when the brothers clashed. It didn't matter that the Seine dock was only a strip of scenery set on edge, or that La Frochard's hideaway was the house curtain hung prison side front, and the cubbyhole to imprison Little Allie were the stage steps nailed to a plank in the wings. With hideous malevolence, La Frochard encouraged her pampered offspring to acts more dastardly than his sluggish mentality could imagine, while poor Pierre, shielding his sightless protegée, chose a knife from his machine with the admonition:

"Remember, brother! We come of a family who kill!"

Delightful though it was, the duel ended all too soon. Frail Rush was entirely eclipsed by his hulking adversary, and the outcome was inevitable despite our heartfelt prayers. Even the arrival of indomitable Picard with his rescue party could not compensate for the cripple's death, for Pierre died in the Spooner version. Their audience demanded a finish fight and no favors, let the dead fall where they may. So amid cheers and hisses, the Frochards were hustled away and Ma Spooner clasped Little Allie to her bosom.

What bothered Joe and me was that the philanderings of a Buffalo attorney should be memorialized in song in the days of Louis of France. The audience accepted it as just another dramatic idiosyncrasy, but we put it up to Uncle Bee. He suggested that Pa Spooner probably was a goddam Republican desirous of blackening the reputation of the only decent President this country had elected in years. But since Grandfather Babcock had just joined the Democratic ranks, this opinion may have been somewhat biased.

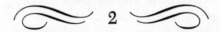

2

Though Joe and I were weaned upon the adventure stories of Captain Mayne Reid, we never associated his novel, *The Quadroon* with *The Octoroon*. So thoroughly did Dion Boucicault revamp plot and characters that I doubt if Reid himself would have recognized his offspring. Some say it was a rewrite of Shirley Brooks' *The Creole*. We only knew that it was one whale of a show and accepted it as such.

Way down in old Louisiana, Colonel Peyton ended his years discussing planter's punch and bloody Kansas while Plantation Terrebone went to the dogs. He bestirred himself sufficiently to beget a beautiful daughter by one of his quadroons and Zoe, the octoroon, was flowering into womanhood when the Bay of Naples rolled up to disclose Terrebone Manor overlooking a vista of northern pine and maple underbrush. You see, the house curtain was created by Ed Hohl, a local painter, whose aesthetic heart was with those damyankees and to hell with all southrons.

George Peyton, the colonel's nephew, pursued the beautiful Zoe (and Ma Spooner was a fine looking woman) while Dora Sunnyside, from a neighboring plantation, mooned over George. Mrs. Peyton was forced to disclose the facts of life to her nephew, warning him that in addition to being illegal, miscegenation was not accepted by the flower of southern chivalry. Old Man Peyton's diversions were quite *au fait* but no real gentleman, suh, allowed such digressions to shackle him with marriage vows. That, at least, was the conclusion we drew.

Through studied misapplication and continuous libations, old Peyton lost most of his property to Overseer Jacob McClosky (the Jacques of the night before) whose appearance was a dead giveaway to anyone not punch drunk. But Jacob was pegged the minute Salem Scudder appeared. Scudder was the silky mustached character man and so was bound to embody all that was pure and noble. Which he did. A persistent inventor, he berated himself for talking the old nitwit into promoting his contraptions instead of paying his honest debts, including McClosky's wages. Casually whittling, he classified Jacob as something lower than a rattlesnake's belly, jabbing his bowie knife against the other's abdomen with the warning:

"Take your hand down, Jacob! Take it down, I say! I know the bowie knife you carry down the back of your neck and whenever I gets into company like yours, I always starts with the advantage on my side."

Then McClosky destroyed the hidden papers giving Zoe her freedom and brought down the curtain with:

"If it takes every dollar I've got, I'll own that octoroon!"

Weenee Paul (Little Allie in sepiaface), grandson of faithful, white-wooled Pete (J. Ashley Rush in blackface), with his Indian shadow, Wahnotee (Pa Spooner in redface and war bonnet), met the mailboat while Mrs. Peyton waited for funds to save the old plantation. Scudder had contrived a weird camera from a Royal Baking Powder tin, a Smith Brothers' Cough Drops carton, and four laths. While Paul posed before it, McClosky knocked him over the head and rifled the mail pouch. Wahnotee found the body and in simple aboriginal fashion concluded the camera did it. Therefore he smashed it, which explained the Royal Baking Powder Tin, the Smith Brothers' Cough Drop carton and the four laths. The camera was built to be destroyed.

Both Joe and I regretted Paul's untimely demise. For a second time, Little Allie had quit cold without even giving us "I Believe It For My Mother Told Me So," a new motto song by that up-and-coming young minstrel, Paul Dresser.

By this time Beaver Dam's stagestruck youths were assembled in the big house. Pa Spooner had washed his face, donned string tie and long coat, and was ready to auction Wilbur Henninger and "Young Joe" Shoemaker ("Old Joe" lived up to his name as the village cobbler) both recognizable under their burnt cork and both welcomed with derogatory comments from envious cronies in the rear of the hall. After a bitter session, Pa Spooner announced.

"Zoe, the Octoroon! Gone and sold to Jacob McClosky for twenty-five thousand dollars!"

And when the gloating McClosky started to claim his prize:

"Jacob McClosky! In my opinion you're a damned scoundrel and horse thief! And (*producing a pair of Colt pepperboxes*) here are the documents to prove it!"

No declaration in Concert Hall ever received a more enthusiastic endorsement.

After the auction, while the Spooner ensemble promoted a lynching bee to avenge Weenee Paul, Pa Spooner had time to reincarnate Wahnotee and get him all but hanged by enacting his assault upon the camera which everyone interpreted as an attack upon the boy. But the photographic plate was found showing McClosky clubbing Weenee Paul and he was dragged aboard the Magnolia, snubbed up off stage, from which he escaped amid an impressive blaze of red fire burned on pie tins by company members not otherwise engaged.

Henninger and Shoemaker, having resumed their local identities, opened the hall windows to let out the smoke and as the spectators recovered from their coughing, McClosky fled for his life while Zoe secured poison from Old Pete, who proved something of a conjur man. McClosky was run down in the heart of Hohl's woods by Scudder and Wahnotee, who chased him to the footlights while he begged for mercy.

"Mercy? What mercy did you show that poor boy?" Scudder asked. "Take that knife and defend yourself for there stands your executioner!"

He threw down his bowie knife, took Wahnotee's war bonnet (turkey feathers are frail things and must be protected), and the stage was left to the duellists. This disappointed Joe and me for we favored the spectators sticking around to watch the fight and perhaps place a few bets on the outcome.

Now Pa Spooner was six-feet-one and proportionately lanky, while McClosky if not Mr. Five-by-Five at least was Mr. Five-by-Four. But neither weight nor height counted. They grappled and rolled about the stage, perilously close to the footlights, then up against the backdrop. It was all very exhilarating, particularly when McClosky lost his knife and dropped to one knee, head bowed, hands clasped, awaiting his death blow. But Wahnotee picked up the knife and threw it to his enemy so that it stuck quivering in the stage.

Then the Indian lost his knife and McClosky kicked it into the wings and prepared to carve his adversary into the semblance of a totem pole. More skirmishing, and McClosky lost his knife again. Wahnotee pinned the man's hands, bent down and picked up the knife in his teeth. Gripping McClosky's two wrists in his left hand, he stabbed his writhing adversary, placed his foot on the dead body, raised his bloody knife on high and let out a whoop of triumph that shook the very windows.

During all this, Zoe had time to drink her poison and was found on her deathbed, surrounded by Peytons and Sunnysides, imploring them, as she died to "Hearts and Flowers":

"In your happier days, give a thought to poor Zoe, the octoroon."

Another burst of red fire and the backdrop rose to show Wahnotee still poised above his fallen victim. This time it wasn't necessary to open the windows. The audience sped down the stairs by leaps and bounds.

Joe and I wondered how a western Indian came to wander so far afield. But Uncle Bee told us that since the plantation was bankrupt with its real and personal property in a mess, Wahnotee, no doubt, was an Escrow Indian; and since Uncle Bee was deep in Blackstone's *Commentaries* preparatory to studying law at the University of Wisconsin, it behooved us not to dispute him.

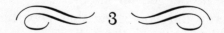 3

The joint efforts of Boucicault and Reid produced *The Octoroon* but Bartley Campbell turned out *The White Slave* alone and unassisted—unassisted, that is, but for his debt to the Boucicault–Reid combination since the semblance between the two plays was of proportions to arouse the choler of eastern critics. But the public liked it. The plot was similar but, paradoxical though it seems, the story was different. There was a heroine

BARTLEY CAMPBELL'S
PICTURESQUE SOUTHERN ROMANCE

THE WHITE SLAVE

A STORY OF 1857
ORIGINALLY ACTED APRIL 3, 1882

"THE WHITE SLAVE"

"The Death of the Master."

"The lamp of life is just flickering like a tallow dip in the west wind. A little breath from the angel of death, and he is gone."

"Hours are sometimes centuries when counted by the beating of anxious, weary hearts."

Bartley Campbell's Picturesque Southern Romance

The White Slave, A Story of 1857 was the billing on this throwaway, and again there is the appeasing sub-title to ameliorate the curse of the theater which many small town citizens shunned as the work of Old Nick himself.

This four-page booklet was far more elaborate than most of the advertising matter distributed by rep shows. More often than not, they ran off sufficient single sheet programs to supply this need.

The second page showed "The Death of the Master," facing "My Old Kentucky Home Far Away," with "The White Slave" proclaimed again on the back. The quotations are excerpts from the text. These scenes are from the big-time production; any similarity to sets and players of the small time rep companies is purely coincidental.

New York Public Library Collection

presumed to bear the color taint; a lecherous slave trader who bought her; a burning steamboat; an escape into a swamp; and the violent death of the villain.

Old Judge Hardin of Big Bend Plantation was dying. No doubt about it, for his house servants said so and sent word to the cotton patch for the no-good fieldhands to stop messing around and snake themselves to the big house to sing ole massa into Paradise at the end of Act 1.

Clay Britton, nitwit hero and Hardin's adopted son, was losing his shirt to Bill Lacy, who traded exclusively in horses and niggers and whaled hell out of both. Britton spent his days gambling with Lacy who dealt not only from the top and bottom of the deck but from the middle as well. It seemed nonsensical that such a weakling could have been given this responsibility, but Uncle Bee explained that this had to be so, else no plot; no plot, no play; no play, no white slave.

Lisa, the heroine, a reputed octoroon, was the judge's illegitimate grand-daughter, the result of an absent-minded overindulgence in continental courtesies between his daughter and a French Marquis on an amorous holiday in Florence. The judge meant to fix things after his daughter died, but the documents were mislaid and before he got around to it he passed on with a blackface quartette standing over him singing "Massa's in the Cold, Cold Ground." No doubt this was intended as a great consolation, but more likely he found welcome relief from it in death.

Being set upon the legal profession, it was inevitable that Uncle Bee should assimilate everything smacking of law. So it was he who pointed out some of the more obvious conclusions in the matter of justice as dealt out behind the footlights. His authority was that eminent historian of stage-land, Jerome K. Jerome, whose digest of dramatic statutes summed up something like this:

The accidental loss of a marriage certificate annulled the marriage.

The evidence of one prejudiced witness of shady antecedents was sufficient to convict the most irreproachable gentleman of crimes for which he had no possible motive.

A conviction could be quashed years after by the unsupported statement of the comedian.

If A forged B's name to a check, B must serve ten years in the pen.

A mortgage could be foreclosed on ten minutes' notice.

If a man died intestate, his property went to the nearest villain.

If he left a will, all of his property went to anyone who got possession of the document.

The last two citations confused Joe and me, for Clay, with power of attorney, had mortgaged the plantation not once but three times, and to get out of the mess sold all the slaves to Lacy and signed the bill of sale without reading it. Atop all this, he calmly announced that he was a good lawyer. How good was disclosed when he discovered he had sold Lisa.

CLAY

Lisa in tears? What has happened?

LACY

I have just told her of my purchase.

CLAY

But she has her freedom papers!

LACY

I had a mortgage on her when they were made out. She is my slave under the law!

CLAY

The first man who places a hand on that poor girl, I'll kill with as little mercy as I would a reptile! Lisa, come here!

LACY

The law—

CLAY

Law! There is a higher law—a law of right, mercy and justice, a law written on the throne of God and in the hearts of men. All others I despise!

This convinced us that Clay Britton was fully qualified to practice law behind the footlights, as was completely proven when he ended up in jail for interfering with a slave sale while Lisa was whisked off to Lacy's plantation on the Mississippi. Lacy had an octoroon mistress, Daphne, to whom Lisa confided her troubles.

LISA

I'll never take your place, Daphne. I am a miserable wretched octoroon like yourself, but sooner than become the mistress of this man, I'd die!

DAPHNE (*quite unnecessarily*)

Then you don't love him?

LISA

I despise him!

She repeated it in detail when Lacy approached her. Why such a consummate villain didn't rape her and have done with it was one of the imponderables. Instead, he argued with her.

LACY

Ever since I first saw you, I admired you and if the law would permit it, I would marry you gladly. But it don't. But of this house and land, a full mile along the river and three back to the bayou, with cane and cotton fields, you shall be mistress.

LISA

And Daphne?

LACY

I'll send her away. I'll fix up Osceola like a bit of fairyland. There shall be new carpets, soft laces and silks for yourself and you can gallop over all these acres on the best horseflesh the blue grass region ever bred.

LISA

And pay for it in the degradation of my womanhood? It is too much! I can't afford so high a price!

LACY

Remember! You are my slave!

LISA

Were I ten thousand times your slave, the answer would be no!

LACY

I can send you to the fields to work all day—a hoe in your hand and rags upon your back.

LISA

Rags are royal raiment when worn for virtue's sake! Rather a hoe in my hands than self-contempt in my heart!

LACY

You'll crawl to me for mercy yet. Under the blazing summer sun you shall toil from dawn till dark! You shall be fed on corn! Sleep on straw! Lodge in the humblest hut! You have made your choice. Let us see how bravely you will bear the burden!

Just then the Belle Creole came round the bend bringing a repentant Clay, who smuggled Lisa aboard the steamboat pursued by Lacy and his minions. Judge Harden by now had time to resurrect himself in the person

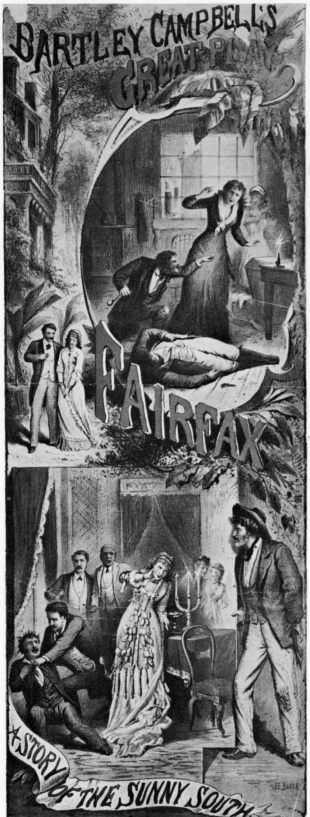

This publicity for Bartley Campbell's *The White Slave* was a colored postcard distributed in limited numbers to patrons and friends.

of Natchez Jim, a noble gambler; and when the fugitives were about to be taken, he saved them by throwing a lighted lantern into the cotton bales. Of course the Belle Creole burned to the water's edge with plenty of red fire and acrid fumes, but Lacy and his victims were saved, as were all the principals necessary to complete the play. The rest probably drowned in the Mississippi. At any rate they never appeared again in the guise of passengers of the Belle Creole.

By degrees everybody got back to Osceola Plantation, where Lisa's identity was established along with her freedom. Somewhere during the play, Lacy had found time to shoot his creole mistress Daphne, for which he was arrested and led away. His punishment established an all time record for expediency and thoroughness. As he walked off stage, two shots were fired. Job, the house servant, entered.

CLAY
Well, what has happened?

JOB
Massa Lacy tried to shoot the sheriff and the sheriff killed him.

Which brought the play to a quick conclusion amid general rejoicing.

Being a drama of many scenes, *The White Slave* was a diamond dye show. But to us it lacked the punch and intensity of *The Octoroon*. The dialogue, too, puzzled us, since virtue and vice alike spoke in numbers more or less tinged with poesy.

Joe and I commented upon this to Uncle Bee, contending that nobody ever talked as did these people. He admitted this cheerfully but remarked that it would be wonderful if they only could. Which left us more puzzled than before.

No adverse omen portended the outrage to be inflicted upon us. It was a fine Saturday morning with a smart breeze bespeaking the great out-of-doors of spring freshets and popping maples. Mother summoned me from the woodshed where Willie Frey and I were fashioning willow rods with intent to commit mayhem in certain frog ponds.

The Streets of New York

The Streets of New York was also called *The Poor of New York*, and was played by rep shows under both titles. Prolific Dion Boucicault fashioned it after a translation of a French play.

The plot was laid during the commercial panic of 1837 and twenty years after. Fairweather, a sea captain, preparing to leave on a long voyage, deposits his entire fortune with Banker Gideon Bloodgood, not knowing that the bank is insolvent and that its proprietor is planning to abscond. Growing suspicious, he demands his money. It is refused, and in the ensuing quarrel Fairweather dies of apoplexy.

Badger, banker's clerk, witness to the scene, helps carry the dead man into the street. His death is attributed to natural causes. But Badger has taken the receipt given the dead man and proceeds to blackmail Bloodgood for stealing the deposit.

Twenty years later Bloodgood has become tremendously wealthy. Badger is still hounding him while the Fairweather family, reduced to poverty, are practically beggars. Unable to secure the incriminating receipt, Bloodgood sets fire to the rickety tenement housing Badger and the Fairweathers. All escape, though the building is destroyed.

Badger shows up as a policeman and arrests Bloodgood. Under stage law, and because he is a humorous fellow, Badger's peccadilloes are overlooked and he lives on and on, probably eventually becoming police commissioner, if not Gotham's mayor.

The Streets of New York was as spectacular as *The Octoroon* in its fire scene. It took two shovelfuls of red fire to impress an audience with the enormity of the conflagration.

Harvard University Theater Collection

"Willie's mother wants him," she said. "And you come in here and get cleaned up. We're going to the matinee."

"Jeez!" was Willie's comment. "Good-bye froggin'."

"I don' wanna go to no matinee!" I bawled. "I wanna go tonight and see *The Hidden Hand*."

"Young man!" Mother's tone bided no dawling. "March yourself straight in here before I come after you with the hair brush! Willie Frey, you hustle yourself home! We're going to see Little Allie Spooner in *Little Lord Fauntleroy*."

"Christ!" said Willie Frey. "Little Lord Fauntleroy! That sissy!"

But march in I did, and home went Willie Frey, and two o'clock found us with other unwilling victims in the front row of Concert Hall, washed and combed with stiffly starched collars and Windsor ties.

Under happier conditions, neither Willie Frey nor I would have protested a votive offering upon the altar of Little Allie. We were starting to ponder the mysteries of sex, and both of us hoped at some distant day to become members of her entourage and come to know her more intimately. Unfortunately neither of us was unacquainted with that dream child of Frances Hodgson Burnett, whose mere name raised the gorge of every he-boy. Reginald Birch's becurled moron had marched across the pages of *St. Nicholas* some years before. Such a paragon of virtue as little Cedric had not been imagined since Little Eva. Nor would such another be dreamed until Pollyanna tripped across the stage.

None of us youngsters escaped those monthly installments in *St. Nicholas*, for our elders pounced upon us with each new chapter and drummed it into our ears beneath the evening lamp. But to have this saccharined dough-head flaunted before us in the flesh was too much, and even our beloved Allie enacting the role detracted not a whit from our agony. That she conspired with our betrayers to give life and breath to little Cedric rendered our torment more acute.

Certain incidents alleviated our misery. Ma Spooner was a charming Dearest, the silky mustached character man an admirably gruff old Earl; while Pa Spooner, as Mr. Hobbs, the groceryman, sang:

> A little peach in the orchard grew,
> Listen to my tale of woe,
> A little peach of emerald hue,
> Listen to my tale of woe.
> And it grew—and it grew—and it grew—
> Listen to my tale of woe.

Little Allie obliged too. Tripping to the footlights, she gave us our sop of consolation for the afternoon in a sentiment echoed in every youngster's heart.

> Oh, how can mamas find a joy
> In making such a jackass of their boy?
> For often I grow tired of wearing the sash
> Of Little Lord Fauntleroy.

Throughout that afternoon our interest centered upon Little Allie's blue pants. They fitted her callipygian quarters with a tightness promising a catastrophe at any moment—a consummation eagerly anticipated but never realized. And at five o'clock we left the hall, disappointed in this small boon so earnestly desired.

Homeward bound, Willie Frey pronounced a sinister forecast I was to remember long.

"Jeez, Bunny," he said, "We ain't heard the last of this Little Lord Fauntleroy business. Aw, Christ!"

Sunday proved him correct. First intimation came when I picked up the current issue of *The Ladies' Home Journal* opened at a dog-eared page with this paragraph marked in pencil:

Fauntleroy trousers are suitable for boys from four to eight.

They are made of corduroy and finished with a ribbon and a buckle at the knee.

But that was only the beginning. Mother and Grandmother met in the front parlor with Aunt Sarah. As a girl, she had sewed for the village tailor and understood the mysteries of patterns and cutting. Neither portions of my anatomy were measured. There was a hustling of lapboards, the snipping of black velveteen, the shaping of a ruffled collar. A week later, to my profound disgust, I emerged a Little Lord Fauntleroy.

Not that in any way was I a replica of the Birch coddling. Rather I was a pantywaist devised by three estimable gentlewomen of a mid-western village. My stockings twisted about my legs like stripes around a barber's pole. My protruding feet resembled blacking tins on the end of broomsticks. My hair was at that shaggy stage akin to an unsheared collie fresh from a burdock patch, for Mother had treacherously kept me from the barber's chair. As it grew longer she curled it by sheer strength and much water, twisting it every which way to form ringlets.

It was little solace that the neighborhood was lousy with similarly outfitted brats, nor was the four to eight year limit observed. In fashion far from angelic some twelve-year-olds even sprawled their ungainly limbs and misfit feet in the habiliments of the angelic Cedric. Willie Frey joined me in his new outfit. Eddie Barnley, affectionately dubbed "Shovel Tooth" by his cronies, came from up the street. George Vaughan led the ranks of the elite from Yankee Hill. Beaver Dam's citizens waded knee deep in Fauntleroys—tall and short, lean and fat, freckled, snub-nosed and bespectacled, whose disguise in no manner diminished their enthusiasm for raising hell. Joe escaped the ordeal. He had reached the long pants stage.

A few days later I met Willie Frey. His disguise approximated mine and like it was dirt stained in an effort to ruin it as quickly as possible.

"What do you think," he said in disgust. "The ole woman wants me to call her 'Dearest.' Jeez!"

"They all do," I answered hopelessly.

Time wore on with undiminished pain until the Universalist Society met at our house. Unobserved I crawled beneath the big center table. A pair of shears slipped from an overfilled sewing bag. Satan tempted—or was it the knowledge that Uncle Bee would stand by me. I seized the instrument of destruction and one by one clipped the ringlets from my head.

I emerged from hiding amid muffled exclamations of surprise and horror. Mother met the situation in admirable fashion. She promptly whaled the daylights out of me and sent me supperless to bed. Only Uncle Bee visited me in durance. He came, cast a melancholy eye, and left in silence.

"That boy looks like hell," he announced at breakfast the next morning. "I'm getting him a haircut."

With Mother's hesitating approval he ushered me to the village shop The barber viewed his task with alarm.

"What do you call it?" he asked.

"Take that boy and shave his head," Uncle Bee ordered. "Shave it clean—smooth as a billiard ball. I'm damned if our family is propagating any more Little Lord Fauntleroys."

The other day I visited a barber shop. The barber ran a practiced hand across my head preparatory to a cranial assault.

"Marvellous cowlicks you have," he commented. "You're sure mangy with 'em. Never saw so many before—on a man, that is. Really unusual! It is, indeed!"

"Listen," I explained patiently. "I'm no Ripley exhibit. My Mother spent days making those. She twisted my hair this way and that. She put water on it. She wanted to make it curl. Those cowlicks are her handiwork. They represent hours of loving labor. She tried to make me a Little Lord Fauntleroy."

The barber nodded sympathizingly.

"Mine, too." He spoke as one who shared a profound sorrow. "My mother did the same, peace to her ashes. But, thank God, now I'm bald!"

Together we gloomed in silence.

Chapter 9

MR. TALBOYS
IN
THE WELL

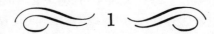

1

HEROINES of those old melodramas were virtuous to the
point of inanity. Either they were battling to ensure their pris-
tine maidenhood or they were grimly determined to retrieve a
character destroyed through the insidious advances of some
despicable adventurer. They always succeeded before the last curtain fell.

But there are exceptions to every rule, and in this galaxy of triumphant
womanhood that exception was the heroine of *Lady Audley's Secret*. For
Lady Audley was a thorough going no-good adventuress, money mad, and
a social climber. She tried her hand at bigamy, murder and arson with a
nonchalance befitting a worthier cause. And her evil doing was made the
easier because of her bewitching beauty.

That, at least, was the explanation given by her associates; and if the
player portraying Lady Audley too evidently lacked the pulchritude attributed to her, that was the fault of the actress and not of C. H. Hazel-
wood, who dramatized Mary Braddon's novel and who could do nothing
about it. Wickedness enshrouded her as a mink coat enfolds a chorus girl.
She lacked only the top hat, riding crop and boots to be marked as the
villain she was.

The curtain rose on the birthday of Sir Michael Audley, a senile old
topper hitting seventy and enjoying every minute of it, for his recently
married second wife, the said Lady Audley, aged twenty-four, was
showing her bemused lord and master the time of his life. All of this is
quickly disclosed by Phoebe Marks in a conversation with her cousin,
Luke Marks, a drunken gamekeeper who devotes more time to poaching
than pursuing the intruders who make free with the Audley preserves.
Two years before, Lady Audley was a governess where Phoebe was a
housemaid; but after snaring the senescent lord, the two women joined
hands, one as lady of the manor, the other as her associate and confidante.
Luke wants to marry Phoebe. Evidently there were no laws against con-
sanguineous matrimony in the England of that day.

Since the birthday celebration is centered about the estate's park, the
wood drop is hung against the rear wall with the woodwings at either side.
An iron garden seat and a couple of the hall's chairs complete the decor.
At right center is a practical well. A practical well was carried by some
companies, but more often a dry goods crate was pressed into service by
knocking out the back, covering the outside with gray crepe paper to
simulate stone, and attaching an iron crank to the side. For it was presumed to be an old-fashioned chain-and-cup well and the handle was an
integral part of the plot. The protecting sides concealed a mattress upon
which Lady Audley's victim landed on all fours and the rear extended
into the wings so that he could crawl off unobserved.

With plenty of laugher off stage, lord and lady make their appearance;
and when Phoebe has explained that her drunken cousin wants to marry
her, Sir Michael generously declares he'll set 'em up in business. This Lady
Audley shushes since it means money out of her pocket. And when they
are joined by Alicia, daughter by the lord's first wife, the merrymaking
continues until word is dropped that Nephew Robert is coming home
today. Robert, it seems, is going to marry Alicia, probably to top off the
matrimonial pairings that were a part of these old-fashioned plots. So Lady
Audley lures Sir Thomas off to the summer house, in which you could

read implied seduction if you possessed an evil mind; and the rest go on other errands; and Robert Audley appears upon the scene.

But Nephew Robert is not alone. He has brought back with him George Talboys, whom he met abroad. Robert has never seen the new mistress of the manor, and Talboys is bemoaning the fact that only two years ago he was left a widower.

In a single breath, he relates the story of his life. Inheriting two thousand pounds, he married, took his wife to the continent, squandered his nest egg and returned to England. Given an appointment in India, he left to carry out his mission only to be notified soon after that his bride is dead.

"And now what atonement can I make?" Talboys asks. "Only this. Seek out her grave and raise a monument over it that shall cause her memory to be respected—her fate pitied."

Alicia comes to greet her suitor and the conversation turns to the new Lady Audley.

ROBERT

What is she like, Alicia?

ALICIA

Oh, a perfect wax doll as regards complexion; fair as the day when in good temper, but black as night if she can't rule anybody as she likes.

ROBERT

And does she rule you?

ALICIA

I should like to catch her at it. I'm as old as she is but I've her likeness here (*shows miniature*) painted on ivory—a speaking resemblance, I can assure you.

ROBERT (*looking at it*)

Fair as the day as you observe. A gentle, innocent looking face enough. Look, George.

TALBOYS (*touching her shoulder*)

Her face! Her's! Good heaven, what can this mean? It is a likeness of my wife! Some fearful mystery is this. Does she live to be the wife of Sir Michael Audley. But let me not be rash. I'll linger in the park and if I have been deceived, woe to the traitress—woe—woe—and punishment!

And having delivered himself of this aside while Robert and Alicia chat unconcernedly, Talboys rushes off just in time to escape meeting Lady Audley.

After a brief exchange, in which the wicked siren starts to work on Robert, and Alicia throws a fit of jealousy, Lady Audley is left alone to soliloquize another clutch of the plot.

LADY AUDLEY

I must stand well with my husband's favorite nephew, I know. I live now for ambition and interest, to mould the world and its votaries to my own end. Once I was fool enough to marry for love. Now I have married for wealth. What a change from the wife of George Talboys to the wife of Sir Michael Audley! My fool of a first husband thinks me dead. Oh excellent scheme, oh cunning device, how well you have served me!

> *(Talboys enters from the rear and comes down silently to her side)*

Where can he be now? In India, no doubt. He is mourning my death perhaps—ha, ha! Why, I have only just begun to live—to taste the sweets of wealth and power. If I am dead to George Talboys, he is dead to me. Yes, I am well rid of him and on this earth we meet no more.

TALBOYS *(touching her shoulder)*

Yes we do!

LADY AUDLEY *(turning with a shriek)*

George Talboys!

TALBOYS

Aye, your husband—the husband of the woman who calls herself Lady Audley. Really, for a woman who has been dead and buried you look remarkably well, my dear.

LADY AUDLEY

I am lost!

TALBOYS

You turn away, a cold welcome from a wife to her husband after a three years separation. You are a traitress, madame!

LADY AUDLEY

Is it to be peace or war between us?

TALBOYS

War to the last till I see thee placed in a felon's dock and sentenced by a judge.

LADY AUDLEY

Oh, spare me! Spare me!

TALBOYS

Spare you—no! I'll expose you, woman—you whom——

LADY AUDLEY

Whom you left here in poverty and dependence—whom you promised to write to from India.

TALBOYS

And to whom I did write.

LADY AUDLEY

Not one letter reached my hands!

Back and forth goes the shuttlecock of charge and counter charge until Talboys plays his trump card. He'll tell Robert Audley. This evident threat hits Lady Audley below the belt.

LADY AUDLEY

Then you will war with a woman?

TALBOYS

To the death!

LADY AUDLEY (*aside*)

Death—death. Aye, that is the word—that is the only way to escape. I have offered a bribe. I have used threats. Now I must employ cunning.

TALBOYS (*seizing her wrist*)

Come!

LADY AUDLEY

One moment. I will accompany you if you will let me have a few seconds to myself so that I may send a few lines in my tablets to Sir Michael saying I shall never see him more.

TALBOYS

Well, be quick then.

(*Music—piano until the end of the act*)

LADY AUDLEY

I will.

> (*Talboys moves over, and as his back is turned Lady Audley goes to the well, removes the iron handle and conceals it behind her.*)

It is mine—one point gained! Now for the second. (*pretending faintness*) Water! Water! For mercy's sake! My head burns!

TALBOYS

This is some trick to escape me but I'll not leave you.

LADY AUDLEY

I do not wish you to. Stoop down and dip this in the well (*gives him her handkerchief*) that I may bathe my throbbing temples! Quick! Quick!

> (*Talboys stoops down to the well. She creeps upon him and strikes him over the head with the iron handle.*)

Now—die! Die!

> (*She pushes him into the well.*)

He is gone—gone! Dead men tell no tales. I am free! Ha, ha, ha! I am free. For none was a witness to the deed.

LUKE MARKS (*protruding his head from behind a tree*)

Except me!

> (*He continues to stare at Lady Audley as she raises her arms in triumph, laughing exulting, as the curtain falls.*)

Six months has elapsed when the curtain rises to disclose the Audley parlor, and while there is some slight speculation as to what could have become of George Talboys no one seems particularly interested except Robert Audley. But by now he is so tied up with his sweetheart, Alicia, that he can devote only a portion of his spare time to this speculation. Luke Marks, however, knows the score. And after waiting these six months, he calls upon Lady Audley and cuts loose. He appears carrying more than half a load of liquor.

LADY AUDLEY

How now, fellow?

LUKE

How now, madam?

LADY AUDLEY

You have no business here.

LUKE

How do you know?

LADY AUDLEY (*points off R.C.*)

Begone!

LUKE

Stay! If anyone hears what I'm going to say, you're a doomed woman. I knows what I knows.

LADY AUDLEY

What is that?

LUKE

Enough to hang thee. I saw you push him in. Dead men tell no tales but the live ones may, so if my mouth be not stopped I may open it.

LADY AUDLEY

You cannot want money, for when you were married to Phoebe four months ago I put you both in the inn at Mount Stanning and trusted you would do well.

LUKE

We shall do well enough when we have a banker like you to draw upon. Phoebe knows nothing of what I saw thee do, and nobody shall know if you always give me what I want.

LADY AUDLEY

What money do you expect?

LUKE

A hundred pounds will do now.

LADY AUDLEY

I'll bring it to your house at dusk. I have not so much with me.

LUKE

I must have thy money or the world shall have the secret.

With which he takes himself off. But Lady Audley has not reached the end of her troubles. Robert renounces his wooing long enough to give a thought to what happened to Talboys.

ROBERT enters, *dressed in mourning*

Six months have passed and no tidings of George. He can not be living or he must have seen the advertisements that I have inserted, begging him to communicate with me. If he had died suddenly, some-one would have given me information of his death.

LADY AUDLEY

Any news of your friend?

ROBERT

None.

LADY AUDLEY

Let me see. What was his name?

ROBERT

George Talboys, ma'am.

LADY AUDLEY

I knew it was some boys but whether Talboys or Shortboys I really couldn't remember.

ROBERT

George Talboy's wife was very like you, Lady Audley.

LADY AUDLEY

She died very young, I believe.

ROBERT

I question whether she died at all.

LADY AUDLEY

Why?

ROBERT

Because she lives again in you!

LADY AUDLEY

Pray, did you ever see George Talboys' wife?

ROBERT

I never saw her but among my poor friend's luggage I found this miniature. Madam, this is your likeness.

LADY AUDLEY

Prove it!

ROBERT

I have remarked your handwriting closely and compared it with this letter found with this likeness! You can tell me of George's fate, for you are Helen Talboys.

LADY AUDLEY

Take my advice and keep your suspicions to yourself. Are we to be friends or foes?

ROBERT

I will give you until tomorrow to reflect. You must leave here. No one must know your destination. Agree to this and I will be silent. Refuse, and I will tell all, and let the law take its course.

So Robert wanders away to find Alicia, but Lady Audley spikes his suit by telling her husband that his nephew has been making advances to her. Whereupon Sir Audley, knowing the lady's weaknesses, sends Robert packing while Alicia declares the engagement null and void.

Robert ends up at the Castle Inn, Luke and Phoebe Marks, Props. This affords a novelty set—a divided scene of two rooms arranged by placing a practical flat against the kitchen backdrop. Since this practical flat possessed a practical door, it had to be carried by the company because such a piece of scenery was a rarity with the small time houses.

Robert and Luke indulge in a drinking bout, for Robert hopes to wrest the secret of Talboys' death from the gamekeeper turned landlord. But Luke drinks himself into a stupor, his head on the table. Lady Audley arrives to pay her blackmail. Phoebe is with her.

LADY AUDLEY

Not a word to Robert Audley that I am here. Send your husband to me.

PHOEBE

I will if he's in a fit state.

LADY AUDLEY

Fit or not, I must see him. I must have no more visits to the Hall. Go!

PHOEBE (*enters the other room*)

Luke (*shakes him*) Luke.

ROBERT

He's too far gone in drink to pay any attention, my dear, and since I don't find him lively company, I'll go to bed.

PHOEBE

This way, sir. (*Both exit*)

LADY AUDLEY (*peeping through the doorway*)

So Robert Audley sleeps in yonder room—would he slept his last.

PHOEBE (*reentering*)
I wish you would call in the morning or have Luke go to you.

LADY AUDLEY
I want you to walk part of the way with me. Go on the road and I'll overtake you.

PHOEBE
I'm afraid to leave Luke. He may set the house on fire.

LADY AUDLEY
(*Aside*) Fire. A good idea. (*To Phoebe*) Go, go Phoebe. If your husband is too far gone to listen to me, I'll follow right after.

PHOEBE
Whatever can she have to say to Luke. (*exits*)

LADY AUDLEY
(*Takes candle and looks off stage*) The hayloft!

> (*Music to end of act. She exits. Fire starts off stage. She returns, locks door which parts the room and leaves hurriedly. Fire increases. Luke wakes.*)

LUKE
Fire! Phoebe! Help! Fire! (*tries door*) It's fast! Great Heaven! I know I've been bad but save me, someone. I choke—I die. Mercy. Help! Help!

> (*Luke staggers and falls.*)

Curtain.

The curtain is the wood drop, and as Phoebe enters from one side of the stage, Alicia enters from the opposite. They meet center stage.

ALICIA
Oh, Phoebe, I'm so glad to see you. My poor father has been struck down by a terrible fit. His speech is fast leaving him. Where can Lady Audley be? Where is Robert? His only wish is to see them. They tell me Robert was seen going toward the inn. Is he there?

PHOEBE
Yes—yes.

MR. TALBOYS IN THE WELL

ALICIA

Go to him—quick—quick. Pray do. I must hasten back for I am in suspense—in agony—away from my father. Oh, haste, Phoebe, haste.

Alicia turns back, and Lady Audley arrives to learn the news from Phoebe, who is ready to go after Robert. Not until then does she pay any attention to the fire which has been merrily burning off stage.

PHOEBE

Oh, look, my lady. There is a fire in the direction of our house.

LADY AUDLEY

Nonsense. It is quite a contrary way—in the direction of Brentwood, I should say.

PHOEBE

I am certain it is Mount Sterling, my lady. I must go and be satisfied.

LADY AUDLEY

Come with me to the hall. Did you not say that Sir Michael was dangerously ill?

PHOEBE

But I have a husband, Madam, and bad as he is, it is my duty to see to his safety.

LADY AUDLEY

Let the drunken sot perish if he will. He is a curse, a disgrace to you and——

PHOEBE

And therefore not fit to die. Why do you hold me? Why do you wish to prevent me returning home. You have some wicked motive. I can see it in your eye.

LADY AUDLEY

You are mistaken, girl.

PHOEBE

No! I see it all now! Luke was the possessor of some terrible secret. You wished me out of the way and Mr. Robert, too. That was your motive in wishing me to leave you alone at the inn. Oh, cruel, wicked woman! What did my husband know that you should wish him dead?

LADY AUDLEY

He knew too much and now he is silenced.

PHOEBE

But I am not. I will denounce you to justice! I will proclaim you a murderess! Help! Help! Murder! Help!

LADY AUDLEY

Silence. Come with me to the Hall. I am your friend.

> (*Lady Audley starts to drag Phoebe after her. Robert Audley rushes on and tears Phoebe away.*)

ROBERT

Away to your husband, girl, and see if there is any help for him.
(*Phoebe rushes off*)
And now, Lady Audley, we have come to a reckoning!

LADY AUDLEY

Alive!

> (*Chord in G*)

ROBERT

Aye, to punish and expose you. I live to be your fate and the avenger of my friend!

LADY AUDLEY

I have wealth—boundless wealth—and I will use it to crush you, Robert Audley.

ROBERT

How?

LADY AUDLEY

Thus!

> (*Rushes toward him with a dagger. He wrenches it from her hand.*)

ROBERT

Thus do I rob the serpent of its sting!

> (*Enter Luke followed by and supported by Phoebe.*)

LUKE

Thank Heaven, I am spared to do an act of justice before I end my guilty life. I accuse this woman of——

ROBERT

Hold! It will be better not to cast a stain on my uncle's name. Say nothing, I entreat you.

LUKE

Then I will be silent for ever—ever—ever

(*Luke falls back unconscious*)

LADY AUDLEY

He is dead and I shall triumph over them all.

(*The great bell of the castle starts to toll as Alicia enters*)

ALICIA

Robert—Robert. My father is dead. Oh, pity me—pity and protect me.

ROBERT

Sir Michael dead! Now vengeance take thy own! Friends, hear me. I accuse this woman of the murder of George Talboys.

LADY AUDLEY

How and where?

LUKE (*reviving*)

She pushed him down the well. But it will be useless to search there for George Talboys——

TALBOYS (*entering*)

Is here.

OMNES

Alive.

(*Chord in G. Luke falls back dead*)

TALBOYS

Back woman and thank that man (*pointing to Luke*) that you have not my death upon your soul. The blow you struck rendered me an invalid for months. I have been silent until today because I gave my word to that poor wretch. But now I am free—free to tell all. Speak to her, Robert, and say that I forgive her.

ROBERT

Do you hear, woman?

LADY AUDLEY (*vacantly*)

I hear! But I do not heed. I have a rich husband. They told me he was dead—but no—they lied. See, he stands there. Your arm—your arm, Sir Michael. We will leave this place—we will travel. Never mind

what the world says. I have no husband but you. It is time to depart.
The carriage is waiting. Come—come—come.

                    OMNES (*retreating up stage*)
She is mad—mad!

            LADY AUDLEY
Aye, mad, mad. That is the word. I feel it here (*Places her hands
on her temples.*) Do not touch me—do not come near me—let me claim
your silence—your pity—and let the grave, the cold grave, close over
Lady Audley and her Secret.

                    (*Falls. Dies. Tableau as George
                    Talboys kneels beside her*)

            CURTAIN

Joe and I were somewhat confused as to just what was Lady Audley's
secret. She was involved in so many things that you had your choice of
the whole gamut of crime. But Uncle Bee settled it once and for all.

Lady Audley's Secret, he said, was how a person could write such a bad
play and why anyone in his right mind would want to act in it.

It was a certainty that each season would bring the same crop of familiar
plays. A new offering was introduced from time to time, but each rep
company stuck to the old favorites best fitted to its players and all of us
would have been disappointed if denied our yearly visit with *East Lynne,
The Two Orphans* or *The Octoroon,* or any of a dozen other favorites whose
appeal never seemed to wane. This same tolerant attitude was found in
later years when vaudeville flourished and its people returned year after
year with the identical act.

Less frequent—and awaited with keener anticipation because of it—
was the visit of *Our American Cousin.* Tom Taylor's three act drama was
played in Ford's Theater the night John Wilkes Booth shot President
Lincoln and that tragedy was still well remembered. Grandfather was one
of the first to join the infant Republican party when it was organized in
Ripon, Wisconsin, and he was all out for Honest Abe from the beginning.

The mourning bunting that bedecked our home when Lincoln died lay mouldering in our attic and the story of that fatal night was familiar to Joe and me through family discussions.

So we always went to see *Our American Cousin* with something of awe in our approach. Tragedy is very real to the young and we visualized the death scene with the vividness of imaginative youth. But the play itself soon caused us to resume our critical attitude and to appraise it at its true value. It was no whit better or worse than a dozen other comedy dramas except that situation was piled upon situation to no good end. Some plays

Our American Cousin

Laura Keene and E. A. Sothern

Florence Trenchard and Lord Dundreary

New York Public Library Collection

When *Our American Cousin* was first produced, Laura Keene took it as a stop-gap when she prepared a Shakespearean revival. E. A. Sothern was given the role of Lord Dundreary, a silly ass Englishman, which he built up until he dominated the play. Joseph Jefferson won stardom as Asa Trenchard. But Miss Keene found herself almost lost in the part of Florence Trenchard, and never was entirely satisfied with her choice of a role that proved a secondary one instead of an outstanding part fitted to the abilities of a stellar actress. On the night of Lincoln's assassination, Miss Keene was playing Florence, but the part of Dundreary was taken by one of the members of the John Ford stock company.

had a disputed will; some an impending mortgage; some a threat of a forced marriage. But *Our American Cousin* had all three, with plenty of skullduggery thrown in for good measure.

The American cousin was Asa Trenchard, a Vermont Yankee and a distant relative of old Mark Trenchard, head of the Trenchard clan and owner of Trenchard Manor. After rowing with his family, Mark went to America, where he died, conveniently leaving Sir Edward Trenchard putative head of the family and all its incumbrances. For the old home is shot full of holes with liens, mortgages, notes overdue, judgments, impending

executions and what not, until Sir Edward is driven to it to keep his wine
cellar up to standard.

But debt-ridden though he is, Sir Edward is overrun with the guests
necessary to the plot. There is Lord Dundreary, the original silly-ass Englishman; Mrs. Mountchessington and Daughter Augusta, seeking an ad-
vantageous marriage; Capt. De Boots, an eligible bachelor; and Harry
Vernon, naval cadet and suitor for the hand of Florence, Sir Edward's
daughter.

Sir Edward's sublime disregard for financial details is evidenced by his
signing every document presented to him and by his infinite trust in
Mr. Coyle, recognized by any knowing spectator as a first class villain.
His sneer was as evident as his unctuous complacency. Besides he sported
a sinister beard, trademark of the stage miscreant, and his plotting was
expressed in loud soliloquies heard all over the house. He was out to marry
Florence or else foreclose one of a half-dozen mortgages that would have
wrecked the place. We could only conclude that Sir Edward was a hero
grown old. Nothing else could account for such utter imbecility.

Apparently impressed by Asa's bucolic naïveté, Old Mark made him
sole heir and when the curtain rose on the parlor set, representing the
grandeur of Trenchard Manor, Asa barged into the party with an insolence
that made him objectionable from the very first. His loud-mouthed introductory rantings partook more of the routine of a Mississippi river bully
than a fugitive from the Vermont hills. As family representative, Florence
Trenchard welcomed him.

FLORENCE

Ah, then it is our American cousin. Glad to see you—my brother told
me to expect you.

ASA

I guess you do b'long to my family. I'm Asa Trenchard, born in Vermont, suckled on the banks of Muddy Creek, about the tallest gunner,
the slickest dancer and generally the loudest critter in the state.
You're my cousin, be you. Well, I ain't got no objections to kiss you as
one cousin ought to kiss another.

FLORENCE

In the old country, Mr. Trenchard, cousins content themselves with
hands but our hearts are with them. You are welcome—there is mine.

ASA

Now if you'll have me shown to my room I should like to fix up a bit and put on a clean buzzom. (*All start*) What on earth is the matter with you? I only spoke because you're so go-to-meetin' like.

Asa freshens up and returns for further gaucheries.

ASA

There were so many all-fired fixin's in my room that I couldn't find what I wanted.

FLORENCE

What was it you couldn't find in your room?

ASA

Soft soap.

OMNES (*singly*)

Soft soap?

ASA

Yes, soft soap. I reckon you know what that is. However, I struck a pump in the kitchen, slicked my hair down a little, gave my boots a lick of grease, and now I feel quite handsome. But I'm everlastingly dry.

FLORENCE

You'll find ale, wine and luncheon on the side table.

ASA

Wal, I don't know's I've got an appetite. Comin' along on the cars, I worried down a half dozen ham san'wiches, eight or ten boiled eggs, two or three punkin pies and a string of cold sausages. I can hold out until dinner time.

BINNEY (*the butler*)

Luncheon.

ASA (*viewing the sidetable*)

I don't want to speak too plain but this is an awful mean set out for a big house like this.

FLORENCE

What's wrong, sir?

ASA

There's no mush. Nary a slapjack. No pork and beans. And where on airth's the clam chowder? Here's to your health. (*Takes a drink and spits it out*) Do you call that a drink? See here, cousin, you seems to be the liveliest critter around here so hurry up the fixings.

FLORENCE

What do you mean—fixings?

ASA

Why brandy, rum, gin and whiskey. We'll make them all useful.

FLORENCE

Oh, I'll hurry the fixings. (*Giggling*) What fun! (*Exits*)

Florence and the butler bring on decanters, glasses and, most miraculous of all, green mint and straws. None of us knew much about mint juleps and so we concluded that the distant English people must be still more ignorant. As it was strictly a southern drink to be consumed on a spacious veranda while happy Negroes strummed the banjo and patted juba, it was equally bewildering that a Vermont Yankee should know the secret of the making. But make them he did, and all were quite happily jingled by curtain time.

Back in his room, Asa discovers a strange contraption that puzzles him. It was supposed to be a shower bath, an effect attained by sticking a tin washtub in from the flies and attaching a sprinkling can to a stepladder off stage so that its nozzle protruded. Asa managed to get under it fully clothed and the first act concluded with him completely drenched, which Joe and I approved most heartily. We hoped it would put him in his place.

While the plotting of Coyle runs on and on, and Sir Edward continues to sign incriminating papers, and Florence appears occasionally to let the audience know she is still alive, we are introduced to Mary Meredith. All of the household are out playing at archery but Mary sticks to her dairy, which happens to be the kitchen set dressed up with some milk cans and a pail. Mary, it seems, is an abused member of the family, a Cinderella deprived of her birthright and ignored by everyone except Florence.

MARY

Grandfather was rich but he must have had a bad heart or he never would have cast off poor mama. Had he adopted me I should never have been as happy as I am now. Uncle is kind to me in his pompous, patronizing way and dear Florence loves me like a sister and so I am happy. I am my own mistress and not anybody's humble servant. I sometimes find myself singing as the birds do.

So while she is singing "The Maid With a Milking Pail," Florence and Asa arrive. Asa by this time has dropped some of his crudeness and evidently is impressed with little Mary's innocence. Florence and he discuss the girl after she leaves.

ASA

I rather think I'm keeping that everlasting angel of a girl out of her fortune all along by this bit of paper. (*Takes paper from his pocket*)

FLORENCE

What is that?

ASA

Old Mark's will.

FLORENCE

Don't show it to me! The fortune should have gone to Mary. She is the only relative in a direct line.

ASA

Say, cousin, you haven't told her that the darned property was left to me, have you?

FLORENCE

Do you think I have the heart to tell her of her misfortune?

ASA

Well, darn me if you didn't show your good sense at any rate.

The bailiffs come to arrest Sir Edward, and by this time we are informed that Abel Murcott, Coyle's confidential man and a drunkard of no mean capacity, knows what is going on; and if he can sober up long enough to tell the story, Sir Edward may be rescued from his financial doldrums.

Asa has fallen for Mary and meeting her in the dairy goes into his big scene. He tells how Old Luke is on his death bed. Asa is beside him.

ASA

Will you excuse me for lighting a cigar? The story is long, awful moving and I don't think I could get on without a smoke. (*Strikes match*) Wal, he says to me and his voice was like a whisper: "Asa boy," said he. "I feel that I've sinned against my own flesh and blood. But I will not wrong the last that is left of them. Give me a light."

Wal, I gave him a light and he says: "When I die this sheet of paper would make you the heir to all my property in England." And he took a sheet of paper just as I might take this (*draws will from his pocket*) and he twisted it up as I might this (*twists it*) and he lights it just this way (*lights it*) and he watched it burn slowly and slowly away.

And he says: "Asa, boy, that act disinherits you but it leaves the property to one who has a better right to it—my own daughter's darling child, Mary Meredith." And then he smiled and sank down on his pillow and that was the last of poor Mark Trenchard.

Ezra Kendall

Some small time stars traveled from coast to coast and one of these was Ezra Kendall, who later graduated to the big time.

Born on a small farm in Allegany County, New York, Kendall tried out his hand as a printer and reporter for the New York *Herald* before he took to the stage. He made his debut in 1880, and for twenty years played small time before he landed on the main stem. He adopted a makeup patterned after that of Sol Smith Russell and never varied it. No matter what the part, his Lincolnian top hat and bagged trousers were in evidence. Kendall wrote many of the comedies in which he appeared, among them *A Fool and His Money*, *We, Us and Co.* and *A Pair of Kids*. Later he was seen in *The Vinegar Buyer*, *The Land of Dollars* and *Weather Beaten Bronson*.

For a time he was featured in vaudeville and turned out a number of paper bound books that contained the gist of his rapid fire monologues. They were *Good Gravy*, *More Good Gravy*, and *Still More Good Gravy;* and were popular with the younger set who memorized many of the gags and passed them off as their own.

Then Mary realizes that Asa loves her, and it remains only for the couple to pair off, and drunken Murcott to sober up sufficiently to denounce Coyle for the unscrupulous plotter that he is, and for Florence to pair off with Vernon, the cadet, and Dundreary to indulge in some more inanities, and the curtain falls with everything straightened out to the satisfaction of everybody.

We knew that this play established Joseph Jefferson as a star in the part of Asa Trenchard; and that E. A. Sothern went on and on playing Dundreary, whose whiskers were adopted by England's young social set; and that Florence Trenchard was a comparatively small part that Laura Keene liked none too well. And we knew, also, that there was the scene in which Mrs. Mountchessington discovered Asa was penniless and denounced him as a person bereft of good manners. (In which she was absolutely right.) And that Asa answered her back with:

> "Don't know the manners of good society, eh? Well I guess I know enough to turn you inside out, old gal—you sock-dologizing old mantrap."

This speech, we were told, was the last ever heard by Lincoln, for while it was being spoken that fatal night, Booth crept into the box and put a bullet in the President's brain. There were a number of old soldiers ready to confirm this. For they said they had been in the theater and had actually heard the words spoken by Harry Hawks, who played Trenchard.

With time, more and more of them remembered the incident, as is often the way with oldsters when their associates have died and they are freer to draw upon the well of imagination. But one who said little played a tremendous role in the great tragedy. He was William Coxshall and he was one of the four executioners who helped hang four people convicted of joining with Booth in his assassination plan.

When Edmund Ruffin fired the first shot upon Fort Sumter and Abner Doubleday retorted in kind to open the Civil War, Concert Hall became the gathering place for Beaver Dam's recruiting. There the boys met to drill until the enlistment roll was filled and they entrained for the front.

While they were gone, wives and mothers worked there making bandages, gathering supplies and relieving the strain with amateur entertainments to raise funds for the cause. When those who lived through it came back again, they were welcomed at the hall with a monster banquet and endless speeches and a plenitude of oratorical flapdoodlery.

For a time Concert Hall was the assembly place on Decoration Day when the women fashioned bouquets of peonies and lilacs, and veterans and school children marched behind the Beaver Dam Silver Cornet Band to place their tribute on the green mounds in Oakwood or the Old Cemetery.

By the time I was old enough to learn about them, most of these men were old codgers, at least in my opinion, wearing their G.A.R. hat and plodding along with a cane. Men were old at forty then. At fifty they were decrepit, and ten years later they were ready for the Soldiers' Home. But there was one who seemed much younger than the others.

He was a tall, spare man with a mustache of indeterminate shade and a reticence which his business emphasized the more. He ran a butcher shop; and butchering in our town was associated with men like John Hensler— strapping fellows of florid complexion who bantered their customers into paying top prices and threw in a hunk of liver for the cat.

William Coxshall was none of this. Quiet spoken and efficient, he made his sales with a paucity of conversation. But he prospered and in time sold his business and became a cattle buyer, shipping his stock to the Armours, Cudahy, and Swift.

As a boy it was my daily errand to pick up the family meat for dinner, and when I peered over the counter's edge, the butcher's hands came into direct view. What intrigued me was his left hand. The forefinger was missing. Not that it in any way interfered with his dexterity, but I wondered just how it came about.

I knew he was a veteran of the Civil War. But not until years later did I learn of the significance of that missing digit. For William Coxshall incurred the loss upon the field of battle and because of it was fated to spring the trap that hanged two of the conspirators in the assassination of Abraham Lincoln. And he told of the incidents of that execution when he hanged Mrs. Mary Surratt and Lewis Payne on that hot July day in 1865.

Coxshall was twenty-two at the time. He left the farm to enlist in 1861, was in the service for nine months, and was discharged for disability. In March, 1864, he was in his front yard when a friend hailed him.

"I'm going down to enlist," he called. "Come on along."

"Wait till I get my coat," Coxshall answered.

By such small things are tragedies created. To town they went and enlisted in Company K, Thirty-seventh Volunteer Wisconsin Infantry. Three days later they were before Petersburg, and Coxshall was ordered to work as a miner. During the skirmishing his friend was shot down, a bullet through his head. Coxshall's finger was shot away. It was rudely amputated, gangrene threatened, and he was invalided to Washington.

One of Company F, of the Veteran Reserve Corps, he found himself mingling with veterans from Wisconsin, Michigan, Illinois and Indiana for the greater part. Members of the Invalid Corps were placed on duty at the United States arsenal. From 100 to 120 men reported each morning and were given their orders. Two hours' service with four hours' relief was the customary stint. The work offered little relief from monotony, and anything for a change was eagerly welcomed.

John Wilkes Booth paid for his crime at Garrett's Farm, and eight persons were convicted of complicity in the crime. Dr. Samuel Mudd, Michael O'Laughlin, Samuel Arnold and Edmund Spangler were sentenced to the Dry Tortugas. Mary Surratt, Lewis Payne, George Atzerodt and David Herold were sentenced to hang. Mrs. Surratt had kept a boarding house where the conspirators gathered. Payne was all but successful in an attempt to assassinate Secretary of State William Seward. Herold accompanied Booth on his flight from Washington and was in at his death, and Atzerodt was told to kill Vice President Andrew Johnson but backed down at the last hour.

On July 5, the sentence was confirmed by President Johnson. Execution was set for July 7. On July 6, the Invalid Corps reported for duty at the arsenal prison.

"Of course we were ignorant of the findings of the commission," Coxshall said. "Only the officers and those actually engaged in erecting the scaffold knew the details. On that day when we reported for service, Colonel Christian Rath came in when we were assembled.

" 'I want four able-bodied men to volunteer for special duty,' he said.

"None of us waited to hear what the duty was. We were ready for anything to break the monotony. Plenty of us stepped forward. Rath looked us over and walked down the line. He stopped before the man next to me and looked him over critically.

" 'Where's your cartridge belt?' he asked.

" 'I got doctor's permission to leave it off,' the soldier said. 'I've been sick.'

" 'I don't want you,' Rath told him. Then he looked at me. 'What ails you?'

"I held up my hand to show the missing finger.

" 'Anything else?' he asked.

" 'Not a thing,' I answered.

" 'All right,' Rath said, 'You're elected.'

"He looked us over some more and picked out the likely ones. We followed him into the yard of the arsenal and there we had the first hint of what we were to do. The gallows was standing, ready for the execution.

"First of all we were put to work cleaning up the litter and debris that scattered the place. Then Rath told us off for service. D. F. Shoupe and I were chosen to knock out the posts beneath one of the drops. G. F. Taylor and F. B. Haslett handled the other one. Three others were chosen to bring in the prisoners, Lieut. Col. McCall being delegated to escort Mrs. Surratt.

"And then that morning, a rehearsal was held in the prison yard—one of the grimmest things I have ever known. Four 140-pound shells were attached to the hanging ropes with chains. For two hours we were drilled in dropping these exactly as though the prisoners were there.

"The gallows had been constructed by the arsenal carpenters under Rath's direction. He had been a sheriff back in Michigan and so had been appointed to this task. It was a broad platform with two hinged leaves at the front, each leaf for two of the quartette. These leaves were each supported by a timber at the front. Half way back were two parallel upright timbers through which ran another timber horizontally, suspended by a rope from the gallows platform.

"It was up to Shoupe and myself to see that the supporting timber in front remained firmly in place until the signal was given. Then by pulling back the swinging timber, thrusting it through the parallel uprights and knocking out the front prop, the drop was shot. For two hours we rehearsed with the shells. Then men were told off and four graves were dug. After that, Rath dismissed us.

" 'I want you boys to do a good job tomorrow,' he said. 'Don't make any mistakes and when it's all over, I'll give you each a canteen of whiskey.'

"But he didn't. The truth is, we never got that drink.

"We reported early on the day of the execution. It was July 7, 1865, a terrifically hot day with the thermometer close to a hundred degrees. Before nine o'clock we were in the prison yard. We were told that the execution would take place around two o'clock. The first floor anterooms of the prison started to fill up with officers who watched proceedings from the open windows.

"Newspaper reporters were on the job, and I picked up scraps of information from them. Three or four of Davy Herold's sisters had spent the night with him. There were six girls, I believe, and Davy was little more than a boy. Mrs. Surratt's daughter had attempted to reach President Johnson to plead for her mother but had been stopped on the way. She was trying to get an order preventing her execution. George Atzerodt had been visited by a woman with whom he lived. None but his lawyers and a minister had been with Lewis Payne. All this gossip helped to pass the time while we stood about and sweated under the boiling sun.

"Payne, they told us, attempted to save Mrs. Surratt in a statement in which he said she knew nothing of the murder plot. It was hatched at 7:30 o'clock before the attempt and he did not believe that she knew anything of the kidnaping plot of which this was the outgrowth. Gen. Winfield Scott Hancock had overall charge of the execution and he waited as long as he could hoping for a reprieve.

"About 11:30, Rath wanted to give the drops a final tryout. One worked all right, but ours stuck. So they called the carpenter to saw it down a bit. We tried it a second time, and though it worked perfectly, we had no great confidence that it would come off all right. Four arm chairs were placed on the scaffold and all was ready.

"A little before one o'clock, Hancock came into the yard and called Gen. John F. Hantraft, his immediate subordinate.

" 'My God, not the woman, too?' Hantraft exclaimed.

" 'Yes, the woman too,' Hancock answered.

"The prison door opened and the condemned came in. Mrs. Surratt was first, near fainting after a look at the gallows. She would have fallen had they not supported her. Herold was next. The young man was frightened to death. He trembled and shook and seemed on the verge of fainting. Atzerodt shuffled along in carpet slippers, a long white nightcap on his head. Under different circumstances, he would have been ridiculous.

"With the exception of Payne, all were on the verge of collapse. They had to pass beside the open graves to reach the gallows steps and they could gaze down into the shallow holes and even touch the crude pine boxes that were to receive them. But Payne was as stolid as if he were a spectator instead of a principal. Herold wore a black hat until he reached the gallows. Payne was bareheaded but he reached out and took a straw sailor hat off the head of an officer. He wore it until they put the black bag on him.

"The condemned were led to the chairs and Rath seated them. Mrs. Surratt and Payne were on our drop, Herold and Atzerodt on the other. Umbrellas were raised above the woman and Hantraft, who read the warrants and the findings. Then the clergy took over, talking what seemed to me interminably. The strain was getting worse. I became nauseated, what with the heat and the waiting, and taking hold of the supporting post, I hung on and vomited. I felt a little better after that, but not too good.

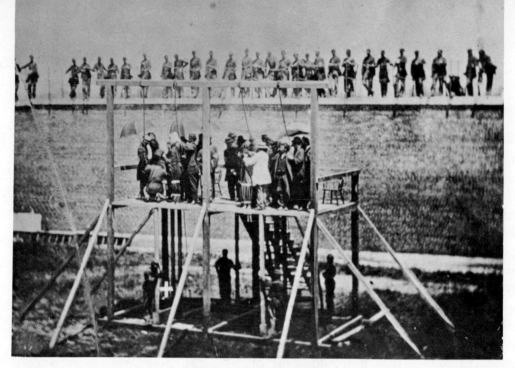

William Coxshall

This photograph of the execution of the Lincoln conspirators was taken by Brady, famous war photographer, while the prisoners were being bound. Mrs. Mary Surratt is seated at the extreme left, and Lewis Payne stands next. David Herold is being bound by Colonel Christian Rath, in direct charge of the executioners, while George Atzerodt is at the extreme right.

Leaning against the cross-bar (x) is William Coxshall. At the back is D. F. Shoupe, assigned to work with him. G. F. Taylor and F. B. Haslett are at the other side.

The platform was hinged at the front into two drops, marked by the center upright. The front of these was supported by a timber against which Coxshall leans, nausated by the heat and the distasteful duty assigned him. The two timbers behind him guided the swinging bar suspended from the rope. On signal, this bar was swung against the front support, knocking the prop away and allowing the drop to fall.

"Much has been made of what Mrs. Surratt said as she was being bound. I know what it was. They tied the bands pretty tight and she complained.

" 'It hurts,' she said.

" 'Well,' was the consoling reply, 'It won't hurt long.'

"Payne stood forward at the very front of the drop. Mrs. Surratt was barely past the break as were the other two. Rath came down the steps and gave the signal. Once-twice-three times—he clapped his hands. On the third clap, Shoupe and I swung with all our might. Mrs. Surratt shot down and I believe died instantly, Payne was a strong brute and died hard. It was enough to see these two without looking at the others, but they told us both died quickly.

"Ten minutes later we cut them down, put them in the pine boxes and buried them. Rath attended to the Surratt body. When the signal was given, a soldier dashed forward and slashed the rope on Atzerodt. The body crashed to the ground as the man snipped off a piece of rope as a souvenir. In each grave we placed a bottle with the name of the occupant."

Chapter 10

WHEN FORTY-COUNT 'EM-FORTY-MARCHED DOWN FRONT STREET

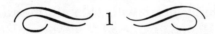

1

THE tall windows of Concert Hall looked down on Front Street, and in an emergency their wide sills became a seat or a catchall. Just now they were the latter. Grandfather was disgorging.

For Grandfather this process was something of a function. The capacious pockets of his long-tailed black coat concealed surprises surpassing a magician's production box. First came a red bandanna with his false teeth. They fitted poorly since small town dentistry was crude, and they spent more time in his pocket than his mouth. He unwrapped them, polished them off and slipped them into place.

Came a book of prescription blanks with "Peter Buel—Druggist and Pharmacist" lettered above the Rx that topped the perforated pages. Followed

153

his folding scissors, a package of long-cut chewing tobacco, another bandanna and the pocket medicine case without which no country doctor left home. After a hasty survey, he called me to him.

"Harlowe," said he, "scoot up to the house and get my turnkeys. Get an ounce of chloroform and some absorbent cotton at the drugstore and tell Pete to charge it. And get a move on."

Hi Henry's Minstrels were in town. A decaying molar had caught up with one of the troupers, and Grandfather was preparing to operate. Beaver Dam had its full quota of dentists, but this was a personal issue. A trouper was ailing within the sacred precincts of Concert Hall, and Grandfather was prepared to deal with it.

Early that morning, Uncle Bee and I had opened the hall, swept the floor, filled the lamps, polished the chimneys with old newspapers and set up the floor—chairs in front, benches next, and chairs supporting planks in the rear. Just now I was giving them a final going over. Not that they needed it but by so doing I could touch the hem of romance that enrobed these kings of minstrelsy. Reluctantly I laid aside the feather duster and headed for home.

I was back in record time. Grandfather planted the ailing minstrel in a chair facing the wall, a wise precaution since sight of a turnkey suggested torture worse than an aching tooth. The black leather case held three rounded pieces of metal the size of a man's middle finger with a hinged claw at the bottom, each angled to reach a different part of the jaw. Grandfather packed the aching molar with chloroform-saturated cotton, picked his turnkey, fitted its diamond shaped top into a black wooden handle—it suggested an oversized corkscrew—and held it behind him.

"Sit down on the floor," he ordered.

Occupying the chair himself, he gripped the patient's head between his knees. By now the others had knocked off work and with dubious comments were forming a vulturous circle. Grandfather removed the cotton, clamped the claw home, took a firm grip and twisted. Something had to give. Something did. It was the tooth.

"Get some water and rinse your mouth out," Grandfather said. "You'll be all right in a little while."

Wondering what had hit him the bemused man staggered away while Grandfather wrapped up the debris.

"What's the damage, Doc?" Hi Henry asked.

"To him—mostly," Grandfather answered. "It ought to be four shillings."

The Clark House

The Clark House, Beaver Dam's principal hotel, was typical of the small town of its day. The Lawrence Boys, Bill and Tom, were its proprietors; and its regular patrons were traveling salesmen who stopped overnight. Some of the more prosperous rep companies put up there, though most of them found accommodations in the cheaper boarding houses. Most minstrel shows had their own private car, but the entertainers could be found any noon lounging on the veranda and nibbling at toothpicks filched from the registration desk. Not that they ate there; most of them filled up on free lunch and a beer at Pete Veling's or Henry Hopf's saloon.

He had never renounced the currency of his boyhood. "But I'll call it all square if you'll give us 'The Bell Goes A-Ringing for Sarah' tonight."

"That you'll have," Hi Henry promised. "Lucky he's the bass drum and not one of the windjammers. Toothache never crippled a man's arm. All right, boys. All ready for the street parade."

The circle drifted away for uniforms and instruments while I hurried to pick up my sign:

TONIGHT
HI HENRY'S MINSTRELS
CONCERT HALL

Toting it in the parade assured me a pass to the show, though Uncle Bee pointed out I could get in anyway since we owned the hall. What he didn't understand was that I wanted to head the parade, even ahead of Hi Henry himself, beside the musket-juggling drum major, Sergt. Cummings, while other youngsters must be content to trail behind.

Candidly, I wanted to show off. And I did.

2

All shows arrived in Beaver Dam on the ten o'clock train from the east and all left the same way. The builders of the Chicago, Milwaukee & St. Paul road became confused at Horicon Junction, ten miles to the east, and wandered onward, laying a spur track to Beaver Dam, ending at Portage, to the west. They hit the junction with a loop through the business district that dropped passengers at the main depot and picked up express and freight on the swing back. Down by the Upper Woolen Mill, a side track was reserved for the visiting troupers.

Hi Henry's Minstrels had its own private car. The name was emblazoned the length of the long yellow coach and through its dusty windows one could glimpse bits of bedding and odd clothing and the brassy gleam of a bass horn or a sousaphone. It was a mousey joint, but it attracted curious villagers who gawked and speculated on what was within; which, after all, was only berths, baggage space and toilet facilities. The visitors ate at the Clark House or the Milwaukee House, or filled up on beer and free lunch at a convenient saloon.

By the time the car was shunted into place and the props and trunks loaded on to Tom Bowes' dray, it was well along toward noon; and the minstrels, grips and instruments in hand, came straggling up the steep stairs. Their salutation never varied.

"Say, lad, what town is this?"

"Beaver Dam, Wisconsin."

"Um—so? Not so bad. Say, where's the water?"

"There ain't no water."

"This is one hell of a hall."

With which declaration, they wandered on to get set for the street parade.

The noon parade was the opening wedge with which a traveling company burst upon the quiet life of a community. Minstrels and Uncle Tommers offered the best display, particularly the latter with its Great Danes, Eva's pony cart, and Marks the Lawyer astride his mule bringing up the rear.

All minstrel parades followed a single pattern. The drum major—in this instance Sergt. Cummings, the musket-juggling Zouave—led the way, a boy with a banner by his side. Next came Hi Henry, a portly man with florid face, closely cropped mustache and gray hair. With his top hat, Prince Albert coat and striped trousers, he exuded an atmosphere of affluence belied too often by the box office returns. His was a commanding personage.

Followed the band and then the minstrels two by two, stretched out to make the line more impressive, with small boys at intervals lugging signs proclaiming the virtues of Hi Henry's Minstrels. A cymbal player added to the musical total, and one unfortunate youth was impressed to lug the bass drum on his back.

The parade uniform was a top hat, a long coat, more or less gaudy, and a cane. Trousers and shoes didn't matter so much, but the cane was indispensable. It set the tempo, marked the step and without its measured swing the procession would have become a rank of stragglers. Swing up! One-two-three-four! Swing down! One-two-three-four! Swing up! One-two-three-four! Swing down! One-two-three-four—while the band blared "The Pillsbury March" with plenty of schmaltz from the trombones.

The parade was an easy one and I got back to the hall somewhat winded but ready for what might come next. It was a brisk early November day, clear and dry. When there was snow or rain, a parade was sadly different. The bedraggled marchers picked their way along the roadside, avoiding ruts and dodging mud puddles, taking to the plank sidewalks, wandering aimlessly while the band dissembled its melancholy with a dispirited tune. If he came along at all, Hi Henry rode in Bill Wade's hack.

By the time I had parked my sign, theater trunks were brought up and properties piled about ready to set up the show. This was a tricky business, so Uncle Bee took charge. From beneath the stage he produced two posts, black curtains and a bundle of canvas. The ten foot posts were fitted into square holes at either front corner of the stage. Each top had a large eye-bolt with a corresponding eyebolt in the proscenium arch. A long hooked rod connected them and braced the uprights. The front drop was moved forward for full stage depth and black side curtains were put up.

The canvas was stretched from each post to the side of the hall, forming a dressing room at either side. Water barrels were filled and rolled upstairs. Pails and sponges were laid out. A minstrel's trunk was his dressing table and these were ranged in line with chairs to match.

It was my job to crawl under the stage and hand out a half-dozen stout saw horses. Built up with planks and covered with the ground cloth, they elevated the orchestra upstage. Chairs for the circle were disguised with elaborate slipons, footlights were checked and in the two dressing rooms, costumes and properties laid out.

Most of the company wandered off to lounge up and down Front Street and pick up some of the town girls. In this undertaking, sad to relate, they were most successful, for no Lothario ever surpassed a blackface minstrel man in his conquests. A couple of the less fortunate were assigned to pick up a cigarbox full of corks at the drugstore and burn them over lighted candles. Prepared cork had not been invented, so you burned your own or went without.

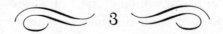

I lugged the family dinner bell down to the hall that night. It was a fine brass piece, eight inches high, with a clang that carried four good country blocks on a quiet day. Grandfather considered it a necessary adjunct for his request number, and it had been used for that purpose before. I sometimes suspected that he asked for "The Bell Goes A-Ringing for Sarah" solely that it might be sounded again.

At seven o'clock the kerosene lamps were lighted and Uncle Bee gave the two stoves an extra stoking of hard coal. The minstrels straggled in, nibbling contentedly on toothpicks while the bandsmen, not bothering to don uniforms, gave their concert in the street below. Hi Henry opened the box office and arranged his pasteboards. His ticket taker camped at the head of the stairs along with Grandfather. The first patrons showed up as the winded musicians took it at the double-quick to blacken up and get into their costumes.

By eight the hall was filled. A measured stamping of impatient feet and shrill whistles of the town's youngsters mingled with an occasional outburst of voices behind the canvas and the exasperating thumping of some moving object. But these were stilled by the first dissonant whimperings of the orchestra tuning up on stage.

Chandeliers were lowered and lamps turned down, leaving a single watch light by the stairs. The footlights were turned up. There was a blare of music and the Bay of Naples rolled up, disclosing the entire company and "over three hundred yards of the costliest Silks, Satins and Velvets used in our Gorgeous First Part Decorations." These were the standby of every minstrel show. Like diamond dye stuff they were quickly packed in a trunk. With properties and a trick set or two they rounded out the equipment.

Minstrel shows all followed the same pattern. The orchestra was banked in back, the circle of blackfaces broke either side of the white-faced interlocutor, otherwise "the middleman." There were six endmen, introduced in pairs at intervals: the bones to your left, the tamborines to your right. Each dragged on his own chair to assure himself an end seat.

After crossfire by the first pair and interlocutor came a tenor solo, the "second edition of premiers," more crossfire and a baritone solo; the top endmen, a comic song by one of them, crossfire and the quartette. More crossfire, a solo by the star "contra-tenor," crossfire and a bass solo by the interlocutor. A general ruckus by the six endmen, interlocutor participating, and a song by them, in this instance, "The Bell Goes A-Ringing for Sarah."

Like many other minstrel favorites the song came from the British music halls. An endman ducked off stage to don wench makeup. His recital concerned the trials of a serving maid on the jump all day to answer the bell. Then the chorus:

> The bell goes ringing for Sarah, for Sarah, for Sarah,
> The bell goes a-ringing for Sarah,
>   All the livelong day.

First it was a small table bell that was rung. As the song progressed, others were added, increasing in size and din. Then came the family dinner bell and finally a deep throated bell on wheels borrowed from the Beaver Dam Fire Department. What it lacked in harmony it surely made up in noise. While the stage was being cleared, the orchestra filed out in front for a couple of selections. The remainder of the program was a variety of acts: banjo solos, songs and dances, the ubiquitous quartette; Sergt. Cummings, who had performed his musket drill, dropping the sergeant for a time to appear as Mr. P. F. Cummings in "No One at Home," juggling this, that and everything; a blackface monologue and then Monsieur Albo LaTour appeared "In Picturesque and Unique Exercises with Roman Implements of War." We suspected him to be the doughty sergeant again since burnt cork and change of costume covered plenty of doubling in a minstrel show.

Hi Henry reserved next to closing for himself. An expert cornetist, he featured a "gold instrument," triple-tonguing the variations of "The Blue Bells of Scotland" and "Home, Sweet Home." He may have known other numbers, but if so he never played them. Year after year, he stalked to the footlights and bugled away as if it was a new experience.

The customary close for a minstrel show was its afterpiece. *Lucinda's Beaux* needed an interior with a closet door, a bed and numerous exits. Every company carried an expert at playing wenches. No female impersonator in any sense, he wore a mother hubbard, buckle shoes and a sunbonnet and specialized in wielding a broom and in pratfalls. *Lucinda's Beaux* brought on most of the company as her suitors, piling in one after another, each concealed in turn beneath the bed, in the closet, behind a chair or curtain, to spring out occasionally and beat up one another with slapsticks or stuffed sausages. It offered no sense but plenty of action.

But Hi Henry for his climax staged a Transformation Vampire Clog. Three pairs of pedestals of graduated height formed a triangle to the backdrop. On the first, Rowley Brothers opened with a clog routine. Whalen and Gorman followed on the second with trick solo work. On the last and highest, Cary and De Lancy did a fancy waltz clog, joined in by all for the finish. They wore close fitting green costumes with skull caps, and draperies hung from their arms. At the finish, they wheeled about, facing the backdrop, raised their arms and were transformed into red-clothed demons with plenty of red fire in the wings. The Grand Transformation Tableau, Hi Henry modestly announced, was "one of the most sensational and elaborate features ever offered on the minstrel stage."

During the performance, I had been deputed by Sergt. Cummings to peddle the famous Hi Henry Songster. I was all blown up by the confidence imposed in me until Uncle Bee pointed out that the sergeant had taken my hat to ensure my making an accounting to him.

Six Brown Brothers

Although Adolphe Sax invented the saxophone in 1840, it was not recognized as a legitimate musical instrument until years later. Among the first musical groups to use it was the Musical Nosses, who varied their programs of mandolin, guitar, violin and banjo music, with saxophone solos and quartettes.

The Six Brown Brothers carried it on to popularity during the late eighties and nineties. For several seasons they were with Gorman Brothers Minstrels. The sextette was the backbone of the orchestra, and they were featured in noon and night concerts before the theater. The brothers went on to win recognition on Broadway—they were an intrinsic part of *Jack O'Lantern,* in which Fred Stone was starred—and their phonograph recordings for Victor made the trade-mark pooch sit up and take notice.

The boys were versatile, as this photograph proves. They played string and wind instruments from childhood, but won their fame when they concentrated on the despised saxophone and helped to make it the popular instrument it has become.

Over the years about every minstrel show on the road visited Beaver Dam. McIntyre and Heath came with Spencer's Minstrels long before Broadway knew them in *The Ham Tree*. They were doing the same routine then. There were the Georgia Minstrels, and Shephard's Great Minstrel

McIntyre and Heath in "The Georgia Minstrels"

McIntyre and Heath

Probably the greatest blackface team of all time was that of McIntyre and Heath, who played small time houses for years before they made the grade in vaudeville and went on to *The Ham Tree* and *In Hayti*.

James McIntyre and Tom Heath are remembered as Alexander, the pessimistic, gullible colored boy; and the boasting, domineering fakir who led him on and on. Soon after their association, they had their own specialty company and joined later with Lew Spencer as Spencer, McIntyre and Heath's Minstrels. After a term with Lew Dockstader they worked out their routine of their famous Georgia Minstrels, went on to vaudeville, to musical comedy, and back to vaudeville again.

McIntyre was given to the bottle, and toward the last it was necessary to carry an understudy to replace him when the wine was too red. They saw little of each other off stage. McIntyre was the one who gave the newspaper interviews, possibly because he was the more genial. He had a routine that was as good as any performance the two gave on the stage. McIntyre told me that they had worked together so long they could go on and on for two hours or more and never repeat themselves.

McIntyre and Heath were truly great. Amos and Andy followed their pattern when they won fame on the radio.

Jubilee, and Gorman Brothers Minstrels with an orchestra built about a saxophone quartette. These were the Six Brown Brothers, early favorites of the gramophone.

Over the years came Thatcher, Primrose and West; William N. West with Billy Emerson, singing "I Feel Just as Happy as a Big Sunflower"; Simmons and Slocum, Delahenty and Hengler, Dan Bryant, Cool Burgess and practically every minstrel show on the road hit the town at one time or another.

The minstrel show was a family institution and its effect upon America's popular music was far reaching. There was no Tin Pan Alley and at first phonograph and radio were unknown. The piano occupied a prominent place in the parlor and much of its sheet music came with the minstrel show. The troopers visited a town annually, bringing with them the songs they sang in sheet music and song books.

Because each stand was a certain sales spot, Ed Christy willingly paid Stephen Foster that he might sign his own name as the composer of "Old Folks at Home." Dan Bryant claimed "Dixie" for the same reason, though Dan Emmett composed it. Mother's pile of music increased with every show and in it was the song accredited to Christy; "Willie, We Have Missed You," autographed by Foster; and a number of old songs with Christy's signature which, incidentally, he signed "Chrysty."

Banks Winter wrote "White Wings" and sang it with W. S. Cleveland's Minstrels. Paul Dresser was heard in "I Believe It For My Mother Told Me So," and "The Pardon Came too Late," both of which he composed long before he took his decrepit organ to New York to produce "Just Tell Them That You Saw Me" and "The Banks of the Wabash."

Contemporaneous with Foster was Will Hays, who divided his time between piloting a Mississippi steamboat and working in a music store. "I'll Remember You, Love, In My Prayers" was a standby for contra-tenors while much parodied was "Mollie Darling," and for many seasons the circle joined lustily in his:

> Angels meet me at the crossroad—meet me!
> Angels meet me at the crossroad—meet me!
> Angels meet me at the crossroad—meet me!
> Don't charge this sinner any toll.

Hays considered himself a legitimate rival of Foster and even charged him with lifting many of his tunes from a manuscript book of an old German composer.

A great debt is due those minstrel shows for those who enjoy the old time songs. Had it not been for Christy, Steve Foster might never have attained his great fame. Lackadaisical from youth, he was whipped to production through Christy's demands with the certainty of a ready market. The same was true of James A. Bland, the colored genius, whose seven hundred compositions include "Carry Me Back to Old Virginny," and "In the Evening by the Moonlight." Paul Dresser started singing his compositions in a minstrel show, and many a lesser composer wrote his songs and ballads for the blackfaced crew.

They were a happy-go-lucky band, those minstrel men, good dressers on and off, though too often they lacked the price of a square meal. Their skins had a rich olive complexion from years of burnt corking and on their faces, wrinkled by the wind, the moldboard of laughter had marked its genial furrows. Nor rain, nor hail, nor flood, nor sudden death ever discouraged them in the conviction that things would be better at the next stand.

Eternal optimists they had to be as I found when Mrs. George Primrose showed me the little memorandum book that her husband carried to record the night's receipts. Primrose and West had dissolved, and after four years, George joined Lew Dockstader. In 1902 he struck out on his own. His was a full complement befitting his tradition, with forty people playing cities and one night stands. It must have been disheartening for even such a hardened trooper as he to enter receipts of $30, $60 and $70 a night, with an occasional $100 or better.

George Primrose carried his own show and backed another for Dan Quinlan, famous interlocutor and the first to leave his position to carry on with the endmen, an innovation necessitated by a larger circle. Quinlan lost money, too, and Primrose ended up doing a vaudeville turn. His soft shoe routine to "Lazy Moon" was a classic.

With passing years I returned to Beaver Dam to find that the famous old minstrel show of Beach and Bowers was no more. They came each year, sometimes in the winter to play the hall, sometimes in summer under a tent. Their manager, a man named Smith, was clerking in Concert Hall Drugstore and his son-in-law, Doc Blair, had opened a dental office across the way. Smith came to me with a proposition.

"Otis Bowers has passed on," he said, "and Bobby Beach died in Watertown. Beach and Bowers Minstrels belong to me. Tent, stage, stringers, light plant, poles, scenery, costumes—they're all stored where I can get at it. I can get the old company together with an ad in *Billboard*. Doc's

Title-pages of First Editions in Foster Hall Collection

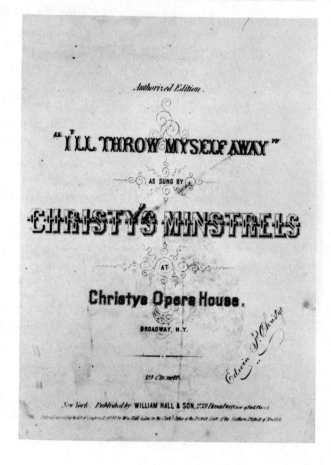

willing to go out again. Let's you and me take out the show again. It won't
cost much and we can whip it together in no time."

"What's the nut?" I asked.

"The storage fee and such. It's in an old building over in Columbus, ten
miles away. I'll start booking and you dig up the storage fees. And we'll
need $100 in reserve."

"What's the hundred for?"

"That," he replied, "why, that's to get us back home when we go broke."

Verily the blackface monarchs of minstrelsy played for the pure love of
it and let the money go hang.

Stephen Collins Foster

Though he wrote his Ethiopian melodies for the blackface minstrel—George
Christy was his principal patron—Stephen Collins Foster was far from popular
with the minstrel companies of the eighties and nineties. "Old Black Joe" and
"The Old Folks at Home" might be sung occasionally, but times had changed
and a new crop of minstrel men were not only writing their songs but singing
them as well.

With Billy Rice's Minstrels, Paul Dresser was a featured tenor, singing his
motto song, "I Believe It, For My Mother Told Me So" and "The Pardon Came
Too Late." Banks Winter wrote and sang "White Wings" with Thatcher, Primrose and West; and Raymond Moore came up with "Sweet Marie," his musical
setting to Cy Warman's poem. And the interlocutor, always a basso profundo,
might take a turn at "The Old Sexton," "The Bell Buoy," or "Rocked in the
Cradle of the Deep."

Foster's melodies were popular before and after these twenty years, but during
these two decades they were largely relegated to concert and lyceum performers. Most of this music was carried by the minstrel shows as a sideline, and
Foster's were prime sellers for Christy. The composer thought so little of "The
Old Folks at Home" that he allowed Christy to present it as his own composition for a payment reported anywhere from $15 to $500. The true amount probably was somewhere between these extremes.

To further the sales, some of these compositions were signed, as "Willie We
Have Missed You" and "I'll Throw Myself Away" shown here.

"ANGELS MEET ME AT THE CROSS ROADS."

SONG AND CHORUS.

By WILL S. HAYS.

Will S. Hays

Eccentric genius and prolific songwriter contesting for minstrel popularity was Will S. Hays, born in Louisville, Kentucky, and bespoken for a literary career by the middle name of Shakespeare. Hays opposed Foster bitterly, claiming that the Pittsburgh composer stole his songs from the composition book of a mysterious German. Hays also claimed that he wrote *Dixie* which caused Dan Emmett no end of raucous laughter.

Hays divided his time between newspaper work and song writing. During the late sixties and seventies he worked the Mississippi from New Orleans to Pittsburgh as a pilot. Then he became marine editor of the *Louisville Courier Journal* but continued to turn out his songs until some three hundred of them had been published. "I'll Remember You, Love, in My Prayers" was a favorite with minstrel tenors, and "Molly Darling" continued on and on and still is heard from time to time.

"Angels Meet Me at the Crossroads" was a standard number with minstrel men. It

had a rousing chorus with a soloist taking off and the entire circle joining in on each "Meet me!"; a quartette rounded it off with "Don't charge a sinner any toll."

In the late eighties, Hays grew ambitious and backed his own company in Louisville, advertised as "the Crème de la Crème of Negro Minstrelsy." It flopped. Saddened and wiser, he returned to his song writing and in the late eighties published a book of songs and poems.

Foster died not knowing that his melodies were to become classics of American folksong, but Hays lived on to realize that the man he had belittled had become a national institution.

COHAN AND HARRIS' MINSTRELS, 1908.

Minstrelsy—Its Beginning and Its End

Of all entertainment, only the black face minstrel is original with this country. It was on Feb. 6, 1843, that the Virginia Minstrels made their first appearance at the Bowery Amphitheatre in New York. Dick Pelham rattled the tambourine, Dan Emmett obliged with the fiddle, Billy Whitlock played the banjo, and Frank Bower manipulated the bones, which in those days were the shinbones of a horse. Whitlock claimed the conception as his own idea, and all evidence seems to bear him out.

From such a humble beginning came the great minstrel shows. Greatest of all were the Cohan and Harris Minstrels who toured the country in 1908. George Cohan staged the show with "Honey Boy" George Evans as the star and "One Hundred Honey Boys" in his support. That cast included among the endmen Eddie Leonard, Alf Gibson, John King and Ernest Tenney. Julian Eltinge, famous female impersonator, adopted sepia makeup to sing "Don't Go Near the Water, Daughter," "The Gibson Coon," and a half dozen other numbers. Eddie Leonard led the dancing crew and there was a one-act musical comedy, *The Belle of the Barbers' Ball*. George Cohan wrote the entire show and much of the music, with other numbers by William Jerome and Eugene Schwartz.

This was the most elaborate minstrel show ever to tour the country, surpassing even those of Al G. Fields, Primrose and West, and Primrose and Dockstader. Since it was a short-lived special production, dyed-in-the-wool blackface troupers looked upon it disdainfully. After all, they trouped in all sorts of weather under all sorts of conditions, and their livelihood depended upon continuing in their chosen field.

Woodcut of quartette from "Gentlemen Be Seated," by F. Dailey Paskman and Sigmund Spaeth, Copyright Doubleday, Doran, 1928.

All others from Edward LeRoy Rice's "Monarchs of Minstrelsy," copyright 1911, Mrs. Emma L. Rice Kenny Publishing Co., 22-24 N. William St., New York City.

DICK PELHAM   DAN EMMETT   BILLY WHITLOCK   FRANK BROWER

THE VIRGINIA MINSTRELS ("BIG FOUR")

AS THEY LOOKED TO AN ARTIST OF THEIR DAY

Scenes From
THE ORIGINAL CHRISTY MINSTRELS
AT MECHANICS HALL, 472 BROADWAY N.Y. IN 1847

J. W. RAYNOR   JERRY BRYANT

CAMPBELL'S MINSTRELS (1848)

The original company was organized in June, 1847. Jerry Bryant and J. W.
Raynor were two of the original company. The other photos represent minstrel
scenes of that day.

A PROMINENT BOSTON COMPANY; 1859.
LON MORRIS
J. T. TROWBRIDGE   BILLY MORRIS   JOHNNY PELL

A FAMOUS NEW YORK ORGANIZATION; 1865.
BILLY BIRCH   DAVE WAMBOLD
WM. H. BERNARD   CHARLEY BACKUS

Chapter 11

WHEN THE BROWNIES CAME TO TOWN

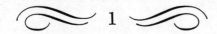

1

WHEN we put on *The Brownies in Fairyland* for the benefit of the Episcopal Church, I was drafted for the Brownie dude, Cholly Boutonniere.

The McClure Girls were responsible for that. They lived down the street in a low, rambling brown house opposite the Methodist Church. This proximity to Wesleyanism in no manner affected Dr. McClure, like his brother practitioners something of an agnostic, nor did it influence his daughters, who were enthusiastic workers in the Episcopal cause. Kate and Dot and Josie sang in the surpliced choir, to which I contributed my boyish soprano, and planned various small enterprises to raise money toward the rector's salary.

MUSIC - HALL,

FRIDAY AND SATURDAY,

APRIL 10th and 11th, 1896.

CAST OF CHARACTERS.

Prince Aldebaran, Ruler of the Brownie Band..................Miss Mabelle Lander.
Cholly Boutonniere, the Brownie Dude..........................Harlow Hoyt.
Chauncey Quoter, familiar with the poets.....................Sammy Groose.
Major Telloff, of the Brownie War Office......................Leonard Keefe.
Patrolman Moveon, the Brownie Police Force...................Bert Shipman.
Billy Tuckabout, who has weathered many a gale...............Ernest Edgerton.
Tutti,   } The Twins................................Ray Vaughan.
Frutti,   }...Bertie Bates.
Uncle Sam, of the Land of the Free.............................Edmund Poetter.
John Bull, from "Lunnon"......................................Herbert Peck.
Donald MacCraggie, from the Highlands.........................Ira Rowell.
Dennis O'Rourke, from Killarney...............................Willie McGill.
Prof. Katchakoff, a Russian Ex-Nihilist.......................Clarence Conigdon.
Afraid-of-the-Day, not Afraid of the Night....................Arthur Beule.
Fur and Skins, an Esquimo......................................George Edgerton.
Wah Sing, in the Laundry Business.............................Roy Moon.
Beatle,   }.......................................Fred. Dean
Wasp,   } Leaders of the Enemy.................Raymund Wilcox
Hornet,   }.......................................Hugo Rossman
Queen Flora, Goddess of the Flowers...........................Pearne Peake.
Toddlekins   }.......................................Mabel Wilcox
Tippytoes   } Wee Attendants of the Queen..........Clara Waldeck
Aesthetica, with a love for the beautiful....................Gertrude Lewis
Sunshine,   }.......................................Edith Congdon
Dewdrop,   }.......................................Louise Richardson
Starlight,   }.......................................Ethel Mohr
Zephyr,   }.......................................Cora Martin
Roseleaf,   }.......................................Alma Poetter
Hyacinth,   } Ladies in Waiting to the Queen.......Leone Keefe
Eglantine,   }.......................................Mertie Beule
Morning Glory }.......................................Bessie Hastings
Columbine,   }.......................................Florence Lander
Heartease,   }.......................................Louise Bellows
Goldenrod,   }.......................................Janet Tefft
King Cole   }.......................................Casey Griffis
The Old Woman } Mother Goose Characters..............Eva Harvey
Simple Simon, }.......................................Ray McClanathan

With many other Brownies and Faries not named.

Everybody's Favorites Are Coming!

THE BROWNIES IN FAIRYLAND.

A Musical Entertainment
IN TWO ACTS
BY PALMER COX.

ORIGINAL MUSIC,
By Malcolm Douglass.

SPECIAL COSTUMES,
Designed by Palmer Cox.

GIGANTIC PRODUCTION,
By Home Talent.

See Date and Cast of Characters on Last Page.

THE FAT POLICEMAN.

☆ ☆ ☆ ☆

ONE OF THE TWINS.
Tutti or Frutti?

SYNOPSIS.

ACT I. Scene—Garden of Queen Flora in Fairyland. Tableau (after Dore) "Sunrise in Fairy Dell." Chorus, "Flowers, Pretty Flowers." Queen Flora tells a tale of woe. The insects have conspired to destroy the flowers. To whom shall we appeal? Brownies' big balloon is sighted. Its bursting and parachute drop. Fairies arrange toilets. Entrance of Prince Aldebaran and Brownies. Chorus, "We're a Band." Return of Fairies. A love scene. Song by Aesthetica and Dude, "They're Different, Yes Different, from Others of Their Kind." Italian organ grinder and his trick bear. Discovery of lost Twins. Brownies prepare for war upon the insects. Mother Goose characters, Old King Cole, Simple Simon, The Old Woman who Sweeps the Cobwebs from the Sky. Return of Brownies armed for the fight. Grand march of Brownies. Chorus, "We're off to the War." Tableau.

ACT II. Tableau, "Brownie Carpenter Shop." Chorus, "We'll Build a Tank." Entrance of Fairies. Song by Fairies, "In a Big, Big Town." Fearful skirmish with the enemy. "The Irish Brownie's fighting with his fist!" "Poor Boutonniere! he falls and will expire!" "No, no; he stoops to roll his trousers higher!" Flight of vanquished Brownies. Council of war; "this trusting to main force will never do." Resort to strategy. Uncle Sam, in disguise, goes to enemy's camp. Uncle Sam returns with thrilling news. "We'll fold them in a net." Chorus, "Mending the Nets." Brownies off to battle again. Song of Fairies, "A Perfumed Fan." Grand victory for the heroic Brownies. Capture and banishment of the enemy. The Fairy Queen also surrenders to the Brownie Prince. Aesthetica and the Dude decide to follow their example. Grand revel of the fays. May pole dance.

"Oh, many a year and trying age
May pass away, ere on the stage,
Another band like this will rise,
To please, to puzzle and surprise."

Wait for Them.   Don't Miss Them.

When Dr. Myron T. Johnson took over the living of St. Mark's, naturally enough he made his home with the McClures. And it was quite logical that insinuations of the drama should mingle with the intimations of immortality for Dr. Johnson had a flair for the stage—his services soon crowded our little church—and he had played cello in a string quartette. Arthur Johnson, his son, visited us with William Owen in *Romeo and Juliet*. Arthur became one of the first movie idols with Biograph and Kalem, and a grandson was to ride Hollywood's lush merry-go-round as Nat Pendleton.

Palmer Cox had been drawing his fanciful sprites for many years when the Columbian Exposition hit Chicago in 1893. *The Brownies in Fairyland* and Hanlon's *Fantasma* played the season with elaborate ballets and spectacles, delighting the visiting yokels. Cox furnished the book and lyrics and the music was turned out by Malcolm Douglas, an author known to us through an occasional verse in *St. Nicholas*. The exposition folded, the Brownies scampered off stage for the last time, and the operetta was taken over by an outfit staging amateur performances in small communities. Their prospectus fell into the hands of the McClure girls and the ham was in the fire. Dr. Johnson may have brought it to their attention for he heartily approved and contributed a benign supervision from the background.

All three sisters started us off but before long Dot was left alone to act as producer, business manager, director, advertising solicitor, ticket agent and general factotum. By then half of Beaver Dam's youth were rehearsing in the McClure spare parlor. Dot had been warned—or her common sense may have told her—that adolescent sexes can't be mixed when there's work to be done. So she separated the fairies from the Brownies and worked with them at different times.

Each of us was given a complete copy of the operetta at the first rehearsal and for three weeks all of us met more or less faithfully with Dot. By that time we knew not only our own lines but the entire show, backwards and forwards, and were heartily sick of it all. To hearten us, Dot let us rehearse with the girls on occasion, though it slowed things down and filled the room to overflowing, and from time to time, suggestions by mail arrived as to new business or an addition, such as "The Serenade to the Moon," which we welcomed as something to relieve the triteness of lines grown old.

Then came the big day bringing Mr. Milton to take over. Mr. Milton proved a young fellow of slight build and sparrow-like alertness with a wisp of mustache and an aura of equal parts enthusiasm and optimism, probably some college student filling in his summer vacation. As an added wallop to our fading endeavors, he moved us to Music Hall where our interest revived with props and scenery on a real stage with real footlights.

The company was to furnish our costumes, and though all of us clamored incessantly to try them on, Mr. Milton dodged the issue by explaining that they would be here in plenty of time. That he had them with him was never suspected until two days before the performance when he dragged his big trunk out of a corner and disgorged our trappings. Then we understood. The costumes were too small. They were cheap cotton cloth. Props were papier maché and the hats shiny oilcloth.

In planning the outfits, the company must have counted upon a cast of ten-year olds. Dot had a flock of infant prodigies—plenty of them—but most of her principals were recruited from the Beaver Dam High School. Vestry-man of St. Mark's and consequently prejudiced, Professor Hubbell aroused patent enthusiasm when he announced that all participants would be ex-cused from classes to attend rehearsals of The Brownies. The entire enroll-ment volunteered in a body but finally settled for the two upper classes. Since these numbered the school's best athletes, including the entire foot-ball team, they contributed a poundage avoirdupois far beyond the pro-ducer's expectations.

When the cries of anguish subsided, Mr. Milton offered a mild suggestion. He was, he admitted, nonplussed by the situation, especially when it was too late to do anything. So he suggested they call the whole thing off.

The proposition was received in stunned silence. For six weeks or more, tickets for the two performances had been hawked far and wide. Hall rent had been paid. There was a printing bill for programs and tickets. Mr. Mil-ton's conditions were accepted none too graciously, and the ladies of St. Mark's Guild retired to scissors and sewing machines to fashion cambric outfits for the oversized volunteers. By some legerdermain known only to herself, Grandmother as usual outfitted me from the attic, down to a shiny top hat whose origin she refused to divulge.

So rehearsals continued and the great day came at last. Though the cur-tain was set for eight o'clock, five o'clock of the opening night found us at the hall as Mr. Milton had ordered. We hustled into our costumes and lined up before the kitchen table with its outlay of lining pencils and fleshing sticks. Mr. Milton drew a black circle about each of our eyes, gave an upward tilt to the brow and told us to fill in the circle with white grease paint. Thus, theoretically at least, the eye itself became the Brownie's eyeball.

Since we numbered more than fifty, and since some of the youngsters only recently had deserted the diaper stage, he delegated the older boys to help out with the whitening. This resulted in frenzied yelps of pain and reddened eyeballs as these unfortunate youths were forced to submit to this newest form of sadistic ingenuity. When the bedlam finally ended, Mr. Milton gave us his final formal inspection.

"Keep your cheeks puffed out when you're not speaking and look as cross-eyed as you can," he cautioned. "Take things easy. Don't fool around and don't muss up your makeup. Don't miss your cues. And if any of you start to show off, I'll strip off your costume and throw you out of the show."

Since he was a slight undersized individual, the final threat was indulgently overlooked by the football team of Beaver Dam High School.

Queen Flora's entourage came streaming in. There was no makeup problem here. All of the fairies dressed at home and the bevy of white frocked maidens were presented without rouge or makeup. Convoyed by a fleet of doting mothers of assorted shapes and sizes, they engulfed Mr. Milton with a whirlpool of questions and demands which he escaped by blithely ignoring them.

"Later, ladies, later," he threw over his shoulder. "Excuse me now. I must set the stage. Almost curtain time, you know."

In some inexplicable fashion the back wooddrop was hung, the fairies corralled and grouped about their queen, the Brownies lined up in pairs in the off stage dressing room, the wings crammed with anxious mamas who managed to get in the way most of the time, and the orchestra given the go-ahead.

The orchestra consisted of a piano presided over by Dot McClure, and of Doc Wagner, the local musical prodigy, whose ability as a violinist exempted him from the theatrical draft. Dot played the introduction, Doc joined in and a rising curtain revealed the crowded stage with all fairyland centered about Queen Flora and a frieze of mothers' heads peeping from the wings at either side. Piping childish voices filled the auditorium.

> Flowers, pretty flowers, blooming ev'rywhere,
> Filling all around you with your perfume rare.
> Would the world we live in be as fair and bright,
> Life itself without you have the same delight?
> Just a simple posy brings of hope a ray;
> Oftentimes a rosebud care will drive away;
> Dainty little creatures of the sun and dew.
> Oh, the love we cherish in our hearts for you!

The chorus ended and as Queen Flora started to address her followers, came the first untoward interruption, untoward but inevitable.

Here, my beloved subjects, let us rest
And each can tell the flower she loves the best.
"Wah! Wah!" from the littlest fairy.

Quickly the suppliant was passed from hand to hand off stage but the suggestion was contagious. In the face of infantile expostulations, the individual fairies bravely undertook to extol their preference for violets, heart's ease, morning glories, columbine or whatever flower they were named for. Three more dampish youngsters were turned over to their hovering mothers who shushed their outcries and hustled them off post haste to the ladies room. All of this to the accompaniment of acidulous remarks from those mothers whose prodigies were doing their utmost to ride the storm.

The hubbub of the praise to the flowers finally subdued and the embattled mothers sternly silenced by Mr. Milton, Queen Flora was able to get down to the business of the innocuous plot with announcement that:

Some wicked monster that we know not of
Is waging war upon the flowers we love.
If this destruction is not stopped, I fear
No flowers will be left our hearts to cheer.

Suggestions to meet the emergency were interrupted by the approach of the Brownies. The doughty band was presumed to arrive by air since for some undisclosed reason they were traipsing around in a balloon blithely looking for trouble. Which they found when the big bag burst, conveniently depositing them near the fairy ring.

See—now they're falling faster than at first!
(*Boom!*)
Oh—what was that? The big balloon has burst!

Mr. Milton consummated this offstage effect by smashing a chair on the floor. Brought down squarely on all four legs it produced a convincing crash that drove the fairy band off upper left, leaving the stage bare for the arrival of the Brownies. The indomitable band marched on in pairs led by Prince Adelbaran followed by myself, as Cholly Boutonniere, the Brownie dude, and Officer Moveon, who served as bodyguard representing the finer things of life protected by the law.

Here again the subterfuge of Mr. Milton in withholding the costumes until the last hour had created a crisis of major proportions. It was intended that the Prince should be played by a boy; and while I had been considered for the part—due, no doubt, to my surpliced service in St. Mark's choir— Dot McClure finally passed me by for a girl from the woman's section. She was confronted with two applicants for the part of Queen Flora and with Solomonic astuteness solved it by dividing the leading roles between them.

Prince Adelbaran was a buxom lass, well endowed in the right places considering her years, and the outfit that Mr. Milton handed her left no doubt that it was intended for one of masculine persuasion. There was a small sword, a plumed hat, an all-too-brief close fitting doublet—and tights. Not only were they fleshings *au naturel* but they were silk besides—fine, delicate silk in a day when silk of that sort was confined to ladies' unmentionables in the privacy of their own boudoir.

As a sort of tour de force, this was the last costume handed out, for Mr. Milton evidently foresaw the ensuing row since, in the opinion of Beaver Dam's churchly, tights were associated only with circus performers and the bedizened hussies of the burlesque stage.

Nor was he disappointed. Not only did the feminine princeling raise her voice in frenzied expostulation, but half of the St. Mark's Guild joined in to make the night hideous. Mr. Milton shrugged his shoulders and waited patiently until exhaustion brought quiet.

"If the young lady cannot see her way to play the part," he declared softly, "there's only one thing to be done. I'll shave off my mustache and play the part myself."

Since it was the only decent costume in the entire outfit, this thunderclap was of Jovian proportions. The dismayed guildites reeled back before the shock but quickly reassembled their forces for a counter attack. They would accept the outfit subject to changes to be made with and under the approval of Dr. Johnson. Well rid of annoying detail, Mr. Milton bade them go to it and turned his attention to matters more pressing.

The compromise disclosed by Prince Adelbaran as we marched forth into the glare of the pitiless footlights was something to behold. The sword and plumed hat remained with their rhinestone decorations glittering magnificently. The pink fleshings were there too, but the brief doublet had been replaced by an ill fitting blouse that reached halfway to the knees.

Something of the contour of a mother hubbard, reminiscent of a man's nightshirt minus the tails, it stood out like a shoemaker's thumb, loudly emphasizing that which it sought to conceal. Nor did it lessen the curse of the tights since the young lady's legs, shapely as they were, were displayed far above the ankle line that marked the limit of decency in that era of propriety.

Fortunately the buzz of criticism was covered by the Brownies' opening:

> We're a band, hand in hand,
> Coming fresh from Brownie Land!
> All for fun round we run,
> Everywhere beneath the sun.
> In the night we delight
> To come forth and show our might;
> Hide away in the day,
> That our motto is alway.

Before its gladsome tidings, Prince Adelbaran's legs were discounted while those parents who comprised most of the audience set about sorting out their own offspring. Overlooked though they were temporarily, the prince's legs were not forgotten. Word was passed and the next night witnessed an influx of the town's younger bloods who came to see and remained to admire.

The plot of *The Brownies in Fairyland*, if it may be dignified as such, concerned the enlistment of the little sprites to capture certain wicked monsters who threatened to destroy the flowers, an assignment completed by the final curtain. Meantime each and everyone was given a line or two to say, and several specialties were staged. Adelbaran won the fairy queen, and the dude walked off with the leading lady-in-waiting, the Fairy Aesthetica.

One scheme to entrap the enemy introduced "Mending the Nets," the nets in question being a half dozen hammocks dragooned from one of Front Street's stores whose unwilling proprietor contributed them under the baleful influence of a half dozen determined guildwomen. Some of the Brownies draped themselves in them and twisted the meshes while the remainder gathered about to carol:

> Mending the nets, mending the nets,
> To sail at the break of dawn,
> While many a prayer for the loved ones there,
> Will follow the fleet that's gone.

It was all very cozy and chummy until Prince Adelbaran dispatched the twins, Tuttie and Frutti, to reconnoitre. As an Italian organ grinder and his trick bear, the two engaged in a wrestling match as a bit of diversion until bystanding volunteers joined in not only eagerly but so enthusiastically that the business was eliminated at a rehearsal that ended in a free-for-all and a tearful bear who resigned forthwith and was coaxed back only by the assurance from Mr. Milton that there would be no more monkeyshines.

"The Serenade to the Moon" was enhanced by a Japanese lantern suspended from above as the only light in the hall. Not only did this convey the illusion of a new moon but it effectively concealed the secret that the serenade was being sung by Queen Flora in the wings while Prince Adelbaran took stage center and made faces. The queen could hit the high notes in this somewhat pretentious number while the prince invariably came a clinker or two.

Anticipating an easy victory, the Brownies constructed a tank in which to ship their captives overseas. The tank was an oversized wooden box contributed by one of the town's stores and about it the workers gathered busily, singing lustily and whacking away at its sides with tack hammers.

One of the Brownies, a freckled, redheaded brat of revolting disposition, clambered into the box and sought to distract his associates by sticking his wriggling finger through a knot hole in the side. Identifying the prankish youngster, an imaginative Brownie bent the finger down, holding it securely, at the same time signalling an associate to bring his tack hammer into play.

The result was eminently satisfactory. Throughout the chorus declaring the band's intention of ridding Fairyland of its curse by the water route, the anguished bleatings of the assailed youngster rose clear and high over the massed chorus. Released at last, he retired in sniveling anger, duly chastened when the curtain finally descended, and the incident would have been forgotten but for Professor Hubbell. From his spot at the door where he was taking tickets, the professor hastened backstage to ask who it was that contributed that wonderful tenor to the ensemble. It was, he declared, something unheard of among youngsters of our age and he prophesied a great future for the unidentified virtuoso. When no less than three of us took the credit, he retired in dignified discomfiture before he learned the truth.

Came the second night and with it an aplomb pervading the entire cast, now considering themselves experienced troopers. Mr. Milton was on his toes the first night and everything came off on the dot. But at this second performance, the doughty band kept falling and falling with no accompanying crash to announce the Brownies landing. There were a number of odd characters with brief scenes—King Cole, the Crooked Man, The Old Woman who Lived in a Shoe, Simple Simon and Mistress Mary among them—and the Simpleton was dispatched to the dressing room where the director held court.

He returned all ajitter and bubbling over with information, hotly followed by Mr. Milton and soon after by one of the older feminine members of the cast. Overlooking their disheveled state, Mr. Milton brought down the chair with a prodigious thump and the show went on.

The Brownies in Fairyland was voted an immediate success. As top soprano in St. Mark's choir, it became my duty to return the hammocks used in the net number. To my disgust, I discovered that the little stinkers had tied them into hard knots, ruining them beyond repair. At least that was the storekeeper's contention and he made it stick, too. The Guildladies paid him full value for the articles.

Mr. Milton left next morning, bag and baggage, on the first train. Simple Simon's simple tale of what he saw was bruited about and aroused more than passing comment.

Through the years, from time to time, I have paused to wonder if Simple Simon really told the truth. Since he was a guileless youth who quite lived up to that appellation, I have reluctantly concluded that he must have done so.

 2

The McClure girls were ever on the alert to promote some sort of exhibition for the benefit of St. Mark's Episcopal Guild and its rector's salary. And since it needed little preparation and no rehearsal, Rogers Statuary became a yearly standby.

John Rogers' statuary was riding high, and practically every family owned one of his homely productions. Years before, Rogers had experimented in clay and found it good. He looked upon the classic contributions of the sixties and found them bad. They ran to oversized feminine nudes whose nudity was made the more conspicuous by a shielding hand and to masculine distortions craftily emphasized by an undersized fig leaf. So he set out to produce groups of figures that told a story, appealed to the simple tastes of the average family and came within the limit of its budgeting.

The man had little training for the job, but he proved an adept once he got under way. He devised a form of casting with a material known as

"Rogers Patent," and produced his groups with an intimate detail comparable to the prints of Currier and Ives. Working with a gelatin mould and a bronze master cast, he reproduced his originals at prices ranging from five to fifty dollars.

Most of these were of red plaster on a metal frame. They were dipped in gray paint and averaged twenty inches in height. Bottles of "Refreshing Color" went with them; the contents not only retouched faded colors but filled in cracks and chipped edges. For most of the statuary was placed on a stand in the front parlor window along with the family Bible, where it could be admired by the passersby. As the rear was viewed by the casual visitor honored in the parlor, this was as complete in detail as was the front. It was, in truth, as complete as the cast-iron statues in the park honoring the heroes of the Civil War. And since it was subjected to daily dusting, there was plenty of need for the "refreshing color."

Rogers Statuary was eminently adapted for amateur reproduction, for his product was roughly divided into three groups. There was the Civil War group, including "The Council of War," for which Lincoln consented to pose. There was a group devoted to literature and the stage, which included a Hamlet posed by Edwin Booth and a Rip Van Winkle for which Joseph Jefferson sat. The third group was made up of general reproductions— "Checkers Up on the Farm," Rogers' initial effort; "Coming to the Parson," "Fetching the Doctor," "Amateur Theatricals," "The Courtship of Miles Standish," and any number of others dealing with simple country scenes or familiar poems and stories.

Presenting a Rogers Statuary program necessitated rounding up a group of volunteers that could be trusted to show up at the appointed place at the appointed time. Rehearsals were not necessary. The volunteers had only to appear in plenty of time, get into their outfits and makeup, take a pose and hold it for two curtains, and then leave as quickly as possible to make way for another group.

The genius who promoted this form of living statuary furnished the committee with gray outfits of cotton cloth, the necessary wigs and plenty of dusting powder, and large photographs of the groups to be presented. The committee saw to it that the volunteers were outfitted, properly prettied up, and posed according to the pictures. The program was divided into three parts according to the classification of the groups.

Usually the show opened with the children's groups in order that the youngsters might be disposed of as quickly as possible and sent on their way before they raised too much cain. The dramatic groups were alternated

Rogers Statuary

From the early seventies through the ninetie
and on, statuettes made by John Rogers grace
the parlors of most of the Americans of th
well-to-do class.

Three of the most popular of these tableau
were *Rip Van Winkle*, posed by Joseph Jeffer
son himself; *Playing Doctor*, which gave th
youngsters a chance to appear; and *The Schoo
Examination*, a companion piece.

with the folk presentations building up to the finish with Hamlet, Miles Standish, Rip Van Winkle and Lincoln's "Council of War." Each group was introduced by a master-of-ceremonies, a task usually delegated to Professor Hubbell, giving time for its successor to get properly set.

Dot McClure outdid herself with the piano accompaniments. Her selections were represented by a hugh sheaf of instrumental music. "Reuben, Reuben I've Been Thinking" themed "Checkers Up on the Farm"; "When You and I Were Young Maggie" set off Rip Van Winkle; and Lincoln and his associates brought down the curtain to the strains of "We're Coming, Father Abraham."

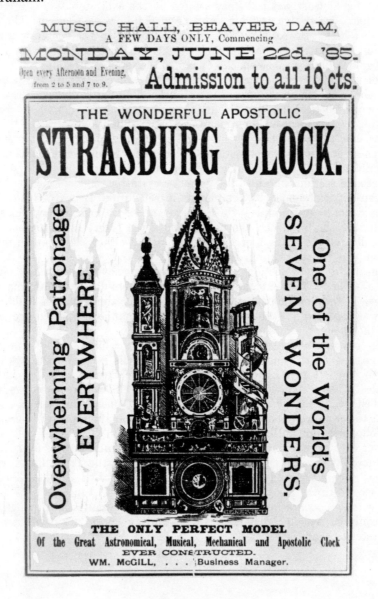

The Strasburg Clock

The Strasburg Clock was a mechanical novelty exibited throughout the country in the eighties and nineties as a replica of the famous astronomical clock installed in the Strasburg (Germany) Cathedral in 1574.

According to the legend, the maker of the clock was blinded by order of the Strasburg authorities that he might never duplicate his masterpiece and stringent laws were passed against anyone attempting to do so. Ulric Goldschmidt, a young watchmaker, set himself to the task and after many years, succeeded in reproducing it in every detail. His model was taken from him and he was banished. However, he managed to return in disguise, secure the model and take it to England where he died in poverty in London. His widow sold it to an English promoter and in time it was brought to America to be displayed throughout the states. This at least was the story related by the exhibitors.

The clock was twelve feet high and divided into three sections. The base was three feet high, six feet long and three feet deep. In the center was the grand calendar, calculated for one hundred years from 1800 to 1900, with years, leap years, golden numbers, the epacts, Dominical letters, months, days of the months, days of the week and the day of the week on which any date fell from 1800 to 1900. Above the dial were seven heathen deities, seated in chariots drawn by animals dedicated to them. These changed daily.

In the compartment on the right were three pendants, illustrating the equation of time, and the geocentric northern and southern declination of the sun. To the left was an ecclesiastical computation calculated forever. On the ends were paintings emblematic of the beginning and end of time.

The second section contained the grand orrery after the Copernican system with a golden sun surrounded by the planets in revolution. Beneath this a small dial indicated hours and minutes. On the right, a cherub held an hour glass; on the left another cherub struck the hours. Above the orrery on a semi-circular dial were indicated the changes of the moon. Lions at either side guarded the arms of Strasburg and of the church directors.

In the third upper section was the automatic movement. In the lower niche stood a skeleton. In front passed the four ages: childhood, youth, manhood and old age. At the first quarter, the cherub struck the time, and the child advanced. This was repeated at each quarter with youth, manhood and old age advancing. Then the skeleton struck the hour.

In the opening above were seven doors through which came the procession of the Apostles. At the quarter hour, a chime of bells rang and the Apostles came through the left door. From a center door, the Savior appeared blessing the Apostles as they bowed before him in passing. Satan appeared as Peter approached, tempting the apostle not to bow. Peter turned his back, a cock on the weight tower crowed and flapped its wings. Satan again appeared watching Judas and following him until the door closed after them. The great bell that tolled once for each apostle gave a final chime, and the exhibition was over.

On the right of the weight tower were paintings of the Three Fates; of Urania, muse of astronomy; and portraits of Copernicus and J. B. Swilgue. To the left, a staircase led to the clock.

The complete exhibition took place every fifteen minutes and though the clock was exhibited repeatedly, it never failed to draw spectators desirous of viewing its mysteries again.

Chapter 12

GRANDMOTHER HAD SOME HAD SOME VERY FINE DUCKS

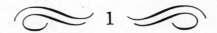

1

AT NO time was our household freed from fowl and livestock. Our corner lot stretched away in either direction a good half block; and with two barns, a chicken house, flowers and a vegetable garden, there remained room for a croquet court. Later Joe and I were able to squeeze in a standard tennis court to the expressed disgust of neighbors and passersby. Tennis was an effeminate pastime which graduated into the he-man classification only when golf became an old man's game.

Uncle Bee laid claim to being the most earnest gallinologist in the state—a term coined on the instant during an argument with "Chicken" Johnson, whose living depended largely upon his flocks and friers. But Uncle Bee was putting it mildly. The barn cote housed a flock of tumbling pigeons who demonstrated at sunset high above the housetops. He tried his hand at laying hens and some new breed of assembly-line producers were always cluttering the chicken run. For a time he fancied gamecocks but gave them up as cruel under pressure from Grandmother.

Grandmother herself had some very fine ducks. Each spring saw a new flock of fluffy yellow butterballs running about the back yard or paddling in the tin watertrough to the dismay of the hatching hen who couldn't appreciate their aquatic inclinations. Along in the late fall the full grown ducks passed on to be replaced with another hatching when winter ended.

Across the street from us lived Mrs. Lawrence, a comfortably compact Englishwoman and an ardent teetotaler, with more than a neighborhood reputation for her homemade cherry bounce. Each cherry season she put up untold quantities and throughout the summer bestowed her largesse upon favored friends as something akin to Jove's nectar for which Ben Jonson sighed.

Grandmother received her annual donation from Mrs. Lawrence and put it away against the winter's dullness. But when she opened it late in the fall, the poorly capped Mason jar had fermented. She dumped the contents into the backyard where the ducks fell upon it and gobbled it down without batting an eye. The luxury was too much for fowl unaccustomed to the finer things of life and next morning disclosed most of them, cold and stiff.

Dead ducks may be dead ducks, but duck feathers do not lose their value because of it. The corpses were brought into the house and stripped of their down by Grandmother and Aunt Sue. By the time the last one was plucked, the first was prancing about as lively as a Mexican jumping bean on a hot griddle. The entire flock had been suffering from a hangover.

This pious tipple of Mrs. Lawrence's was fifty percent cherries and fifty percent high powered French brandy. It carried the authority of a baseball bat and was hard enough on a human being to say nothing of an unsuspecting duck, now deprived of its outer garment.

Naked ducks could not survive the rigors of late fall. So Grandmother and Aunt Sue fashioned cute little red flannel underwear for the shivering flock, sewed it on for keeps and sent them forth, quacking their gratitude. But it was a feckless kindness, for the last one was eaten before their feathers were grown in again. So Grandmother and Aunt Sue washed and ironed the little red flannel coverings and laid them away as patches for our underclothes.

This pious tipple was imbibed freely by the White Ribbon Band when they foregathered at the Lawrence residence to raise their voices in protest against King Alcohol. The more they tested, the more eloquent they became, a not unwarranted result when one considers the proof of the decoction.

Because they were bound together in a noble cause, the Lawrence house became the rallying place for these ambitious musicians and frustrated elocutionists. They looked upon Mrs. Lawrence's cherry bounce and found it good. Each week guitars and mandolins and violins paraded up the street, and music and declamations continued long into the night—sometimes, in fact, until ten o'clock.

From such beginnings were spawned many of the young hopefuls who helped out in Christmas cantatas or played in amateur productions in the smaller assembly places. Disciples of Delsarte and strict adherents to "Fenno's Favorites, Principles of Gestures," most of their endeavors were ridiculous by any standard and were so recognized by everyone but the participants and their doting parents.

There was no Little Theater movement in Beaver Dam nor were there any earnest torch bearers intent upon improving the drama by presenting plays no one wanted to see. The Little Theater was something far in the distant future when mechanical entertainment had given the Perpetual Invalid another sock in the solar plexus and these faith healers began to administer panaceas as efficacious as a duck in a thunderstorm.

There were as many potential actors then as there still are in every country town. Each one knew he was the best of the crop and wanted to prove it. Showing off before the home folks is an innate trait from the day the little stinkers start to make nuisances of themselves until later years when their indulgent parents, continuing in their wonted rut, are certain their talented offspring are better than any star in the movies, on radio or TV.

Some youngsters outgrow this Narcissism, and those who don't, continue on to find a living as professionals or to bask in local adulation in some Little Theater. Most of them end up very bad actors, though occasionally some make the grade.

So it was in our town. For those who proved the best actors, elocution and Delsarte went by the boards. They just wanted to act. So they got together and put on a show. By and by they were sorted out after a fashion and each became associated with a group by social environment and daily contact. Also each became associated with a certain line of parts to which he was best suited. The result was something like a loosely strung stock company with a variable personnel, since all were on call for any play any time.

Dramatic groups were formed not through necessity of casting but because the players were associated socially. The Revera Club, Company K, the Arions, St. Mark's Episcopal Guild, St. Patrick's Sodality—each managed to line up enough more or less talented members to cast an average play.

The first step in any dramatic project was to select a suitable vehicle. Just as in big time productions, entertainments ran in cycles. Following the Civil War and during the next twenty years, there was a tremendous trend towards musical shows and operettas. Though they didn't call it that, vaudeville had been the mainstay of the Women's Sanitary Commission and it continued until well along in the seventies. They referred to them as "entertainments" and they continued to fight the war and wave the bloody shirt again and again. One of them introduced Uncle Bee to the stage at the tender age of three.

The program opened with a bevy of young ladies dressed in white with corsages of red roses, singing "Tramp, Tramp, Tramp, The Boys Are Marching." The blue ribbons that tied their hair completed the patriotic motif, and they marched about very prettily. Then Uncle Bee made his appearance.

Uncle Bee and a half dozen other curly pated youngsters were put on early in the evening so that they might be hustled home to bed. Besides it was next to impossible to keep them awake. They ranged across the stage wearing nightshirts and carrying lighted candles to join in a plaintive lullaby.

> Oh, birdie, I am tired now,
> I do not care to hear you sing,
> You've sung your pretty songs all day,
> So hide your head beneath your wing.
> Come, sister, come, put me in my bed,
> When my evening prayers I've said.
> You know what mother made me promise,
> Before she went away,
> She made me promise to be good,
> And never, never go astray.

Those old song writers were happy only when someone was dead or at least stricken with some progressive disease like consumption. They were strong for lost loved ones, mourning doves whooping it up in a weeping willow tree above a lonely and neglected grave; and a child's number, even as simple as this one, wasn't complete unless mother had passed away.

But by now it was time for the Beaver Dam Musical Academy to take over, so a mixed quartette assembled about a piano on the stage for close harmony in "Lilly Dale" and "The Hazel Dell."

> In the hazel dell my Nelly's sleeping,
> Nelly loved so long,
> And my lonely watch I'm keeping,
> Nelly's lost and gone.
> Here in moonlight often we have wandered,
> Through the silent shade,
> Now where leafy branches drooping downward,
> Little Nelly's laid.
> All alone my watch I'm keeping
> In the hazel dell,
> For my darling Nelly's near me sleeping,
> Nelly, dear, farewell.

And when defunct Nelly had been mourned for two more verses, the spectators were primed for something lighter. So young Al Burns was next on the program. Al was not so long back from the wars where he had served as drummer boy for Bragg's Iron Brigade. He was, the whole town agreed, "a great cutup," for he could dance a bit, sing better than average, and had a sense of comedy that made him top endman in most of the amateur minstrel shows. Al had selected "Et Cetera," billed as "A Comic Song, Written and Composed by J. H. Hewitt," and since it was his first appearance after his return, he elaborated it into a production number.

Dressed in skin-tight pants, patent leather shoes, with top hat, gloves and malacca cane, Al minced on to the stage in the best dude fashion. Lord Dundreary and his whiskers had set a run as chappy impersonations and this was Al's conception of how it should be done. Favorite that he was, he bowed to the enthusiastic applause and then, like Casey at the bat, raised his hand, the multitude was stilled, and he went into his act.

> The bloods who lounge about the streets,
> Or with their ponies dash on,
> Are always sipping luscious sweets,
> From off the lips of fashion.

They rise at twelve (*yawning*)
Then pick their teeth (*picking with gold toothpick*)
Or puff a mild cigar
(*Hunts for cigar and after fumbling, produces a stogie—a sure fire
laugh getter.*)
Then yawn a bit (*yawning*)
And talk a bit
(*Business of animated conversation after tipping hat, prodding
with cane and slapping imaginary companion on the shoulder*)
And swear (*starts to swear—hand over mouth—horrified*)
Et cetera

At night when charged with wit and wine,
Through street and alley reeling (*drunken business*)
Then while they're groping in the dark
They know they're men of feeling.
A row or two is all the go,
A black eye or a scar,
They love a bout—a yell—a blow—
A fight.
(*This afforded a ferocious battle in pantomine, throwing hat on
floor, pulling off coat, sparring and finally landing flat on back
from a knockdown*)
Et cetera

Then to a lockup off they go
(*Policeman enters swinging nightstick*)
All swearing—shouting—yelling—
The chappies fare the worst, you know,
Black eyes and noses swelling
(*By this time he is engaged in fisticuffs with the policeman*)
They tip with silver
(*Pulls loose and gets dollar from pocket. Policeman takes it and
exits*)
                              Soon the charm
Heals up each bruise and scar.
(*Brushes off, gets hat and cane, spruces up*)
Then to their nightly home they go
To sleep
                    (*Leering*) Et cetera!

This concluded the first part of the program and none too soon, for the good ladies in the front row were somewhat miffed at the implication of Al's tag to the song. Like Mae West's amorous invitation, it wasn't what he said but the way he said it. However, ten minutes intermission gave everybody a chance to regain their complacency and get ready for the second part.

The second part opened with another delegation of village belles in a fan drill. In contrast to the opening number, they wore black silk dresses with white ribbons in their hair. The leader added a Spanish shawl and a high back comb, and her Spanish folding fan was like the others except, perhaps, a trifle larger.

Black was worn to set off the gay colors of the fans, and against this background they gleamed the more brilliantly. The fan drill was the outgrowth of a discussion years before of fan flirtation by Addison in *The Spectator* and some inventive genius had hit upon it for just such an occasion as this. "The Pittsburgh March, Composed and Dedicated to the Officers and Members of the Du Quesne Grays," was the music to which they marched and countermarched, bringing their fans into various positions and in the trio of the composition, which introduced a bugle solo, the trumpeter of the Burchard Guards joined in offstage. It was the hit of the evening.

Next Al Burns displayed his versatility in a clog dance. For this he put on a minstrel corking and donned short silk pants, white shirt and Windsor tie. And then in compensation for the sad songs that had gone before, one of the elder members of the Beaver Dam Musical Academy puttered on to the scene in a maternal makeup with white wig and woebegone countenance. On her arm she carried what proved to be a pair of short trousers with a red patch in the seat. Her's was a plaintive tale of woe of her son, Jimmy, and what happened when the cruel draft called him.

> Our Jimmy has gone to live in a tent,
> They have grafted him into the army,
> He finally puckered up courage and went
> When they grafted him into the army.
> I told them the child was too young, alas,
> At the captain's forequarters they said he would pass,
> They'd train him up well in the infantry class
> So they grafted him into the army.

Drest up in his unicorn—dear little chap—
They have grafted him into the army,
It seems but a day since he sot in my lap,
When they grafted him into the army;
And these are the trousies he used to wear,
Them very same buttons—the patch and the tear—
But Uncle Sam gave him a brand new pair
When they grafted him into the army.

Now in my provisions I see him revealed,
They have grafted him into the army;
A picket beside a contented field,
They have grafted him into the army.
He looks kinder sickish—begins to cry—
A big volunteer standing right in his eye;
Oh, what if my ducky should up and die—
Now they've grafted him into the army.

Chorus.

Oh, Jimmy farewell! Your brother fell
Way down in Alabarney.
I thought they would spare a lone widder's heir
But they grafted him into the army.
(*Exits weeping, necessitating three encores of the chorus*)

The Civil War produced two types of composers. George F. Root favored the highly patriotic numbers: "Tramp, Tramp, Tramp, the Boys Are Marching" and "Just Before the Battle, Mother." But H. C. Work was a chap more cheerful who turned out "Wake Nicodemus" and "Grafted Into the Army." He did slip once in producing, "Father, Dear Father, Come Home With Me Now," but this was the only black mark on record, and his followers tended to overlook it when the temperance crowd took him to their respective bosoms.

The Grand Finale was ushered in by Al Burns, all washed up and wearing his army uniform, drumming away for dear life while the trumpeter played assembly on his bugle. The pair marched to the center of the stage and the black and white bevy of personable misses entered from either side, two by two, to execute a well planned drill to "Rally Round the Flag, Boys." They ended paired off, black and white alternating, while piano, drum and trumpet joined in a final fanfare with a flag dropped from the flies to the center of the stage.

On the face of it, the program appeared all too brief. But as is ever the way with amateur productions, each individual performer was not averse to encores. Luckily the planners had limited these to one each, and since preparations were not allowed for more than that, the entertainment was concluded at the reasonable hour of ten-thirty.

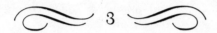

About this time Concert Hall was given a thorough overhauling. Stage boxes had proven impractical and were torn out to increase the seating capacity. The interior was redecorated, frescoed, and the new curtain with the Bay of Naples was hung. There was a batch of new chairs to fill in the extra space and a grand opening was in order. This was assigned to the Beaver Dam Musical Academy.

The Beaver Dam Musical Academy, like most of the small towns of the seventies and eighties, had its professor of music who taught voice, elocution and piano and more often than not tuned the instruments on the side. Our academy was the project of Professor Myron Hawley, a self bestowed honorary title, who made it the center of culture for ambitious youngsters who believed they were destined to become entertainers.

The Academy participated in any number of entertainments. Indeed, the annual concert was one of many inducements to keep the Hawley registration up to standard. If you weren't a member of the Academy, you just didn't rate; and if you didn't rate, no power, political or monetary, could place you on the program. So when a four day gala entertainment was bruited, the Hawley enrollment became the greatest in its history.

The rebuilt Concert Hall was at its best and when it had been inspected and the spectators welcomed by the mayor and board of aldermen the first night's program got under way. It was a concert by the advanced classes of the Academy supported by the Beaver Dam Cornet Band. The last night was devoted to its graduating exercises but in between were two performances in which Mother played a leading part.

Lily Bell, the Culprit Fay, an operetta by Herman S. Saroni, had been seen before but, it was explained, "the labor, expense and trouble of getting up such an entertainment is our only excuse for its repetition." Professor

Professor Myron Hawley

Conducted the Beaver Dam Music Academy and produced *The Twin Sisters* and *Lily Bell, the Culprit Fay*.

Hawley didn't intrude the fact that the cast included most of the town's young people, either in leading parts or the chorus of fairies and naiads, and that their presence ensured attendance of the families of each, assuring capacity houses on both nights. For economical reasons, the band was dispensed with and Aggie Bogart occupied her accustomed seat at the piano.

The plot dealt with Fairyland and the husky young belles, though anything but ethereal, tripped about and sang and rattled castanets—a must in every musical evening—while Titania, the fairy queen, sat in judgment on Lily Bell, her favorite, who had strayed off the fairy ring and taken up with a mortal man. Mother was Thistledown, the favorite's rival, and she gave it her all, out of frustration because she had not been cast in the leading part. That Susan Boomer had it was rank favoritism, Mother was sure, since Susan took more lessons at the Academy and consequently increased the Hawley revenues.

Lily Bell is ordered to answer three riddles, and while she is mooning about searching for the solution, Thistledown in turn strays away and falls for a mortal on her own account. Unfortunately for her, the evil spirits of the wood get hold of her and proceed to torment and plague her until she is ready to faint.

That was where Mother went to town. There was plenty of action and no end of singing, and while Lily Bell indulged only in plaintive airs the villainous Thistledown could open up and let go. And that is what Mother did so successfully. In fact, she was accorded top honors by all unprejudiced observers, which of course did not include the Boomer kinfolk.

Another favorite of the Academy was Saroni's *Twin Sisters*. That man supplied most of the nation's academies with operettas calculated to serve all sorts of vocalists and furnish material for expansive chorus numbers

Concert Hall

FIFTH ANNIVERSARY
BEAVER DAM
MUSICAL ACADEMY

FOUR CONCERTS,

Tuesday, Wednesday. Thursday and Friday,

JUNE 22D, 23D, 24TH AND 25TH.

TUESDAY EVENING, 22,

Concert of Vocal and Instrumental Music, by the Advanced Classes, assisted by the Beaver Dam Cornet Band. This Concert will be the re-opening of Concert Hall, and we invite everybody to attend. Tickets Free. Let us have a grand jubilee.

Wednesday and Thursday, 23 & 24.

HERRMAN S. SARONI'S

NEW AND BEAUTIFUL OPERETTA—IN THREE ACTS,

LILY-BELL, THE CULPRIT FAY.

"Lily-Bell will be given with appropriate Costumes and Scenery. The Scenic and Musical effect of this Operetta will be a feast to the eye and ear, and should be witnessed by all, both old and young. The labor, expense and trouble in getting up such an entertainment is our only excuse for its repetition. Concert Hall has been reconstructed, frescoed and painted, which makes it a first-class Hall, and will add much to the beauty and effect of this Operetta.

FRIDAY EVENING, JUNE 25,

Concert by the Graduating Class. To conclude with a Grand Re-Union, Sociable and Promonade, with Strawberries, Ice Cream, Lemonade, Oranges, Lemons, Confectionery &c., furnished by Geo. Sipplein. Programmes will be circulated through the city.

Thankful for past favors bestowed on this "Home Institution," we would say to the citizens of this city and surrounding country, that we have spared no pains in making the coming Anniversary worthy the occasion, the place, the times, and patronage of an appreciative community.

PROGRAMME,

For Tuesday Evening, June 22d.

PART I.

Music by the Band.
1. CHORUS GLEE—Forest Festival.
2. PIANO DUET—L'Amarante, F. E. Carrier and L. Armstrong.
3. PIANO SOLO—Rainbow Schottisch, F. L. Gower.
4. SONG—The Tempest, L. Armstrong.
5. PIANO DUET—Les Fifers De La Garde, R. Willard and F. E. Carrier.
6. VOCAL DUET—Under the Beautiful Stars, S. Boomer and L. Armstrong.
7. PIANO DUET—Fille Du Regiment, F. L. Gower and T. Torbert.
8. PIANO SOLO—Wandering Spirit, Rosa Willard.
9. PIANO SOLO—Echos of Lucerne, Olive Bush.
10. VOCAL TRIO—Harvest Day.
L. E. Smith, M. Sherman and L. Armstrong.

PART II.

1. PIANO TRIO—Overture, Barbiera De Sevilla.
S. Boomer, M. Sherman and J. Mayne.
2. PIANO SOLO—Cascade De Roses, F. E. Carrier.
3. VOCAL DUET—Light may the Boat Row,
F. E. Carrier and F. L. Gower.
4. PIANO DUET—Steeple Chase. Gallop.
N. Babcock and L. E. Smith.
5. PIANO SOLO—Love's First Dream, M. Sherman.
6. VOCAL DUET—O come to the Forest,
L. E. Smith and L. Armstrong.
7. QUARTETTE AND CHORUS—The Pacific Rail Road.
8. PIANO DUET—Les Bord Du Rhin, C. Hyland and M. Sherman.
9. PIANO SOLO—The storm, L. E. Smith.
10. SOLI AND CHORUS—Shepherd of Thine Israel Lead Us.

Tickets to Each Concert, Except the First, 25 Cts.
Children - - - 10 cts.

DOORS OPEN AT 7 O'CLOCK: COMMENCE AT 8 O'CLOCK.

Tickets For Sale At The Musical Academy.

Concert Hall

FIFTH ANNIVERSARY
BEAVER DAM
MUSICAL ACADEMY

Director, - - M. Hawley.
Pianist, - - Aggie Bogart.

Wednesday & Thursday

EVENINGS,

JUNE 23d and 24th,

HERRMAN S. SARONI'S

NEW AND BEAUTIFUL OPERETTA—IN THREE ACTS,

LILY BELL,

THE CULPRIT FAY.

DRAMATIS PERSONÆ:

TITANIA, the Fairy Queen, - - LUCY SMITH.
LILY-BELL, her favorite, - SARAH BOOMER.
THISTLEDOWN, a Rival, - NETTIE BABCOCK.
HEART'S EASE, a Fairy in Titania's Train, DOLLIE BOGART.
SILVER SPRAY, - - CELIA HYLAND.
EUDORA, the Naiad Queen, - L. ARMSTRONG.
CHORUS OF FAIRIES AND NAIADES.

ARGUMENT.

Lily-Bell, the favorite subject of Titania, the fairy queen, while wandering outside of fairy land, falls in love with a mortal, which is a violation of the laws of the realm. Her crime is discovered by Thistledown, who is jealous of her. In spite of Lily-Bell's pleadings, Thistledown makes known her faults to Titania, who, loth to banish her from the realm, imposes on her as a punishment the task of solving three riddles. Until this is done she is banished, but may return whenever she accomplishes her task. While searching for the answers she assists Eudora, the Naiad Queen of another dominion, who in turn gives Lily Bell the clue to the information she is in search of.

In the meantime Thistledown, whose feminine curiosity was greatly excited by Lily Bell's account of her experience in love, and feeling a little ashamed of her own conduct in the affair, starts out on an exploring expedition, partly to see how Lily Ball is getting along, and partly to see what this wonderful love is, that has had so great a power over her. Poetic justice of course decrees that she should fall into the hands of wicked spirits, who so torment and plague her that she is ready to faint with exhaustion, when Lily Bell, who is returning to her home with Eudora, forgetting the injuries she has received, comes to the rescue, and the three fays seek Titania in triumph, with the answers to the riddles.

Arriving at the court of Titania, great festivities and rejoicings take place, and the curtain falls on a happy scene.

Tickets to Each Concert, Except the First, 25 Cts.
Children - - - 10 cts.
DOORS OPEN AT 7 O'CLOCK: COMMENCE AT 8 O'CLOCK.
Tickets For Sale At The Musical Academy.

besides. Like *The Culprit Fay*, this was set with a woodland background. And a full stage was assured, free from encumbrances to hinder the cavorting of the dancing group.

It is May Day and Mab Stanley is crowned Queen, but not without a musical introduction worthy an opera more pretentious:

> Come where pleasure lingers,
> Where the gentle woodland fay,
> Weaves with magic fingers wreaths to crown the brow of May.
> Oh come away, come away, come away.
> With lively dance and merry song,
> We greet the joyous day,
> When once again within our throng,
> We crown the Queen of May.
> Hail joyous day!
> Hail, Queen of May!

And so after an interminable repetition of the greeting, Queen Mab Stanley accepts the garland but laments for her sister, Florence.

> Oh, Sister dear, where dwellest thou,
> Where rests thine aching heart.
> Oh, Sister dear, come back to me,
> And never more we'll part.
> And fate perchance will smile on us,
> Have pity on our doom,
> And joys serene accord to us
> Life's journey to illume.
> By wealth and friends surrounded,
> To every blessing born,
> Thou'rt roaming among strangers,
> From loving bosoms torn.

And as Queen Mab exits, two of the girls give the plot in detail, a favorite subterfuge of both amateur and professional productions of that period, since it cut down production costs, saved time and speeded up the action. Three years before, the party held its May Day outing on this very spot, concluding with a torchlight dance. But a band of gypsies had stolen Florence, Queen Mab's twin, and nothing had been learned of her since.

Came an intermission while the gypsies set up camp and then here they were, in the selfsame spot where the merrymaking had taken place. Mother was the Second Gypsy and her bosom friend, Dollie Bogart, was the first gypsy. Their part lines were brief but vital.

FIRST GYPSY
Leora, do you know that this is not the first time we have struck our camp in this spot?

SECOND GYPSY
I well remember thrice twelve moons ago where our band received an additional member in the form of Preciosa.

FIRST GYPSY
And a good card she has proved to us in spite of her unwillingness to submit to our laws. Her performances always bring a shower of silver coins.

SECOND GYPSY
But have you no fear that she will be discovered by her friends in this her native place?

FIRST GYPSY
I will take the precaution and send her on to our next encampment by a footpath unknown to all but us. Come, a song, Preciosa.

With which Mother and Dollie were through for the evening so far as any speaking part was concerned. So were most of the others, for the chorus was working full blast and the plot rambled along until Florence was finally recognized by her sister, which took some time because as a gypsy she was wearing an old dress. And then the two of them exchanged cries of "Sister, dear" for a good three minutes, mounting the scale with each repetition; and Dollie and Mother did a gypsy dance with castanets, which poulticed their disappointment over a dearth of dialogue; and the curtain came down with the entire Academy ensemble crowding the stage, while the littlest ones scattered paper flowers about and for some unexplained reason, Sister Mab crowned Sister Florence Queen of the May, too. And all joined in with:

> Call blessings adown,
> On the Queen of our choice,
> And under her homage
> With loud ringing voice,
> Hail, all hail, hail, hail, hail!

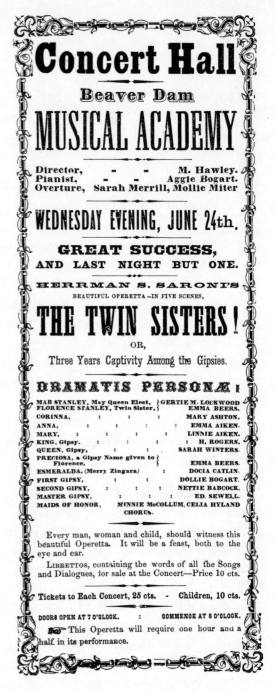

When the Beaver Dam Musical Academy gave its annual students' recital, operettas such as *Lily Bell, the Culprit Fay*, or *The Twin Sisters*, or *Three Years' Captivity Among the Gypsies* might be the presentation. Dollie Bogart (*left*) and Mother (*right*) appeared frequently in these, and here they are in *Lily Bell, the Culprit Fay*. Or it might have been *The Twin Sisters*, since the same costumes served on both occasions. Wardrobes were scanty, and amateurs made the most of what they possessed.

As Mother related it, so outstanding had been her reading of the part of the Second Gypsy that she was cast as the heavy when *The Culprit Fay* was staged. And she paid no attention to Uncle Bee's suggestion that this happy outcome resulted from Grandfather's entering her for added lessons in the Academy.

4

Time passed on, as Time has a habit of doing, and good Professor Hawley went on to join the celestial choir invisible, and the Beaver Dam Musical Academy closed its doors, and its graduates faded away. Some died, some moved to other towns, while most of them got married and had no time to plump at auditionings even if there had been any.

And in the Academy's place came the McClure girls, who went happily on their way promoting entertainments for St. Mark's Guild and the rector's living until they came a near cropper with the lady's minstrel show. The idea was rational enough and they had no difficulty in enlisting Beaver Dam's choicest talent. The trouble began when the talent refused to jell into that give-and-take performance so integral to this peculiar form of entertainment.

When it assembled in the McClure parlor the line-up was about equally divided between the more mature ladies of the town and the up-and-coming generation who had adopted ragtime, the cakewalk and similar innovations. Mother was picked for her mastery of the bones. Cherry McClure, the banker's wife, was a logical interlocutor because of her singing voice, graceful personality and a head of prematurely white hair to deck the center of the circle. Emma Lawrence, whose husband ran the Clark House, and Carrie Buel, wife of the leading druggist, were others of the older menage.

Then there were Winnie Shipman and Jen Richardson, who played banjo duets; and Babe Keyes, and Josie McClure, youngest of the sisters; and a number of others who wanted to pep up the performance while the oldsters stuck out for the conventional minstrel routine. When this had been thrashed out at the first two meetings, circle places were assigned and the rehearsal got under way. As top end man, Mother was given the first chair of the bones section, nearest the left of the audience. That is, she was for a time. Then a change was made and she picked up her bones and went home.

I was pretty much of a youngster, but I can still picture her storming into the house in a fine fury. She had been put into second chair and Josie McClure had been given the choice seat. It was, she declared, rank favoritism on the part of the McClure sisters, and the minstrel show could go hang for all of her. When Dot McClure arrived soon after, palpitating with consternation at such an unheard of display of temper, Mother expressed herself in no uncertain terms.

"But, Nettie, don't you see it is necessary to the success of the show?" Dot queried.

"Why is it necessary?" Mother questioned squarely.

"Why? Don't you know Josie has that joke about the organ grinder and his monkey, and she has to lean over to grind the organ, and if she isn't on the end, no one will be able to see her and the point will be lost?"

Mother considered a moment. Then she delivered her ultimatum. "Maybe so," she said. "It's all right with me. Let the monkey play the bones."

So Mother went back to the first chair. But bickering continued and the McClure girls decided that a stronger hand than their combined ones was needed. So they enlisted the services of unsuspecting John Woodruff, who played the violin and who was to be rewarded with an opportunity to appear as soloist. After which, Dot confined herself to the piano while Josie and Kate took their place in the ensemble and joined in the arguments that followed the attempts of the young to outsmart the old. But when the big night came, the bill was a compromise. There was no olio. The second part took care of that.

In festive mood, none of the participants were listed on the program. Instead each was identified by a fictitious name which the inventors fondly imagined smacked of the old South. I never did get them all untangled but Mother was Smirky Columbine, and Cherry McClure was Mrs. Johnson, and of the rest I could only identify Winnie Shipman and Jen Richardson and then only because they played a banjo duet. There was some reticence among the ladies in disclosing their identity too obviously. It was anticipated that a generous display of bosom would be necessary in the blacking up process and since Mr. Woodruff supervised this part of it, the less said about it the better. Anyway, they were ranged on the stage by 8:30 and as curtain was announced as 8:15, this wasn't at all bad for an amateur show of such proportions. They opened with a grand chorus: "Ching a Ling." It had to do with a flirtatious couple but the music was sprightly and nobody paid much attention to the words.

> Ching a ling, ching a ling, that's how the bells ring,
> Ching a ling, ching a ling, oh you darling old thing,
> I'll be your bride if you'll buy the ring,
> And servants will play on the ching a ling ling.

Then the endmen were introduced and local gags were bandied to the delight of the members of St. Mark's congregation, who constituted the majority of the audience, and Judy Skimmerhorn, an unidentified member of the cast, obliged with a song made famous by May Irwin.

> Mamie, come kiss your honey boy,
> While the sun do shine
> Don't you hear me, Mamie?
> Mamie, come kiss your honey boy,
> While the sun do shine.

In place of the traditional tenor solo, Cherry McClure sang, "Pride of the Ball," a popular waltz number with a chorus:

> Proudly she reigned like a queen upon her throne,
> Cheeks that were flushed like a rose in Heaven grown,
> Graceful and fair, she was loved and wooed by all,
> She stole my heart, the Pride of the Ball.

Then Josie McClure told her story of the organ grinder and the monkey, and went to the center of the stage to grind the hand organ, attracting more attention thereby than if she had occupied the first bones position.

The endmen, all six of them dismissing their personal animosities, lined across the stage to sing "Mary Green."

> Airy, fairy contrary is Mary Green,
> She's the belle of the town it is plainly seen,
> All the boys they are jealous of me, I ween,
> Mary, my Mary, she's just like a fairy
> Is Mary Green.

More songs and persiflage, and the first part ended. The oldsters having had their day, the second part of the program was taken over by the younger generation.

The opening was a lantern drill by a dozen of the girls on a darkened stage. As usual, the good ladies of the guild had put pressure on the town's two hardware stores, and a dozen lanterns had been requisitioned from their shelves. Covered with red and blue bunting, they were carried in formation, swung perilously close together at times, and finally arranged in a pyramid formation. It was all very effective, and the audience drew a deep breath of relief when it was ended without setting the theater on fire.

Shipman and McClure obliged with a banjo duet, "On the Mill Dam," a standard number for the five string banjo. If you tackled the mandolin, your first task was to master "Over the Waves." With the banjo, it was "On the Mill Dam," a gallop with a lively tempo and not too hard to play. It was a sure fire solo for all aspiring banjoists.

The big number was "The Colored Four Hundred," sung by the entire organization in drill formations.

> We're the crème, de la crème,
> Of the colored population and we are a stylish team,
> And as for swells and colored belles,
> None can beat the members of the colored four hundred.

Then when Woodruff had given Wieniawski's "Mazurka" on his violin, the performance closed with an animated square dance with Babe Keyes as caller. It was, one might say, a peaceable melding of the old and the new, for Babe, in this honored spot, was one of the newcomers who wanted to change the established order of things.

So the curtain finally fell, and after an hour or so the ladies had removed enough of the burnt cork to venture home, where they spent most of the night getting rid of the rest. Some of the less audacious wore their makeup home and so far as the general public was concerned, their identity was lost forever.

The Lady Minstrels were voted a success but not until Woodruff and the McClure girls were on the verge of nervous prostration. After that, the sisters contented themselves with lawn parties, soliciting tables and chairs and Japanese lanterns and ice cream contributions. They knew that their greatest worry was in keeping the neighborhood urchins from lugging off the ice cream freezers. But with time, they recovered their aplomb and in due course, with the paternal supervision of Dr. Johnson, they put on *The Brownies in Fairyland.*

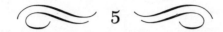

5

Musical shows continued until well along into the eighties. This, no doubt, was due to the fact that every family had a piano or parlor organ, that the sons took to music to join the town band or some orchestra, and that everybody sang after a fashion. Uncle Bee had a fine baritone voice, though he insisted on singing bass. He said it was less offensive. Listening to some of our baritone crooners, I am certain he spoke the truth.

When *The Mikado* was pirated across seas, a veritable Gilbert and Sullivan epidemic swept the nation as thoroughly as ever did the Japanese beetle. Vocalists were always insulting the scales with the "Tit-Willow" song and "I've Got a Little List," and whenever a trio of girls got together they started "Three Little Maids from School." Worse than that they dressed up and did it with kimonos and fans.

But the drama was coming into its own. Even back in the seventies, when concerts and minstrel shows were amateur favorites, the Beaver Dam Dramatic Association survived a brief and tumultuous career before artistic temperament disintegrated the group after one benefit performance for Blind Man Phelps. *Dollars and Sense, a Favorite Comedy in Four Acts* was their offering. But tastes changed with time, and when Joe and I were old enough to participate the groups were "putting on plays."

There was a distinct advantage in being attached to Concert Hall. We could furnish a rehearsal hall scot-free and so were included in the cast whenever possible or spotted in between acts for a banjo solo.

Picking the right play was most important in these dramatic projects. The players had not only to suit themselves but the townsfolk as well if they wanted to break even. Only with benefits did they hope to net anything above expenses. As a rule they were in luck when they got off the nut and on such rare occasions when a balance was left they blew it on a chafing dish party at some member's home.

Westerns and comedies were the best bets. You could bumble along and fake lines if you had to, and no one was really certain whether you had blown or were just adding a few frills for good measure. Lorenzo Lambeck had catalogues of Samuel French, the American Play Company and the Chicago Play Company with a brief resumé of the plot, starting with the cast number and the author's name when he dared admit his perpetration. It ran like this:

THE VAGABONDS, by Charles Townsend. 6 m 4 f. 3 acts. 3 int. 2 ext. Moderate cost.

Act 1—The lawn at the Major's in Old Virginia. Ireland and Africa prepared for war. Yankee Doodle commands the peace. "Guess they hain't so full of fight es they wuz." Chub and Peggy. A scrimmage on tap. Peggy's orders. "The next time I meet you I'll kick the top o' your head off." A jolly old maid. Bascom the Vagabond. "I'm a hoodoo. If I look in a pan of milk it turns sour." "Who—who are you?" Dilworthy the hypocrite. The threat. Bascom to the rescue. The recognition. The price of silence. The hypocrite triumphs. Planning a murder. The unseen witness.

Act 2—Scene 1—Parlor at Dilworthy's, evening of the same day. Father and son. A pair of rascals. "Don't you preach morality." The agreement. A lover's quarrel. "Don't want your candy?" The story of a crime. The forced confession. Dilworthy's threat. Scene II—A road in the forest. A lost coon. Scene III—Bascom's home. "It's better nor outdoors." A threatened quarrel. "Why don't you throw me out. I'm used to it." The plotters. A murderous scoundrel. A rifle shot. The accusation. "Before another night, the truth shall be known."

Act III—Library at the Major's. Time, the next morning. "I'd like jest one slash at dat ole Dilworthy." Taking testimony. "Stick to your story." Charlotte makes some remarks. "Hurrah for Ireland." Ephraim and the ghost. An unexpected arrival. "Dar's de ghost." Cornered at last. A game of bluff. Mother Carew. A startling denouncement. Vindication. Justice asserts herself. Reunited at last. Finale.

Translated, the information showed a cast of six males, four females, three acts, three interiors, two exteriors, all at moderate cost, which meant you could get by with the house scenery and a little imagination. The resumé was printed on the program so the audience could follow the plot if the actors went haywire.

From these sources a choice was made. *Tess, or Beyond the Rockies* smacked of the west as thoroughly as a modern horse opera. *Tony the Convict* was a cinch for a man betrayed, as were most of those dimwitted heroes. *Hans the Cobbler* ensured comedy with a German dialect. Most likely it was copied after one of W. J. Scanlan's Irish plays or Joe Emmett's German comedies. *Topsy-Turvey* of course was the broadest kind of a farce, and *Peck's Bad Boy* was known to everyone since it came occasionally as a road show.

Most of the minstrel shows that traipsed the country hit every small town at one time or another, though most of them confined their routes to their chosen territory where they had built up a following. Though two or three minstrel troupes played the average town annually, home talent broke out with a rash of blackface at least once a year. The Beaver Dam Cornet Band staged this minstrel show in the early eighties. The tambo endman at the traditional right might have been presiding at the drums, for he was Al Burns, Grandfather's brother-in-law, who was one of the many drummer boys who returned from the Civil War to stage exhibitions of their skill.

MINSTRELS
—AT—
CONCERT HALL,
TO-NIGHT!

PROGRAMME:

INTRODUCTORY OVERTURE,
HARDER'S ORCHESTRA
OPENING CHORUS.
COMPANY
COMIC SONG—"*Perhaps*,"
O. F. WEAVER
BALLAD—"*Homeless and Friendless*,"
QUARTETTE
COMIC SONG—"*Summer Sounds*,"
A. M. BURNS
FINALE,
COMPANY

OVERTURE.
BALLAD—(Guitar Acc'pan'mt,) "*My Home in Kentuck*,"
O. M. DAVIS
BONE SOLO.
G. H. HIBBARD
FARCE—"*Backwoods Echo*,"
F. S. LEWIS, O. F. WEAVER, A. M. BURNS
OVERTURE.
SKIDMORE GUARDS—*Marching Song of*,
Introducing the entire Company in military costume, and executing a series of drill unparalleled in Military Tactics.
SONG AND DANCE—"*I want to See the Dear Old Home*,"
A. M. BURNS
FARCE—"*Troublesome Infant*."
Mr. Jenkins, : : : W. H. LEWIS
Mrs. Jones, : : : F. M. VANBERGEN
Little Tommy Jones, (2 years old,) G. H. HIBBARD
Utility Sam, : : : O. F. WEAVER
OVERTURE.
SERIO-COMIQUE—"*Where can the Old Man Go*,"
O. F. WEAVER
PLANTATION SONG—*Duett*,
DAVIS AND HIBBARD
PLANTATION SCENE—"*Walking for dat Cake*,"
COMPANY

"WOLVES! What can save us?" | "The strong arm of a Backwoodsman."

Davy Crockett

Davy Crockett, fashioned by Frank Murdock, was a stellar vehicle for Frank Mayo, who played it until his death. When he had exhausted its possibilities in the larger cities, he continued throughout the country, and one-night stands had an opportunity of witnessing the performance of a big time star.

Davy is the son of the hero of the Alamo who fell before the guns of Santa Anna's Mexicans. He has adopted his father's motto, "Be sure you're right, then go ahead," which also is the subtitle of the show. Untutored child of nature, he had a respect for womanhood which exceeded even that of today's hairpants cowboys. Nellie Vaughan, his childhood playmate, passes through the settlement.

Nellie's guardian has become financially involved with Oscar Crampton, and his nephew Neil is set to marry the gal. Nellie is not at all happy about it, as Davy soon discovers. So he follows the party. A convenient change of weather brings on a terrific blizzard, separating the travelers and leaving Nellie and Neil stranded near Davy's hideout in the woods.

Half-frozen, Neil crawls to the cabin, Davy rescues Nellie from the storm, and while the winds howl and Neil sleeps, the girl reads "Young Lochinvar" from her copy of Scott's poems. Their tête-à-tête is interrupted by distant howling of wild animals.

DAVY

That's wolves. But don't be skeered.

NELLIE

But I am.

DAVY

Aint I here?

NELLIE

But they are so dreadfully near.

DAVY

This door is built of oak. I built it and—blazes—the bar's gone.

NELLIE

Gone? (*Wolves howl about the cabin*)

DAVY

Yes, I split it to warm you and your friend. Rouse him. The pesky devils are all around the place.

NELLIE

Neil! Help!

DAVY

Quick, I can't hold the door agin 'em.

>   (*Wolves throw themselves against
>   the door, howling.*)

NEIL

I tell you, uncle, if the girl says no, that's the end of it.

NELLIE

My God! He's delirious! Nothing can save us now!

DAVY

Yes it can.

NELLIE

What?

DAVY

The strong arm of a backwoodsman. (*He bars the door with his arm as wolves houl louder and their heads appear in openings and underneath the door*)

CURTAIN

He's still at it the next morning, but the rest of the party arrive and drive the wolves away, while Davy, handicapped with a badly swollen arm, sets off for a doctor ten miles away. He makes it, too, and turns up at the wedding of Eleanor and Neil to snatch up the girl and ride away, another Young Lochinvar comes out of the West.

In later years, James J. Jeffries cashed in on his heavyweight championship by starring as Davy Crockett. The best that could be said of his histrionic effort was that he certainly barred the door.

New York Public Library

Frank Mayo as Davy Crockett

Peck's Bad Boy was a mess of surefire hodge-podge on a leisurely string of incidents bordering on burlesque. This loose construction gave a specialty to everybody in the cast, ending with a burlesque on *Uncle Tom's Cabin,* where Mr. Peck played Uncle Tom while the Bad Boy, in mother hubbard and red wig, climbed up a stepladder as the rest of the company stood at the footlights burning red fire on pie tins and singing, "Tell Me Where My Little Eva's Gone."

With a chorus in silk tights for a background—burlesque frowned upon nudity until Ziegfeld and Earl Carroll discovered it filled their theaters—*Peck's Bad Boy* could have played the Columbia wheel exactly as we put it on as a benefit for our basketball team, though such a possibility never entered our minds. We looked upon it as a mess of nonsense with specialties, which it was, and as Mr. Peck I gave my all as stooge for my stage son's jokes, being banged over the pate with an inflated pig's bladder, enduring a dousing from a pail of water, and ending with fistfuls of flour in the face. Mack Sennett had not yet demonstrated the risibility of an expertly tossed custard pie.

The cast was tailored for burlesque, for there was a Jewish pawnbroker; a German storekeeper; Mr. Peck, whose dignity made him the logical butt of the play's mishaps; and a school scene in which all of them suffered with Junior including the ingenue who was pressed into service as schoolma'am; and wound up the melee by joining in "Snitzelbank."

For some reason I never understood I was picked to play genteel old men—Mr. Peck's misadventures were an exception—or eccentric comedians. In *Topsy Turvey* I was a doddering old fossil pursuing an equally doddering old maid and fearing the approaches of an English lord. All of these alleged comedies sported an English lord and enacting this one was Doc Anderson, local veterinarian and a basso profundo. Doc introduced "Asleep in the Deep" in response to the customary request:

"And now, Lord Chumley, how about that song we like so well?"

"Bah Jove, I do believe you must mean that little number—"

"That's it!" from all of us. "Asleep in the Deep."

Doc was giving it his all, growling lower and lower with the warning:

"Many brave hearts are asleep in the deep,
So beware! Beware!"

when our stage manager started beckoning wildly in the wings and the soloist became more engrossed in this offstage demonstration than in hitting the final note on the head. But he did and his exit came soon after. I could see him in animated conversation with an obviously excited individual wearing a flap cap and felt packs. When I reached our common dressing room, both had vanished. Doc had hustled away with the stranger without removing his makeup or changing his costume. Nor did he leave word as to the party which we had planned after the performance. But all this was made plain when I met him on the street next day.

"I bet a veterinarian never delivered a bull calf before with a plug hat on the harness rack and a Prince Albert draped on the side of a cow stall," he greeted me. "Or with his face daubed with makeup streaked with sweat until he looked like a wild Indian. But that's what I did last night. And a damned good job I made of it, too."

Makeup, as we used it, was of the scantiest and for good reason. Since none of us had learned the necessity of a cold cream foundation, we used it sparingly. One inventive amateur bethought himself of cocoa butter as a makeup base, but it proved capable only of clogging the pores and furthering blackheads. Besides it cost too much for our slender purses.

But since the halls were small, most of us got along without any at all, whitening our hair with flour if needed and trusting to luck for the rest. When a production assumed greater proportions we called in Ed Hohl. Besides painting scenery, Ed played in the band and imagined himself something of a makeup artist. He had procured a fleshing, a couple of liners, and a black and red makeup stick, also a makeup book with crude heads roughly diagrammed to show where the stuff should be applied. Following this, Ed daubed us imaginatively, sans cold cream, and we always wore the makeup home, and slept in it more often than not, for it took plenty of soapy water and scrubbing to remove it satisfactorily.

Benefits were selected to satisfy the demands of the chosen group who were to profit from the performance. *Robert Emmet* was a regular for the Catholic groups. It was the only time that the Dion Boucicault show was given, for road companies never seemed to care for it. Possibly they were unable to get hold of the script. *Shamrock and Rose* was another favorite with St. Patrick's Church. Like the other, this play dealt with the Irish uprising of 1798, proving beyond question that every Irishman was a broth of a boy, every colleen was a rose of Killarney, and every Englishman was a deep-dyed villain and hanging was too good for him.

"Hanging!" said one of the old timers after viewing one of these Irish for Ireland dramas. "Hanging's too good for him. He ought to have his posterior booted."

This statement, I blush to admit, was couched in a manner far more brief and much less refined.

ADAM FOREPAUGH, JR., IN HIS SENSATIONAL 30-HORSE ACT.

HORSE BLONDIN CROSSING THE HIGH WIRE.

EXHIBITION of MARKSMANSHIP
BY DR. W. F. CARVER, BEFORE
HIS ROYAL HIGHNESS, THE PRINCE OF WALES,
AT SANDRINGHAM, ENGLAND.
RIFLE.

Moving Objects.—1.—Shooting 75 Glass Balls out of 100. 2.—Shooting Glass Balls thrown very high in the air. 3.—Shooting Glass Balls thrown across in front of shooter. 4.—

with back to object, sighting by aid of a mirror. 18.—Shooting a Glass Ball placed upon the ground, holding the Rifle upon the hip, shooting without sighting. 19.—Shooting a Glass Ball, the Rifle upside down, shooter lying upon his back over a stool. 20.—Shooting 10 shots at a target in 20 seconds, placing the balls nearly all together. 21.—Miscellaneous shooting.

SHOT GUN.

22.—Shooting 100 Glass Balls sprung from two traps, right and left. 23.—Shooting 50 pair of Glass Balls sprung from one trap. 24.—Shooting a Falling Ball. 25.—Shooting from right to left shoulder. 26.—Shooting Glass Ball sprung from trap, shooter standing with back to

THRILLING, SOUL-STIRRING AND MASTERLY REPRESENTATIONS OF WILD LIFE ON THE
DISTANT FRONTIER, AS PRESENTED ON THE QUARTER OF A MILE HIPPO-
DROME TRACK OF THE FOREPAUGH-WILD WEST COMBINATION.

Forepaugh—Wild West Combination

During the last years of the eighties the Adam Forepaugh Show was an unusual combination of circus and wild west which set the pace for Buffalo Bill's Wild West Show, organized in North Platte, Nebraska, in 1882.

Forepaugh's street parade featured elephants, golden circus chariots, equestrians, trained dogs, and Nebo, the largest horse in the world, who stood twenty hands high and weighed 1800 pounds, aged four years. There were bands, of course, with a cowboy band on horseback, and a closed wagon containing "the largest hippopotamus in captivity."

The performance was a strange mingling of circus and wild west. Young Adam Forepaugh, Jr., was starred in the only act of its kind ever attempted. Standing on two horses, he drove a team of thirty others around the arena at top speed. The horses ran in fours, but the wise country spectator noted that the reins ran only to the lead horses and that the entire hitch was kept in line by guide ropes that ran from the lead four to the pair ridden by the driver. But at that, they admitted, it was no small peanuts and something well worth the viewing.

Young Adam seemed to be something of a magician with horses, for he also exhibited Blondin, the horse that walked a tight rope thirty feet above ground. It was explained that Blondin wore a special shoe grooved through the center to fit the rope and that the rest of the feat was dependent upon the animal. This was all very well, but when the time came, the rope was reinforced by a platform nearly two feet wide on which it lay. This was brushed aside as a necessary part of the rigging. Mlle. Marguerite Sivado was a bareback rider, and young Mr. Forepaugh whose magical touch evidently extended to canines, exhibited Jack and Jim, the somersault dogs, while a man raced on foot against a horse. The man always won because he was given a start of half the distance.

The wild west had two stars, Dr. W. F. Carver and "Carazo," the female crack shot of the world. Carver went through the routine that brought fame to Buffalo Bill, performing feats of shooting on horseback with rifle and shotgun; and Carazo, said to be a "belle whose lineage has been traced back to the Aztec race," split playing cards set up sideways, shot the pips from their faces, and proved almost as adept as Carver. Both wore buckskin outfits, and the lady displayed plenty of wampum in belts and decorations.

Custer's massacre was still remembered in 1889, and a big drawing card was participation in the wild west portion by eight gentlemen said to be the only survivors of Reno's command. Custer's detachment had been wiped out to a man, and everybody knew it. But Reno had taken cover and some of his soldiers lived to tell what happened. The oldsters rode in the stage coach, which came straight from Deadwood, and helped to drive the Conestoga emigrant wagon said to have seen 143 years service. The century old harness was too fragile far practical use, but it was an interesting relic.

So, too, was the "canoe that carried Washington." The crude pirogue was said to have been employed by the expedition when Col. Dinwiddie, the colonial governor of Virginia, dispatched Major Washington to the northern outposts to see what encroachments the French were making in the Ohio Valley.

We remembered Adam Forepaugh as a plethoric individual with mutton chop whiskers who posed beside the ticket box at the main entrance; and his son as a slight, athletic young man with close cropped hair, a stubby black mustache and, in his low open collar and shirt front, diamonds that rivaled a locomotive headlight for brilliancy.

The most successful benefits given year after year were those of Company K, Wisconsin National Guard, produced under the direction of Mr. and Mrs. M. G. Dillenbach. As certain as Maytime merged into June, the Dillenbachs were on the scene rehearsing for the big two nights. Success was assured, for the whole company turned ticket sellers and their own families would fill the hall for one performance. There were no passes for anyone and a clean sellout was certain from the first announcement.

Dillenbach himself was a short stocky man who brought his own play with him and on occasion appeared in one of the principal roles. His wife contented herself by whipping into shape the feminine members of the cast. *Our Starry Banner,* or *The Spies of Gettysburg,* was good for two nights, and at the end of his visits *Remember the Maine* was done in the spring following the boys' return from Cuba after the battle of Manila Bay. All of the plays were deliberately framed to introduce all of Company K not in the actual performance but in a big battle scene, uniforms, guns and all. That modern uniforms mingled with those of the Civil War was an anachronism never considered for a moment; and if space permitted, they also went through their manual of arms.

But with few exceptions, benefits were played according to the rules of the game. They gave their audience what they knew it expected. St. Mark's Guild went in for musical programs, drawing upon its big mixed surpliced choir. The guild stuck strictly to this after one misadventure with *A Gilded Fool.* Nat Goodwin had just finished with the comedy on Broadway and it was the only New York success ever presented in Beaver Dam while it was hot from the griddle. It was too much even for an audience sacrificing itself in a good cause; and when it was bruited that the play probably was pirated, the straightlaced church goers who rated stage shows with playing cards and whiskey officially declared it a visitation of Providence upon such goings on.

Production followed the pattern of *The Brownies in Fairyland*. Each player chipped in fifteen cents or two bits for a printed copy of the play and carried it about with him, studying at odd times. First rehearsals were at some home and opposites often paired for private sessions on their own account. These sometimes resulted in marriage.

The ten dollars hall rental included its use for a half dozen last meetings when they went through the show from start to finish, following stage directions and grouping the curtain tableaux according to a ground plan at the end of each act. No one directed nor even tried to do so. Had anyone evidenced such temerity he would have been thrown out of the hall. By the last day everyone knew the play by heart, so there was no need for a prompter. If one person went up in his lines, another picked them up and the performance meandered along more or less intelligently to a final triumphant curtain.

I noted the professionals learned their parts from half-sized letter sheets with only their own lines and business and the last few words of the preceding speech to cue them. I mentioned this to Uncle Bee and he said it was a damned good thing that amateurs didn't try to show off like that.

"Most of the time these professionals don't know what the whole play is about," he explained. "They only know the scenes in which they appear, and half the time the villain is in doubt as to why he should try to kill the hero. That's why they get off the track so often and start off with *Lady Audley's Secret* and end up in *East Lynne*."

He may have been right at that. I've witnessed performances today when I thought the very same thing.

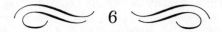

6

One day when Grandmother was recounting the adventure of her fine ducks, Uncle Bee announced that he thought I was old enough to know about his pet hen. And he proceeded to enlighten me.

When he was a small boy, Uncle Bee was the proud possessor of a hen, the first one he had ever owned. Petty, as he named her, showed nothing

Annie Oakley and one of the famed passes that gave her name to all

Buffalo Bill

Buffalo Bill, otherwise W. F. Cody, is remembered for the wild west show that bore his name from 1882 until shortly before his death in 1917. But his first histrionic efforts—for Cody was ever an actor on or off—came long before when he trooped small time theaters in a horrible western melodrama written for him by E. Z. C. Judson, better known as Ned Buntline.

Judson discovered Cody when he was an unknown western scout, christened him Buffalo Bill, and sold him on a stage career with no effort at all. Offhand Judson knocked out *Scouts of the Prairie,* and J. B. Omohundro, otherwise "Texas Jack" was induced to participate, with Buntline casting himself as the heavy. Action consisted largely in awaiting the coming of Indian bands and shooting them down until the stage was piled high with dead redskins. Then the corpses were recusitated in time to die again at the next curtain. "Wild Bill" Hickok came on for a while, but quit after a time because the extras who enacted the Indian roles failed to appreciate his humorous antic of shooting them in the legs with blank cartridges.

After a few seasons of traveling across the country, Cody formed his own wild west show whose featured members were Annie Oakley, affectionately known as

From the collection of Judge D. C. Van Buren, Wauseon, Ohio

"Little Sure Shot," and Frank Baker, expert with the rifle, who shared equal billing with her. Professional jealousy between them seems to have been missing since they married and enjoyed a long and happy life together.

In theatrical parlance an Annie Oakley is a pass to a theatrical performance. It derived its name from the duplicate holes punched in the slip accompanying the seat reservations; since one of Annie's favorite demonstrations of skill was to shoot out the pips of a playing card, the name was adopted.

Frank Baker

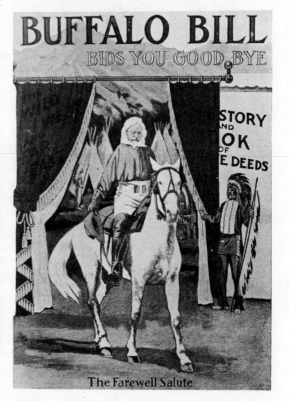

The Farewell Salute

out of the ordinary until she froze her feet, necessitating the amputation of one of them. Grandfather did this very deftly with his jackknife.

Uncle Bee whittled a nice little wooden leg for the hen and renamed her Peggy. Equipped with her new limb, Peggy quickly adopted a superior attitude toward the less gifted members of the flock. All went well until nightfall. Peggy scrooched up on the hen roost with the rest of her companions but her new impedimenta proved inadequate to the demands. She lost her balance and fell down like a trapeze performer, clutching desperately with her lone claw until tired nature gave way and she fell squawking to the floor.

Taking council with himself, Uncle Bee solved the dilemma with a trick roost. He took a lath, whittled down one end for a perch and bored a hole in the flat side. Peggy had only to hop up, grasp the perch, stick the wooden leg in the hole and she was all set for the night. This worked like a charm until one rainy night when the wet wood swelled and Peggy was stuck for good.

Uncle Bee was explaining how he got around this difficulty by breaking the handle off an old tablespoon and using it as a substitute when Grandmother bore down on him. She declared acidly that he ought to be ashamed

Hiawatha

Burlesque was getting a good start, and though it never touched the smaller towns, it held high revelry in the larger cities. At Wallack's Theater, New York, *Hiawatha, or Ardent Spirits and Laughing Water* was given.

Pocahontas, or The Gentle Savage preceded it and John Brougham's burlesque set the ball rolling late in 1855.

The next year, Charles Walton, a member of the Wallack Company, produced this burlesque on Longfellow's opus. Minnehaha, Gitchi-Manito and Wabun were reinforced by mythical characters Poohpoormanni, Nukkleundah, Hinakite, Dammidortur, Minnie's father, and Showandasee, an inquisitive visitor from the South.

These old burlesques were strong on punning and the custom continued when Charles Hoyt wrote his topical productions years later: *A Contented Woman, A Texas Steer, A Temperance Town, A Trip to Chinatown,* and the like.

This burlesque accomplished one thing at least. It discouraged the reading of Longfellow's poem in public, a practice that was becoming a general nuisance. But this never penetrated to small time and the nuisance continued well along into the nineties.

of himself filling Harlowe's head with such nonsense and if he kept on the child would grow up to be a worse liar than Ananias. Uncle Bee retorted that this was no worse than her duck story and besides this was true. Grandmother came back with the fact that he didn't even have the wooden leg or broken spoon handle to prove his claim while she had the red flannel patches from the duck's underclothing. More than that, she announced, he was wearing one of those patches right now and if he doubted it she'd take down his pants and prove it.

That closed the books for Uncle Bee. There was a deal of the matriarch in Grandmother's makeup. Not for nothing had she been a pioneer woman.

Chapter 13

HOW BEAVER DAM TOOK TO CULTURE

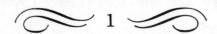

1

CULTURE'S advent in Beaver Dam accompanied the chest-nut bell and the high school's sun stereopticon. It's a far tocsin from the chestnut bell to the sun stereopticon yet these mark the town's renaissance. For they also marked the birth of the Travel Class.

Beaver Dam was peopled for the greater part by down east Yankees and they went after the better things of life, tooth and nail, under pioneer conditions that would have discouraged individualists less sturdy. Until the first library opened in a room in City Hall, each family owned its own. Shakespeare, Thackeray, Scott, Wilkie Collins, Charles Reade, Marietta Holley, Will Carleton, the Irish novelist, and Will Carleton, the Detroit ballad maker; Lover and Lever, the two Sams: all were to be found along with Mark Twain in his entirety. Mark printed his own books and sold them by subscription.

One or two families could afford *Harpers, Century* and *The Atlantic Monthly. Frank Leslies* and *Harpers Weeklies, The Youth's Companion, St. Nicholas* and *Harpers Young People* made up the magazine list with one of Chicago's daily papers. Frank Munsey had yet to start his flood of ten cent magazines and *The Black Cat* had not yet entered the five cent market.

Back from the South after the Civil War, James Redpath decided that talk was not cheap and started to cash in. By 1868 he had convinced the Boston brain trust that it was better to be paid for their dissertations than to waste their breath upon each other. In the west, James B. Pond started the same road with a wife of Brigham Young.

Emerson, Greeley, Henry Ward Beecher, Charles Sumner, Mary A. Livermore, Mark Twain, Josh Billings, Petroleum V. Nasby, Wendell Phillips, Bayard Taylor, Julian Hawthorne, one by one became the forerunners of the chautauqua that would blossom under brown summer tents with everything from William Jennings Bryan to Edgar Bergen and Charlie McCarthy.

Most of these came to Concert Hall, spoke their piece and went on, not forgetting to take a generous check though they might prate of the brotherhood of man and the futility of laying up gold when you can't take it with you. There were diversions too. P. T. Barnum came to talk on temperance and again to display Mr. and Mrs. Tom Thumb, Lavinia Warren and Commodore Nutt.

There were stereopticon novelties and in the mid-eighties, the most pretentious panorama on the road. Prof. H. E. Moore of Brooklyn, New York, presented his "Panorama of Europe and America." The professor also did a little magic and offered his wife in a musical program but the panorama was the attraction. The panorama was a series of curtains on rollers, running across the back of the stage when manipulated by hand. Such scenes as "Niagara Falls" and "Lake Killarney by Moonlight" were quite elaborate with the best artificial lighting the period afforded.

But after a time, as the lecture bureaus became established, they tilted the fees at the demand of the lecturer, who commenced to see that he was as much of an attraction as some of the dramatic stars on the legitimate stage. Local groups sponsoring these visitors thought twice before signing on the dotted line. And the Travel Class resulted.

Professor Hubbell had cozened the school board into purchasing a sun stereopticon. On sunny days, it was demonstrated at the school, illumination being furnished by a mirror stuck out of the window and reflecting the sun's rays against the colored slide. But this could be adapted to oxy-hydrogen lighting. And with this, the Travel Class was formed to fill in open time at Music Hall.

The class was made up of one hundred subscribers who guaranteed two dollars each for a course of eighteen evenings. A bureau furnished the slides and a written lecture. These were parceled out among the more voluble members who acted as lecturers while Saney Lewis, the high school janitor, presided at the stereopticon.

2

Once the Travel Class was started, Culture was under way. But not until Charley Miller and the chestnut bell stepped in did it climb upon the driver's seat, assume a capital C and whip the good people into hauling the battered wagon of information across the hump of ignorance. Charley Miller ran Music Hall and handled the ticket sale.

Charles also ran The Book Store on the middle of Front Street and managed the hall as long as I can remember. When an attraction rated reservations, he rigged a ticket rack behind his front counter. This brought him business, and the younger set rated his shop second only to Wade's Livery Stable and Lorenzo Lambeck's Barber Shop.

Bill Wade's attractions were lithographs of Maud S., John L. Sullivan, the Boston Strong Boy, Gentleman Jim Corbett and Lillian Russell in tights. Lillian was the main attraction. Besides his regular service, Lambeck ran any number of small enterprises. On the second floor was a pool room and baths at a quarter a throw. The basement housed a shooting gallery. Newspapers and magazines, tobacco, pipes and cigarettes, sheet music and the first pay phonograph with an octopus of rubber tubing to pipe the waxed selections at a nickel a head, each contributed its modest bit to his income. As a surety, he had a number of one-armed bandits to coax the nickels from his schoolboy patrons.

But at the Book Store one rubbed elbows with visiting thespians and hobnobbed with the shop's feminine clientele for imperturbable, pompa-doured Charley was a genial host and welcomed the fair sex. When the loungers blocked traffic, Charley chased them out and they moved on to

This Is It!

This is the poster that attracted the boys to Wade's Livery Stable, where it adorned the office wall. It is the only one of Lillian Russell in tights. It was taken early in her stage career, and the print was a colored supplement to Richard K. Fox's *Police Gazette*, which specialized in reproductions of prize fighters, chorus girls and burlesque queens.

the livery stable to give Lillian's tights another inspection while the rest went on to Lambeck's to play the slot machines and listen to the phonograph. "The Bank Has Failed Today" was a favorite as were the "Trinity Church Chimes" and "The Ravings of John McCullough."

The ravings were as authentic as another wax record which was offered as the on-the-spot recital of a southern lynching with the outcries of the burning victim. McCullough, at the height of his career as a tragedian, went suddenly mad while rehearsing his company in Chicago and was sent to an asylum. The record was a mixture of Shakespearean bits, *The Gladiator, Richelieu* and *Douglas*. It began:

"They say that I am mad! What, mad—that terrible affliction?"

Then it continued to end in incoherent babblings. We accepted the explanation that a phonograph had been smuggled into the madhouse to make the record. It was years before we learned that while the name was the name of John McCullough the voice was the voice of Morris Gest, who cooked up this tricky ingenuity to turn a soft dollar and give himself the push up Broadway's slippery ladder that made him a son-in-law of David Belasco and, among other things, the producer of *The Miracle*.

The chestnut bell was a contraption for the coat lapel that Charley introduced the day he opened the Travel Class seat sale. If an ancient wheeze were told, the wearer pressed the bell and all joined in the happy chorus of "Chestnut." If the wearer offended, any listener might sound the alarm. Charley had his so rigged that if another person punched it, a sharp needle pierced his thumb. This created no end of unholy merriment especially when the dupe was a visiting comedian. For them, Charley had accumulated a flock of mildewed gags.

The first night of the Travel Class found the school stereopticon set up with a tank of gas, a box of highly colored slides and a jittery Saney Lewis, who wasn't quite certain whether the experiment would succeed before the whole thing exploded. In keeping with the procedure, and to give it sufficient dignity, the opening lecture had been divided between Attorney James J. Dick, the school superintendent, and Frank Hutchins, the town librarian. "Washington, the Paris of America, Our National Capital" showed the White House, the Halls of Congress, the Department Buildings, Washington Monument, Mount Vernon and Arlington, while both speakers read the lecture which accompanied the showing.

The following week, Professor Hubbell told of "Picturesque Scotland." Since he had visited the British Isles on sabbatical leave, he threw away his script and talked off the cuff. With these two under its belt, the Travel Class settled down to fortnightly meetings throughout the winter. Proceeds went into the school fund to purchase more stereopticon slides.

But through it all, the oxy-hydrogen tank was a horrible threat to Saney Lewis. With practice he became adept in putting in the right slide right side up. Not more than two or three times an evening did he muff it, bringing a click-clock from the speaker's signal and the warning: "Change your slide, Mr. Lewis."

But the tank overshadowed not only Saney but the audience as well. There was an engulfing timidity that it might explode at any second. And the woodenbacked chair travelers breathed a sigh of relief and sped for

the exit the minute the last word was said and the hall lights were switched
on again.

Other groups besides the Travel Class went in for culture in a big way,
too. About the time that appendicitis became popular, Edward Bellamy published his Utopian novel, *Looking Backward.* His prophetic insight into the
future aroused the imagination of our information seekers and out of hand
a Bellamy Club was formed. It vied in popularity with the Emerson Club
and it was neck and neck as to which was the more popular. The Emerson-
ites had the edge, though, since their literary explorations included the
whole Concord group besides Ralph Waldo and even reached over to
dabble with England's Lake Poets besides Byron, Shelley, Keats and
Browning.

The Bellamy Club waned and the Emerson Club grew stale and the
Audubon Club was formed by a younger group under the impetus of *St.
Nicholas.* It was a pseudo-scientific and nature study group encouraged by
the high school teachers and including the older pupils and some outsiders.
Will Snyder, local taxidermist, carried the load and furnished most of the
information. Will had been a member of an exploring expedition into
Alaska and brought back a collection of relics and utensils. When interest
slackened, he dressed up in an Eskimo outfit and suffered the evening in
the cause of science.

These intellectual pursuits prospered mightily until a soap advertiser
started to whoop it up for the Larkin people. His name was Elbert Hubbard
and he originated the Larkin Clubs to further his sales. The town's good
women turned from literature and social reform to huddle together and
purchase the Larkin supplies and pool their coupons hoping to knock off
a gift worth while.

Elbert Hubbard brought culture back again when he quit the advertising field of soap and turned to that of literature. When he copied William
Morris with the Roycrofters and East Aurora, New York, these same persons accepted The Philistine and The Fra as the epitome of erudition. Even
his broad brimmed hat and long hair convinced them of his mentality,
though Uncle Bee said he was a dead ringer for Beason, the Quaker Doctor.

I was dramatic critic of the now defunct *Milwaukee Free Press* when
Hubbard essayed a brief vaudeville tour. His service on the two-a-day was
brief since he talked and talked, proving poor opposition to the opening
risley act or the performing dogs that closed the bill. In describing him, I
wrote that he was a cross between Dr. Munyon and Quaker Oats. An office
ruling banned the mention of advertising names in pure reading matter and

the conscientious proofreader changed it to "a cross between a patent medicine and a breakfast food." I eagerly awaited Elbert's response to the libel, but apparently he didn't believe in reading his own reviews, a habit professed by many actors but followed by few.

The Chautauqua Institute on that lake in New York state started its extension courses and these became the next culture craze. Mothers and daughters met twice weekly to go over the lessons and commit the questionnaires to memory. And with this came a revival of the lyceum courses. A dozen booking agencies had sprung up throughout the country following the example of Redpath and Pond with lesser attractions than the big guns of the east. Some of them were good, some were bad, and some must have paid for the privilege of working. At least this seemed the only reasonable explanation for their presentation.

But good, bad or indifferent, these bureaus filled a vacuum long endured and too rarely satisfied. There were local lecturers like Will Snyder. From Wisconsin University at Madison, Professor John C. Freeman came to the Library Auditorium to talk on Shakespeare, Ignatius Donnelly and The Drama. His quite evidently were classroom lectures, as soporific as they were informative.

Since these bureaus were regional they could deliver their attractions at fees within the ordinary small town budget and reasonably enough since they demanded little more than your right eye for a guarantee. The lyceums worked on the system followed later by the brown tented Chautauquas of summer time. A blanket contract covered the season with a gross guarantee. From ten to twenty substantial business men were jockeyed into signing on the dotted line and each was responsible for the total of any loss. When any of the tent shows failed to clear their considerable expenses, the loss was pro-rated among the signers.

The tent Chautauqua carried an overhead of no small amount. The lyceums needed only hall rental, ticket printing and the fixed fee. Professor Hubbell and Ed Brown, English professor at Wayland on the Hill, signed up for the Star Entertainment Course. And the Travel Class was forgotten. Theirs was no frenzied plunge into the entertainment whirlpool, for each was certain that high school and Wayland students would buy enough tickets to cover the guarantee. And with this backlog, the course paid out year after year.

There were five attractions in the Star Entertainment Course spotted to continue throughout the winter months. A season opened with a Grand Concert by the Patricelo Company: Filippe Governale, violinist, Lillian

Arno, soprano, and Jeanne Shomaker, Delsartian. Dr. F. W. Gunsaulus came next with an inspirational talk. Spedon, chalk talk artist, was third. Louis Favour added a touch of education with a demonstration of "Induced Electricity," and Maro the Magician rounded up the five.

Of the entertainers, Maro was the best. He had been a music teacher in Kansas City and Chicago and appeared as a concert soloist. He took up magic, became adept in shadowgraphy and lightning sketches and introduced all of these in his evening's entertainment. And he was the only magician to make a production of two rabbits, coatless and bare armed, from the midst of his audience.

Another season was opened by Dr. Russell Conwell, lawyer, minister and lecturer, whose "Acres of Diamonds" was delivered by him more than 6,000 times. With the income he founded Temple University. Greatest of the inspirational speakers of that time, he told and retold the story of his Egyptian trip where a native guide impressed upon him that you need go no farther than home to find diamonds in your own backyard. J. Arthur Dunning brought a literary touch with Dickens' impersonations, and once again Louis Favour balanced the season with his scientific talk. Col. L. F. Copeland lectured on "Seeing the Elephant" and Hoyt L. Connary furnished a lighter touch in "Around the Stove," a "Tales of a Wayside Inn" entertainment laid in a country crossroads store.

Reservations for the Star Entertainment course were made at the Book Store, and Charley Miller nearly upset the applecart the very first day. Looking in to check on the ticket sale, Professor Hubbell was induced to forget his dignity long enough to take a punch at the chestnut bell. The excoriation delivered by this mild mannered instructor when blood spurted from his thumb was something never to be forgotten. Charley Miller renounced his plaything forever and Culture continued its way serenely unhampered by practical jokers and ribald jeerings.

Chapter 14

THE NIGHT WAS FILLED WITH MUSIC - AND MYSTERY

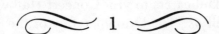

1

FOLLOWING the Civil War, a rash of lecturers broke out over the north and for ten years or more every angle of the late rebellion was discussed from the platform. Generals told how they won the war. Lesser officers told how they told the generals how to win it. And even lowly privates were willing to divide the honor between "me and Grant." The one exception was Robert G. Ingersoll, who agnostically recounted "Some Mistakes of Moses," ridiculing the Old Testament while fundamentally minded listeners awaited the thunderbolt that was to strike the infidel dead.

This phase diminished until the war was won again only at election time when the bloody shirt was brought out and waved on high to continue the

Republican office holders in the seats of the easy. And then they were followed by a swarm of drummer boys.

The northern ranks—and the southern, too, for that matter—had been reinforced with youngsters, some barely ten or twelve years old, who matched their drums against the muskets and Sharp's rifles of the regulars. Sooner or later they were picked up by the lyceum bureaus to become small town attractions in their own right. These men, now nearing middle age, had been in some of the more important engagements and so labeled themselves "The Drummer Boy of Shiloh," "The Drummer Boy of Gettysburg," "The Drummer Boy of Winchester," or whatever title took their fancy.

On the face of it there wasn't much entertainment in listening to hell being beaten out of a snare drum by a mustached, corpulent individual whose bulging midriff made the job more difficult. Though they brought along their original drum and told how they marched and beat until they dropped exhausted and were toted along on the back of a sympathetic soldier, this was old stuff. Every old soldier in Beaver Dam had carried a drummer boy to hear them tell it until, as Uncle Bee remarked, the Union Army must have been recruited equally of drummer boys and privates to have enough to go around. Even Gene Krupa couldn't hold down a solo spot for an hour or more, and as an evening's entertainment this sort of thing would become as nerve-wracking as those jungle drums that made *Emperor Jones* so highly artistic and so entirely irksome.

Canniest of these skinbeaters to visit Concert Hall was Major R. H. Hendershot, billing himself as "The Drummer Boy of the Rappahannock." The original drummer boy·with the 8th and 9th Michigan Infantry, he was eleven when he joined up in 1861, and must have been nearly fifty when he played Beaver Dam. He gave his sponsors more than they bargained for and they, in turn, gave him more than they realized.

Henderson booked himself out of Chicago and his success in lining up dates was based upon sure fire formula so evident that his sponsors entirely overlooked it. He let them give the show.

The major brought with him a noble array of drums and sticks. There was the drum presented to him by Horace Greeley in December, 1862, after the Battle of Fredericksburg. There were the Garfield and Arthur drumsticks, a political reward for his campaigning for them in 1880; the drumsticks contributed by the Honolulu G.A.R. in 1886; and the drum and badge given him by the G.A.R. and the Women's Relief Corps at the National Encampment in Indianapolis in September, 1893. Whatever they

R. H. HENDERSHOT.   J. C. HENDERSHOT.

ROBERT HENRY
HENDERSHOT,

Eleven years of age at the
time he went to the front
with the 9th Michigan
Infantry, October 25, 1861.

....MAJOR....

R. H. Hendershot,

The original Drummer Boy of
the Rappahannock, 8th and
9th Michigan Infantry—one of
the most wonderful drummers
in the world—and his son,
J. C. HENDERSHOT, one of
America's best fifers.

ADDRESS,

Postoffice Lock Box 966,

CHICAGO, ILL.   (OVER)

Major R. H. Hendershot

Major R. H. Hendershot, the original
"Drummer Boy of the Rappahannock,"
was one of many who turned to the
lecture platform following the Civil War
and carried on into his old age,
recounting his adventures, and playing
his drums. Major Hendershot was assisted
by his son, J. C. Hendershot, "one of
America's best fifers."

were, they all looked and sounded alike. For good measure, the major was
accompanied by his son, J. C. Henderson, "one of America's best fifers."
He was prepared to give a full evening's entertainment, the major explained,
but drumming was a strenuous exercise. He needed intermissions to rest. So
the sponsors were asked to contribute "a few pieces of local talent"—not
too many—just a few "eight or nine pieces perhaps so we can rest."

The bait was too tempting to be ignored and every amateur who sang,
danced or recited—or even thought he could—was behind him. Each was
ready and willing to help out and if necessary to fill out the entire evening.
So with a Lancashire clog by Paddy Dolan; a guitar solo by Mrs. McNulty;
Foster melodies by the male quartette; patriotic recitations such as "All
Quiet Along the Potomac Tonight," and "Driving Home the Cows," Hen-

THE HUTCHINSON FAMILY

The Singing Hutchinsons

Of the family groups who toured the country, the Singing Hutchinsons from Milford, New New Hampshire, were best known and lasted the longest. They started in 1841 and some of the original quartette were giving concerts in the mid-eighties.

"The Old Granite State," the "family song" featured on each program, carried the original quartette on its title page. They were Judson, Abby, John and Asa. There were eleven boys and two girls in the family, all of them musicians and singers. Brother Jesse wrote the words to the song, appropriating an old revival hymn, "The Old Church Yard," for the music. Its innumerable verses recounted the family and its doings, commencing with:

> We have come from the mountains,
> We have come from the mountains,
> We have come from the mountains
> Of the Old Granite State.
> We're a band of brothers,
> We're a band of brothers,
> We're a band of brothers
> And we live among the hills.

With time and increased families, the singers divided into The Tribe of John and The Tribe of Asa. They had founded the town of Hutchinson, Minn.; and Asa's tribe traveled from there, while John and his brood returned east. This family picture shows Asa and Lizzie with their children: Dennett; Abby the Second, named for her Aunt Abby; Asa; Lizzie, and Fred.

Even then, the second generation was coming into its own. Dennett was to carry on as "The Tribe of Asa, Young Folks"; and in the east The Tribe of John was to be represented by the Dearborn Male Quartette. Today the family tradition is represented by Mary Hutchinson of Doylestown, Pa., a direct descendant, who has recreated their songs and story on the lecture platform.

The original Hutchinsons were riding high during the Civil War days. They sang for Lincoln whenever they visited Washington and were among the first to introduce "We Are Coming, Father Abraham, 300,000 More," one of the few songs for which Stephen Foster wrote only the lyrics. James Sloan Gibbons composed the tune. And they were the first to realize the possibility of dramatizing *Uncle Tom's Cabin*, a suggestion rejected by Harriet Beecher Stowe, no doubt to her ultimate regret, since she never received one penny of royalty from the play.

derson and Son were lucky to edge in for two appearances. The grand windup saw all assembled on stage to sing "Tenting Tonight on the Old Camp Ground." It is a pleasure to record that neither drum nor fife accompanied this finale.

Patriotic and wholesome were the comings of the Hutchinson Singers to Concert Hall. The Singing Hutchinsons of New Hampshire were a family of thirteen brothers and sisters not only possessed of voices of concert calibre but proficient on musical instruments besides. After them came a second generation, and a third, and today they are represented by Mary Hutchinson, directly descended from and closely allied to the numerous offspring of the group. Mary keeps the name alive with concerts and dramatic recitals recalling the family traditions.

The Hutchinsons became nationally famous during the Civil War. They travelled the country from east to west and not only introduced most of the popular songs of the day but composed many of their own. Rabid abolitionists and stern temperance advocates, they gave voice to their sentiments in their own compositions. The Ranier Family, a Swiss quartette, had broken the ice for four part concerts, but the Singing Hutchinsons soon took over the field. There was a folksy flavor to their programs and they sensed what the people wanted and gave it to them. Today they might have been in Grand Old Opry, singing folk songs and making a fortune with their recordings.

When the family divided, Brother Asa settled in Minnesota, where they had founded the town of Hutchinson. It was the Tribe of Asa who came most often to Concert Hall. The Singing Hutchinsons had been there during the war days but when Asa became practically a neighbor, he came with what was affectionately called his "Tribe." There were Asa himself and his wife, Lizzie, and his three children, Abby II, Fred and Dennett.

The McGibeny Family

Family life was strong stuff in the good old days, which was one reason why the McGibeny Family went on and on. They hailed from Oregon, and this early photograph was taken of the thirteen to prove there were no ringers masquerading under the family name. Drums, violins, cornet and piano were their instruments, with the members bursting into solos, trios, quartets, octets and complete ensembles. Some of the family dropped away. Others married and their children were enlisted as replacements. They remained a standard attraction until the country theater passed its peak. On their last tour "The Anvil Chorus" was featured, and much levity was created when one grandchild, in Little Lord Fauntleroy costume, picked up the anvil and dashed off stage with it. But people were easily amused in those days.

Dick Kohorn Collection

They sang the same songs and were received as family friends whenever they appeared.

Another of these singing groups was the McGibeney Family. Thirteen was their family number, too, with the parents, a married son with his wife, four boys, three girls and the baby. The infant in arms had grown into the Little Lord Fauntleroy stage when I saw them and the family increased by marriages. Some of them had dropped away but there were still around thirteen with musical instruments and vocal numbers. Little Fauntleroy aroused much merriment when at the conclusion of the anvil chorus from *Il Trovatore*, he deftly picked up the anvil from its block and forthwith ran offstage with it.

The Musical Nosses gave a musical program with a saxophone quintette, a mandolin quartette, and a variety of entertainment. They moved on to big time vaudeville and musical comedy and in later years, I attended a theatrical wedding in a Milwaukee hotel. Visiting troupers were married after the last performance and in that small hour wedding, the Five Musical Nosses played the wedding march on their saxophones. It was impressive as any organ recital. This, of course, was before the day when wild blattings and frenzied squeaks of the instruments are looked upon as something superfine in musical transgressions.

2

They stopped in front of the post office one summer's evening, a slight sinewy dark haired man and an older companion who might have passed for Guy de Maupassant. They carried a good sized carpetbag and a roll of carpeting. Under the inspection of the loungers waiting the last afternoon mail, they spread the carpeting in the center of Front Street and the younger man stripped away shirt and trousers to reveal pink fleshings. From the bag his older companion removed a kerosene lamp, which he lit, and a couple of metal rings and a long tin tube.

The acrobat gave an exhibition such as he might have given on the Left Bank. Of the old school, he turned handsprings and flip-flops, forced his body through the rings, and then inched his way through with the lighted lamp on his forehead. Finally from the tin tube he blew a peacock's feather, caught it on his nose and danced about balancing it. De Maupassant took up a collection, the impromptu stage was cleared, carpet rolled, and the pair went on, thanking the crowd for the few coins received.

They showed up again the following winter but prosperity had touched them in the meantime. Their clothes were new. There was a hint of well-being and every indication that they had fed and lived well. They said that they were Charley and Pete Goshen and they wanted to hire Concert Hall for "an exhibition." When they produced $30 for a week's rental, Grandfather decided he had nothing to lose if theirs was a proper show. They assured him it certainly was. Pete, the acrobat, was a mind reader and they proposed to present demonstrations of the peculiar ability with which he was endowed.

Mind reading was the newest mystery to astound and entertain. Stuart

Cumberland had started it and Washington Irving Bishop gave it the dramatic color to make it popular. It was a form of trick telepathy known as muscle reading. The medium would grasp the wrist of a volunteer directing him to concentrate not upon the wording of his message but the direction he wished him to take. Since the message was framed to discover some hidden object or some similar act, this was not difficult. If something were hidden in an adjoining room, the volunteer must think of the direction of the door, the direction of the next room, and so on in order until the discovery was made.

The medium for his part was blindfolded. By attempting to lead the way he kept the volunteer in a state of perplexity. Attempting to think of the direction, he would unconsciously pull in the direction he wanted to go. This involuntary action gave the medium his clue and he had only to follow on.

The Goshens' exhibition was in two parts. Charley made the opening introduction and Pete put on his acrobatic performance ending with "the funny feather dance" as he had in the street show. While Pete changed to street clothes, Charley lectured the audience on what they were to see and how they were expected to assist in the mind reading exhibition.

"The medium will be entirely guided by your thoughts for his is an exhibition of thought transmission proving that mental telepathy is a reality," Charley concluded. "So that he cannot hear, his ears will be stuffed with cotton. So that he cannot see, a black bag will be placed over his head and tied around his throat. So that he cannot taste, a cigar will be given him to smoke. He must be allowed to breathe, else he would suffocate, and he must have the use of his hands that you may transmit your commands by contact. Now will a committee of volunteers come upon the stage and we will prepare the medium."

The routine employed by these muscle readers followed the same pattern. Pete Goshen's was that of Bishop, though not so elaborate. A coin was taken from one man's pocket and concealed somewhere in the hall. Hats and coats were exchanged and identified. For a spectacular finish, a murder was re-enacted. A Dr. Cronyn had been murdered in Chicago and the papers were filled with the story of how his body had been dismembered and dropped through a manhole into a sewer. This served as a background sufficiently lurid to arouse the spectators to a new pitch. A volunteer was furnished with an oversized butcher knife with which he indicated a cross on the back of some unwilling victim. And, of course, Pete followed the course and re-enacted the pseudo-crime.

Titus March.

Titus March

When the Ringling Brothers graduated from a wagon to a train show, they produced their first opening spectacle. Staged by Alf (Alfred) T. Ringling, it was the first of the many elaborate openings that were to follow it season after season.

This was "Caesar's Triumphal Entry into Rome," with the band afoot at the head and dancing girls and armor-clad performers on horseback, in howdahs and two by two, with the display wagons alternating, the high diver who impersonated Caesar seated atop the highest of them.

The spectacle was retained for several seasons and the music for it always was the "Titus March."

The most spectacular exhibitions were the free ones given for advertising purposes. A pin was hidden somewhere within the city limits. Blindfolded and accompanied by a committee, Pete drove Wade's hack about town until he finally located the building and reclaimed the hidden object. Though he never attained the prominence of Cumberland or Bishop, Pete Goshen's blindfold drive was as skillfully executed as was theirs.

The death of Washington Irving Bishop was as macabre as any tale dreamed by Edgar Allan Poe. On March 12, 1889, he gave an exhibition at the Lambs' Club in New York City and soon after went into a state of profound coma. Pronounced dead by the attending physician, his body was taken to an undertaking parlor and a post mortem performed by the bewildered medicos who knew nothing of mind reading and were eager to discover what made Bishop tick. Naturally, they found nothing, not even anything to account for his demise.

In his billfold was found a note warning that he was subject to fits of catalepsy and asking that he be allowed to rest quietly. It developed that Bishop had once lain in a fit of catalepsy for twelve hours and had been pronounced dead by physicians. After this experience he always carried this letter of warning.

His mother believed that he had been killed by the autopsy and brought charges against the physician and his assistant. They were indicted for a misdemeanor but were never brought to trial. That the coroner's jury decided they had acted in good faith may have been a factor in dropping the action.

Chapter 15

"TICKETS A DOLLAR A COUPLE - SUPPER AT ODD FELLOW'S HALL"

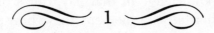

1

WHEN Great-grandmother Mary Whittaker died they buried her in a little windswept cemetery on Clason Prairie. She had come to Wisconsin when the swelling vales were green with spring and the gentle hills and dotting lakes extended a verdant welcome. Worn out before her time by the rigors of pioneer life and the labors of child bearing, she died with the fall and her rude pine coffin was borne down the winding trail from her log cabin, through brushing hazel furze and mellow golden rod, to the little hill where slept a few other lonesome newcomers.

My Great-grandmother's single claim to beauty was her hair. A faded daguerreotype shows her in the strained posture of that embryonic photography, her hair coiled high above a broad brow and intelligent saddened eyes.

Some years later, Grandfather Babcock moved to the scattered log cabins and farm buildings that were Beaver Dam, a distance of some half dozen miles away. He had ridden saddlebags across half of Dodge County, and now he established his home in what was to become a thriving community. When the Old Cemetery was plotted, he bought a family lot and it was decided to bring my Great-grandmother's remains to rest among her own.

Little remained when they opened her grave—a rotted coffin, a few poor bones and her hair. It had reached to her waist and now it coiled about her disarticulated skeleton, a mass of glorious, dusty Titian bronze.

I never knew why the family reinterred the bones but kept the hair. Perhaps it was the desire of my Grandmother in her last hungry grasp for a final contact with her mother. They were a lonely people, those pioneers, and family ties girded the tighter because of it.

Great-grandmother's hair filled a pasteboard shoebox on the top shelf of Grandfather's desk—an austerely plain glass fronted case redolent of formaldehyde and carbolic acid. Surreptitiously, when no one was about, I would clamber up on the desk leaf to open the box and enjoy the shiver of self-induced fear through contact with the dead.

I was a small boy when Aunt Sue died. My great-aunt and my grandmother's sister, she had joined the household during the last year of her losing fight with consumption. Grandfather ministered to her with the best of the crude medical knowledge of that day, but a tubercular victim then was marked for death from the moment the white plague laid finger on him. Primitive treatment and inadequate home accommodations handicapped the wisest doctors.

The day of Aunt Sue's funeral my grandmother took the hair from the shoebox and placed it in the coffin, to be finally buried for the last time.

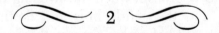

2

My first recollection of Concert Hall conjures the sickish odor of formaldehyde and carbolic acid and the dusty suffocation of my Great-grandmother's auburn hair. That was because in the top of Grandfather's desk, the hall key was kept alongside the skeleton of a Colt's pepperbox—record of Chicago's great fire—and a dainty pearlhandled twenty-two calibre pistol.

Of a cold winter's morning, before the breakfast table was laid, I would take the key and start off for Concert Hall. For the night before there had been a masquerade and a dozen masks might be salvaged before the place was cleaned. Uncle Bee called it the key to the Bastille, and a clumsy iron key it was, a good seven inches in length, fit to serve the village in welcoming a visiting dignitary. The huge iron lock it fitted might have been fashioned in Dick Thomas' smithy. But both key and lock were in keeping with Concert Hall.

It was two blocks to Front Street and a like distance to the hall. But for a little fellow, there was plenty of adventure. There was the confectionary store and bakery of Jake Martin whose daughter Melita, an attractive miss of my own years, was to be worshipped at a distance. Little did I realize when she served me my first ice cream soda years later—it was a new fangled frivolity many eyed with suspicion—that she would grow up to become the mother of Fred MacMurray. For motion pictures and Hollywood were then not even a dream.

There were two particularly nasty bullies who prowled about at all hours without rhyme or reason, and there was Old Man Loomis.

Old Man Loomis was a village character. Beaver Dam had many of them, sturdy New Englanders who had brought west the dress and manners of another time and place. There was J. J. Williams, the banker, who built the Williams Free Library, always decked out in a shiny tall hat, Inverness and shoulder shawl; Billy Drown, obstinately clinging to strapped trousers with "barndoor" buttoning on the side; Ed Hall, amateur actor who looked like Sol Smith Russell, and George Higbee, who might have passed for Joseph Jefferson.

Outstanding men of the village they were. Many of them, like Squire Hosmer, doubled in brass. The squire made harness in the rear of his courtroom when not dispensing justice in the front office. Pioneer demands forced a man to use his hands as well as his head to supply the necessities. And most of them did so.

Old Man Loomis was a humorist of down east mould. He nursed an acquisitive thirst and for seventy years had chased merrily along Time's highway in a futile endeavor to overtake it. Now in the mellowness of years that seemed as countless as his potations, he was the first to bid the early saloon keeper a thirsty greeting when the slatted doors swung open for the day. A friendly soul he always stopped me, and like the Ancient Mariner held me with his glittering eye since I, in truth, was somewhat embarrassed by his attentions.

"Listen, sonny," he would beam. "I'm eighty years old—yes, sir, four-score and some and living on borrowed time. And some day the old town's going to wake up and hear that I'm dead. And do you know what they're going to say then? Do you know, son, eh?"

All this he would emphasize with jabbing forefinger while I gasped silently like a fish out of water, seeking words that would not come. "They're going to say: 'Poor Old Loomis! Poor Old Man Loomis! Too bad! Too bad! Past eighty years—and now he's dead! And whiskey killed him!'"

Brightened by the thought he would chuckle his way through the swinging doors while I hurried on to retrieve the papier maché faces and wrinkled dominoes thrown away at the mystic hour of midnight upon the imperative command: "All unmask!"

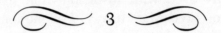

It was a time when elaborate costume balls filled the society pages of the New York newspapers. It gave the Ward McAllister Four Hundred a chance to do their stuff and impress upon America's great unwashed how a bumbling capitalist could throw away his Wall Street money once he set his heart upon it.

Mrs. William Vanderbilt gave a costume ball where Mary Stewart and Queen Elizabeth in an anachronistic revelry rubbed shoulders with "The Electric Light" and Louis XVI. The Bradley Martins broke all records of profligacy and quite outclassed the others in ostentation without taste.

Since New York newspapers never reached Beaver Dam, reports of these high life jinks drifted through on *Harpers* or *Leslies Weekly*. But as only a few subscribed to these magazines, balls were unknown in the community. We called them dances.

Dances were of two classes: impromptu and planned. Matt Peacock and Will Stacey might meet in the post office. It was summertime and but for croquet and an occasional round of whist, things were dull. Both were ardent in their pursuit of simple social pleasures.

"How about a dance?" Matt would ask.

"Count me in," Will would answer. "Next Friday?"

"Consider it settled," Matt would agree; and so it was settled.

These impromptu dances were exclusive affairs confined largely to the residents of Yankee Hill, with its bankers, lawyers, retired moneyed men and their families. The two would consult their select list and when enough couples were run down, Music Hall would be spoken for and a telegram dispatched to Hall's Orchestra at Oshkosh. Hall always played for the Yankee Hill crowd. He brought along a bass viol and a violinist while he alternated between harp and violin. Hall's harp waltzes were famous throughout the state with a rubato that delayed just the right note to make reversing inevitable. It made for uniformity on the dance floor and he spent much of the evening with "I've a Longing in My Heart for You, Louise," "While the Leaves Came Drifting Down" and "Sweet Bunch of Daisies." Twosteps and redowas, a couple of quadrilles, and at least one Virginia Reel and an Old Dan Tucker rounded out the time until one o'clock. Then the party wandered back homeward, most of those who owned them resplendent in white tie and tails.

The Commencement Dance headed the formals. It was called just that— the Commencement Dance—for everyone knew that it was the commencement of the Beaver Dam High School. Being a Baptist institution, Wayland on the Hill put its foot down on such frivolity as some pagan demonstration unworthy the halls of higher learning. The Commencement Dance found a more heterogenous gathering filling the hall to overflowing. Again it was Hall's Orchestra and Hall's harp waltzes, and the select formalities laid aside their inhibitions and shook the mothballs from their evening clothes to join in the dancing on the green. After all, many of them were alumni.

These summer affairs were but time markers for the big winter events. These were the masquerades—two of them—and as they were benefit affairs they brought out the biggest crowds of the year.

One was given by the Revera Club, a group of the town's young bloods whose rooms shared Concert Hall's second floor with the Beaver Dam *Citizen* and Grandfather's office. The other was sponsored by John Harder's Military Band, one of the best town bands of its time due, probably, to John himself and five others of Harder kinship, each one an able performer. The Revera Club's money kept the group going while Harder's profit went to music and new uniforms. Both masquerades had the same catchline:

"Tickets a dollar a couple—Supper at Odd Fellow's Hall."

Your dollar entitled you to take your girl to the dance but the "Supper at Odd Fellows Hall" was extra. That cost you another fifty cents. It might be served by the Order of the Eastern Star, or the Blue Ribbon League, or the Universalist Society, or a church guild, but the place always was the same. Odd Fellows Hall was a few doors up Front Street and was as much an accessory to a masquerade as Concert Hall itself.

With primitive lighting, winter night clamped down at sunset. Coal was costly, fires were banked, and by nine o'clock, most of the good folk were warm in their feather beds. From seven o'clock on, masked figures were scurrying along through the snow, meeting at homes to be on hand when the grand march opened the dance at eight o'clock. By eleven, the dancers were ready to traipse up the street and take their turn at the supper table. Baked beans, potato salad, rolls, pie and cake, preserves, oyster pie, chicken pie, coffee, tea and milk, were among the dishes served family style. After which, dancing was resumed.

There was no dillydallying at a masquerade. People were there to dance and to crowd all they could into the night, so the grand march at eight o'clock came off on the dot. All of the couples ranged around the hall headed by two masked figures whom everyone recognized as Ray Weaver and Jennie Rowell. They were the only pair in town with a grand march routine. Women in one line, men in the other, the figures continued to "Titus March" and you waltzed your partners to their seats.

Waltzes, two-steps and quadrilles were interrupted from time to time with special stunts by prize seeking groups. Cash prizes were awarded for the best costumes, male and female; comic, unique and group. It was almost a certainty that the group award would go to The Three Gypsies. With a sense of the dramatic, they rigged up a kettle and tripod in the center of the hall, burned an oilsoaked sponge beneath it on a tin pan, and lolled on the floor while they sang "Juanita" in close harmony. It never failed to click.

Judging for awards started with the grand march and continued until eleven. Then the announcements were made, winners called to the stage, given their cash in a small envelope and unmasked by the announcer. At midnight, came the order: "All unmask." Supper during an hour's intermission and another two hours' dancing saw the affair breaking up at two o'clock.

When he heard of the Hobby Horse Quadrille at the Vanderbilt ball, Uncle Bee snorted in disgust. Our quadrilles were divided into three sets with a pause between, and change of time; and the caller made himself understood with clear clipped commands instead of the singsong auctioneering chant of today's square dances. The Hobby Horse Quadrille had its participants wearing horses' bodies as they pranced about. This, Uncle Bee remarked, was old stuff. Circus clowns had used it for comedy stunts for many years.

Besides these two sponsors, another promoter was Fred Hippenhauer, who ran a novelty store with everything from books to ice cream to comic valentines and masks. Since he handled masks, he was sure of a neat profit on each dance he promoted.

Few dominoes were worn by the dancers. Most of them settled for papier maché disguises—Arabs, tramps, darkies, Dutch and Irish characters, Indian, Chinese and even monkeys. One of the delights was a group of monkeys, decked out in their red flannel underwear. Many were satisfied to buy a ten cent mask and let it go at that. But the particular, especially the groups, out to win a prize, more than made up for these slackers.

The masquerade had one figure found in no other dance. As they overflowed with good spirits, physical and alcoholic, the "grand right and left" ended the last quadrille. The couples formed a gigantic circle about the hall and were supposed to weave in and out with an interchanging of hands. Properly performed, it was no small effect.

But with the last quadrille, the orchestra went into "Chippy, Get Your Hair Cut." This was the set-off signal and the whole circle, joining hands, jumped up and down, yelling at the top of their voices. The reverberating roar could be heard to the city limits.

As Grandfather often remarked, it was a crucial test to the stability of much maligned Concert Hall.

Chapter 16

"FIFTY CENTS A BOTTLE – FOR MAN OR BEAST"

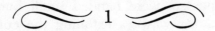

1

SINCE he was the city physician and doctored most of the old timers, Grandfather Babcock maintained an ethical standard as to what medicine shows could use Concert Hall. It was a variable yardstick whose computations were his own secret. For many proprietary medicines were sold and approved by the town's three drugstores.

Dr. Pierce's Favorite Prescription, Electric Bitters, Father John's Remedy, Six-Sixty-Six, Wine of Cardui, Dr. King's New Discovery, Dr. Shoop's Restorative, S.S.S., otherwise Swift's Sure Specific; Fletcher's Castoria— "Babies Cry For It"; Dr. Munyon's "I Am For Men," and Lydia Pinkham's Vegetable Compound, arrayed in yellow and brown and green wrappers pockmarked with type faces best suited to instill confidence in the particular cure-all—all these had a rapid sale and enthusiastic endorsement. The biggest sale was in the most palatable. All proprietary medicines were plentifully spiked with alcohol and the temperance toper who imbibed then picked those that tasted best.

Dr. Munyon and Lydia Pinkham did extensive advertising in the rural newspapers and the patent insides furnished them by the Western Newspaper Union. The doctor's upraised hand with forefinger pointing heavenward was as familiar to country readers as was Lydia's smiling face and gray hair. Small town editors stocked a supply of their cuts, and in an emergency were not above using them to illustrate a news story. Joe made a collection of these from exchanges in the office of *The Citizen* and among others found Lydia's beatific countenance masquerading as Queen Victoria, Sarah Bernhardt and Frances Folsom, recent bride of President Cleveland. Oddly enough nobody seemed to notice the contretemps or if they did they never troubled to complain.

The drugstores were not the only place where these nostrums were advertised. These patent medicines had their harbingers with spring. Pure food regulations were nil and there was no restraint on those solicitors who left their samples on your doorstep. When snow melted and the wooden sidewalks became passable, these emissaries of health and happiness stepped off the train at the Milwaukee depot and conveyed an express load of paper cartons to the Clark House.

A few willing youngsters were handed small burlap bags filled with medicine samples and throwaways extolling the curative virtues of the panacea. These sheets had a rubber stamped imprint of the drugstore where the nostrum could be had. The town was thoroughly and expeditiously canvassed. Samples and advertising were thrown on the front porch to confront the delighted householder when he opened the door. One after another they came from early spring until well along in summer when the medicine pitchmen took over.

Nobody seemed to realize that children might find and consume the stuff with unhappy results. Egyptian Tea was one of the more earnest of these giveaway campaigns. The supply was generous, and when Mrs. Lawrence opened her door to find a half dozen packages awaiting her, she looked upon it as the Israelites looked upon manna. Forsaking her cherry bounce, she gathered in the herb, and true to her British heritage, brewed it as a substitute for breakfast tea.

Egyptian Tea was—and still may be, for all I know—a physic of no small proportions. This fact the family realized shortly after their imbibitions and Grandfather was hastily called across the street to rescue the perishing. Uncle Bee started to say something about a constipation of ideas but Grandmother shut him up in a hurry.

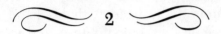 2

With this situation, Grandfather handed down his decisions when medicine pitchmen tried to rent the hall. Not too often was he called upon as most of these pill purveyors either were too pretentious or too insignificant to rate a theater showing.

Many of these made their pitch from Bill Wade's hack on a corner of Front Street. Wade's hack, the only one in Beaver Dam, was an impressive vehicle and the town's show piece. It conveyed the mayor in Fourth of July parades. It transported the governor from the Milwaukee depot to Dodge County Fair Grounds at fair time or when the Old Settlers held their annual get together. In bad weather it headed Hi Henry's minstrel parade with Hi himself resplendant in his top hat and it was hired by patent medicine pitchmen to impress the townsfolk with their impeccability.

One of these street hawkers was Diamond Kit, a painless dentist who sold a liniment to curb anything from rheumatism to sore throat. A middle-aged, blonde-mustached, undersized man with a marked foreign accent, he dressed in a squarecut outlandish costume with a pillbox cap. His coat buttons were set with rhinestones. A huge zircon spotted his necktie, and a circlet of shining stones ornamented his cap.

Kit's dentistry was part of the ballyhoo that set off his sales. When Elmer Staab had unhitched the team and the hack was on call, Kit carefully arranged a display of shining dentist's instruments. Though he never touched anything but a pair of extraction forceps during his operations, these bright steel gewgaws caused a crowd to gather in sadistic anticipation of tortures to come. Oral care was primitive and it was a certainty that in every crowd there was at least one poor soul with an aching or decayed tooth ready to volunteer for a free extraction and save the fifty cents charged by the town dentist.

Kerosene lights had been attached to either side of the hack and when the crowd was gathered, Kit lighted them and began his lecture. His Painkiller, he said, was the most marvellous concoction of the sort.

As a painless dentist, he owed his success entirely to this miraculous remedy. He was willing to demonstrate it, free, for nothing, with no liability on the part of the patient. There was no liability on Kit's part, either, though he glossed this phase over. A patient found, he continued his chatter while he swabbed the man's mouth with cotton soaked in Painkiller. After inspecting the troublesome molar from time to time, he waved his forceps on high, grasped his victim around the head with his hand across the windpipe, eliminating any chance of a strangled outcry, and yanked out the tooth.

The aftermath was the acme of salesmanship. The victim's mouth was stuffed with more cotton to staunch the blood flow and when he had been thoroughly gagged, Diamond Kit asked the sixty-five dollar question.

"Did I hurt you?" he queried solicitously. And while the red-faced sufferer sought vainly to express himself, Kit dropped the bloody tooth over the hack's side with the gladsome tidings: "He says it didn't hurt a bit. And, now, gentlemen, as I was saying, this Painkiller—"

And so on until he turned the tip and made his sales. Then Elmer came up Front Street with the team, hitched it to the hack, drove back to the livery stable with the kerosene flares in the back of the vehicle, and Kit, instrument case in hand and the night's booty in a small black satchel, returned to the Clark House, counting another day well done and another night's repose honestly earned.

Most pretentious of the medicine pitchmen was the Quaker Doctor. At the Clark House he was registered as Beason and it was said that he came from Litchfield, Illinois. He carried a colored quartette with him and set a platform on Front Street in front of the hotel. These pitchmen had a magic formula in addition to a magical preparation. Somehow or other, they seemed never to be questioned by the city fathers or the police, embodied in Constable Ed Powderly, when they expropriated the main thoroughfare for their sales place.

The platform was a big one with canvas backing and sides forming a shut-in stage. Kerosene flares lighted it. There was a table to display the nostrums, and the mixed colored quartette ranged at the back in chairs with a guitar and a five-stringed banjo. The chairs came from the undertaking establishment of McKinstry and Son in exchange for a couple of bottles of his medicine. Uncle Bee surmised that the undertaking outfit probably used it for embalming fluid.

Beaver Dam had no colored families, and since the quartette were outfitted in the latest fashion—the men with bulldog yellow shoes, three inch white collars and wide brimmed fedoras, the women with leg-o'-mutton sleeves, wasp waists, high buttoned shoes and peek-a-boo hats—the four were as much an attraction as the Quaker Doctor himself.

There were several of these pseudo-Quaker practitioners and all of them were said to come from Illinois. Something about their subdued drab clothing instilled confidence in their listeners and their "thee," "thou" and "Brother" were paramount when they started their pitch. Even if this affectation was dropped once the sales talk got under way and the lecture became quite as commonplace as any other ballyhoo, the audience listened entranced and remained to buy at the blowoff.

The Quaker Doctor usually came about Fair time when the crops were harvested and the honest husbandman had time to take stock of his ills and decide which of his pains, real or imagined, was housemaid's knee and which was incipient appendicitis. Most of them were merely imaginary ones awakened by the vivid description of the lecturer. But by the time the victim decided to be less hypochondriacal, the show was far away.

Tent medicine shows pitched their outfits down by the Upper Woolen Mill where private cars sidetracked when an itinerant company could afford a private car.

The Kickapoo Indian shows always played there. Most pretentious of all the medicine outfits, they even distributed handbills throughout the town. They were regulation four and one-half by twelve and one-half throwaways with woodcut illustrations. Announcing a "Free Indian Exhibition," they displayed "Kickapoo Indian Ballplayers" holding modified lacrosse bats; "Kickapoo Indians in a Buffalo Dance"; and "Kickapoo Indians Hunting Buffalo for Tallow to Make Kickapoo Indian Salve."

And there was a portrait of beautiful Little Bright Eye, a genuine prairie flower and daughter of a Kickapoo chief. I've often speculated as to whether she might be the Little Bright Eye summoned by so many a spiritualistic medium to bring messages from the other world. If she is the same, Little Bright Eye is far more busy than when the Kickapoo promoters extolled her virtues. For though they had their whole Indian band in full regalia and warpaint, the beautiful princess appeared only on their advertising throwaways.

Main tent and wigwams furnished the setting for the show that featured a war dance by the Indian contingency around a blazing bonfire. To handle the outfit the management carried a half dozen roustabouts who were much in evidence during the day but mysteriously absent by night. Contrariwise, the Kickapoo band vanished with daylight but at showtime they blossomed anew resplendent as the night blooming cereus. Yet this mild deception was forgotten when the free show started and the good White Doctor told again of how the white sick prospector was saved from death by a Kickapoo Indian medicine man and how, in grateful return, he filched those closely guarded secrets and brought them back to civilization that the white man might hawk the stuff throughout the land to his own profit.

Cassidy the Medicine Man played there, too. His was a big platform show with a full complement of entertainers and a consultation tent where he might confound such victims as saw fit to call during the day.

 3

He said that he was Hamlin himself, and Grandfather never questioned but that he was the Hamlin of Hamlin's Wizard Oil Company. He was the one patent medicine seller allowed to return to Concert Hall to hawk his lotions and ointments season after season.

I suspect the man was welcome because he was an entertainer first and a salesman afterwards. I have read somewhere that the Hamlin who concocted Wizard Oil was a magician who decided that there was more money in scaring people half to death than in amusing them by snatching rabbits from hats.

And this Mr. Hamlin was a first rate magician, a lecturer quite above the average medicine man and withal a gentlemanly individual, well poised and cultured. So he may have spoken the truth. He may have been the Hamlin he professed to be.

Mr. Hamlin—Grandfather always called him that—was a slight, dapper person with a small mustache and an ingratiating manner of one accustomed to the footlights. He was accompanied by Mr. Mack, whose honest moonlike countenance and silver-rimmed spectacles seemed to label him a man of austere wisdom. But to the contrary, Mr. Mack—Uncle Bee said his name was undoubtedly McGillicuddy or McGrogan—was a Dutch, Irish and Negro comedian, and not a bad one either, with a robust baritone and the nerve of a burglar, as he proved while distributing Wizard Oil and all its other accessories.

When Tom Bowes delivered his drayload at Concert Hall, besides the cartons of curealls he left two wardrobe trunks, a portable organ and a package of Hamlin's Wizard Oil songbooks. The trunks carried Mr. Hamlin's magical apparatus and Mr. Mack's costumes and outfits for the modest sketches they presented.

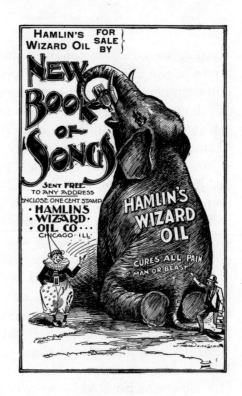

PAT MALONE.
Words by HARRY C. CLYDE. Melody by JAMES J. SWEENEY
Times were hard in Irishtown,
Ev'rything was going down,
  And Pat Malone was pushed for ready cash.
He for life insurance spent
All his money to a cent,
  So all of his affairs had gone to smash.
But his wife spoke up and said:
"Now, dear Pat, if you were dead,
  That twenty thousand dollars we could take."
And so Pat lay down and tried
To make out that he had died,
  Until he smelt the whiskey at the wake.

Then Pat Malone forgot that he was dead,
He raised himself and shouted from the bed,
  "If this wake goes on a minute
  The corpse he must be in it,
You'll have to get me drunk to keep me dead."

Then they gave the corpse a sup,
Afterwards they filled him up,
  And laid him out again upon the bed.
Then before the morning grey,
Ev'rybody felt so gay,
  They all forgot he only played off dead.
So they took him from the bunk,
Still alive, but awful drunk,
  And put him in the coffin with a prayer.
But the driver of the cart,
Said "Bedad, I'll never start
  Until I see that some one pays the fare!"

Then Pat Malone forgot that he was dead,
He sat up in the coffin while he said:
  "If you dare to doubt my credit,
  You'll be sorry that you said it—
Drive on or else the corpse will break you head!"

So the fun'ral started out,
On the cemetery route,
  And the neighbors tried the widow to console.
Till they stopped beside the base
Of Malon's last resting place,
  And gently lowered Patrick in the hole.
Then Malone began to see,
Just as plain as one, two, three,
  That he forgot to reckon on the end.
So as clods began to drop,
He broke off the coffin top,
  And to the earth he quickly did ascend.

Then Pat Malone forgot that he was dead,
And from the cemetery quickly fled.
  He came nearly going under,
  It's a lucky thing by thunder!
That Pat Malone forgot that he was dead.

Words and Music for sale by PETRIE MUSIC COMPANY,
4657 Champlain Ave., Chicago.

All medicine shows followed the same pattern—entertainment to attract a crowd; the medicine pitch to separate them from their money; and more entertainment delayed to keep the crowd until the end. Mr. Hamlin started his show deliberately with a bit of magic. His favorite was presented on a plank supported by two chairs on which he piled an imposing pyramid of tin cups produced from a borrowed hat.

Mr. Mack next seated himself at the organ, facing his audience with a deadpan stare, to render "Pat Malone Forgot That He Was Dead," "Swim Out, O'Grady," "Do, Do, My Huckleberry Do," or any other whose words were in the New Book of Songs of the Wizard Oil Company, sent free to any address for a one cent stamp. The booklet's cover showed a clown pointing at an elephant that zestfully drank a bottle of Wizard Oil while a painter inscribed its broad back with "Hamlin's Wizard Oil, Cures All Pain in Man or Beast." Words to a dozen popular songs were in the book, but most of it was devoted to testimonials and elaborate descriptions of man's ills calculated to scare the hell out of the reader.

Mr. Hamlin promoted the sale of Hamlin's Wizard Oil, Blood and Liver Pills, and Cough Balsam. The Oil was a guaranteed sure cure for more than fifty afflictions from whitlows, to catch the rural trade, to cholera morbus, white swelling diphtheria, deafness and headache. There was no direct claim to cancer cure though the song book devoted a page to a testimonial—unsolicited, it said—from D. Clark of Portland, Oregon, who cured his wife of breast cancer with only five bottles of this miraculous liquid.

When the sales had been thoroughly worked, Mr. Hamlin and Mr. Mack presented a sketch for two people, such as "A Load of Wood," in which Mr. Mack, as a thick headed countryman, tried to sell his wares to Mr. Hamlin while keeping a weather eye on an imaginary offstage mule, shouting "Whoa, January" and snapping a long lashed whip.

Twice a week they had pay night with a ten cents admission to a special performance and a free song book for everyone attending. On these nights, Mr. Hamlin outdid himself. Donning full dress, he delivered one of Robert J. Burdette's lectures with some magic for good measure. Mr. Mack lengthened his song program, and a novelty ending followed the medicine pitch.

Quite often this was comedy magic, in contrast to the opening legerdermain, with Mr. Hamlin as the suave magician and Mr. Mack as the dumb volunteer from the audience. At Mr. Hamlin's command, a cigar box filled with beans was found empty. Mr. Mack then took the box and scattered beans all over the stage, disclosing that it had covers on both sides and a partition in the middle. Or Mr. Mack vanished from a flour barrel into which he crowded himself. Returning to take a bow, he reversed it to show that the back had been removed to facilitate his exit.

The Hamlin show became a standard with Concert Hall though there were a few minor visitors now and then. One of these hawked an electric belt. It was an imposing contraption with metal disks clamped to a red flannel belt with connecting wires to unify the current. It worked, too, when a volunteer was brought to the stage, stripped of his shirt and girded with the band.

There was always a brisk sale after such a demonstration, and the electric belt was no exception. There was a distinct burning, irritating sensation with its application that proved electricity was at work. That is, the effect continued until the capsicum was absorbed from the cotton flannel. For the band had been thoroughly impregnated with this burning unguent and it did its work until the hawker was well beyond the reach of those he had hoodwinked.

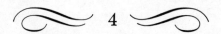 4

Shortly before his death, Uncle Bee wrote me a gossipy report on Beaver Dam.

"One item of interest," he wrote, "is that Mr. Harter, the man in the Gall House, accompanied by his son-in-law, Mr. Chambers, went over to Fall River some time within the week. They had a horse and light wagon. While there, they secured some thirteen sacks of flour, some tea, coffee, spice, mittens and other goods, wares and merchandise.

"You must further know that Mr. Chambers had a postal card in his pocket that had his address, street and number, that he lost out on the floor of the store and mill where the merchant carried on his business. They arrived safely in Beaver Dam and as they had rented no other place for the stuff they took it right to the house.

"The sheriff of Columbia County in returning the lost postal to Mr. Chambers called at his home at the Gall House and he took Mr. Harter and Mr. Chambers to the Columbia County jail and returned the goods to the Fall River merchant. If they had patronized and dealt with their home merchant they would have avoided notoriety. Here is another case where trouble occurred by getting goods away from home.

"Mr. Patrick Powers, a one-legged Irishman in Columbus, is not going to vote the Democratic ticket any longer. He is also going to refrain from the use of all strong intoxicating and ardent liquors. Mr. Powers bought a bottle of good old rye whiskey, drank it all and laid out all night. When his brother found him, everything about the body was frozen except the peg leg and that was stiff.

"I have just been catching sight now and then of this new television stuff. I used to wonder what had happened to those medicine men who played Beaver Dam and sometimes Concert Hall. Now I knew. They have decked themselves out in barber's coats and are passing themselves off as physicians and dentists endorsing toothpaste, cigarettes, hair tonic and everything else they got paid for. Or if it isn't they, I'm sure it's their descendants. Probably all of those old codgers are in the home for the aged or tucked away in some cemetery, unmarked, forgotten and unsung."

Chapter 17
EMERSON (PINK) HAWLEY, "THE DUKE OF PITTSBURGH"

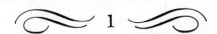

1

ABOUT the time that Music Hall was built, Grandfather saw the writing on the wall. Compared to Concert Hall, the new theater was the latest word, with new scenery and a half-dozen dressing rooms. The seating capacity was not that of our old place, but was fresh with paint and new chairs and a small balcony suspended from rods in the back.

More than that, Concert Hall was becoming outdated. More pretentious shows were on the road, and as Grandfather stuck to his kerosene lamps and scanty scenery, they had been skipping the town, and odds and ends had been slowly replacing them. So when Mattoon and Shean approached him with a proposition, Grandfather wisely decided to forget culture for physical diversions.

Mattoon and Shean came from Waupun, the state prison town some thirty miles away, where they had been operating a roller skating rink. They brought along a packing case filled with Henley skates and took over one of the dressing rooms, lining it with cubby holes and sawing a trap in the door. They sorted out the skates according to size, filed them in the wall boxes and were ready for business.

But one thing remained. A new floor was in order, so one was laid over the old. It was one of the best dance floors in the state and remained so until the old hall finally folded. But Music Hall still feared competition. Looking for something to carp about, they picked upon the new floor. A new floor, two floors, double weight—the building couldn't stand it! The building certainly would collapse! So the story started in an attempt to put a curse on Concert Hall. In time it became a legend more honored in the breach than the repetition.

Mattoon and Shean lasted out the year, then moved on to other promotions, leaving Grandfather with a fullfledged skating rink on his hands. Uncle Bee took over and each winter the public skated on Saturday afternoon and night. He hired the Polish Band from that fast increasing community of immigrants, and while little could be said for its music, one thing was certain. It played good and loud and could be heard above the roll and clatter of the skaters.

Admission was a quarter, and skates could be rented for another two bits, so it was a reasonable entertainment and town patronage was good for a weekly turn around. As the habit caught on—and this was the height of the country's roller skating craze—the rink was opened on Wednesday night. After that, skating continued intermittently throughout the week with Wednesday and Saturday the regular days.

Uncle Bee rounded up three or four helpers who spent half a day cleaning the skates and oiling the wooden wheels. Joe and I helped at keeping the floor immaculate to anticipate possible spills. It was dressed daily by cutting thin slices from a brick of paraffin, a similar procedure to that followed on dance floors. The two of us would don skates and work out until the shavings were ground into the hardwood, giving it a glassy finish. It was quite a trick to keep your skating stance on a newly waxed floor and our labors brought us a dexterity that made us the envy of our youthful associates.

When summer came, the hall was in demand by tight rope walkers. Like most of the middle west, Wisconsin was overrun with small fly-by-night circuses, and when these surrendered to little patronage and bad weather, the abandoned acrobats would start working their way back home. Since they were down on their luck, Grandfather let them have the hall without charge and often brought them home for a square meal.

Concert Hall was only one end of the exhibition, for the rope was stretched across Front Street and tied off on the Old Corner Drug Store. Grandfather arranged for that, too, probably feeling a hereditary right because he had once owned it. The rope was tied off in the hall on one of the iron pillars and ran through the third story open window across the street. Stability was assured by guy ropes fastened to the hitching posts.

The hall was ideal for these exhibitions. It stood at the end of Front Street, not far from the Williams Free Library and the intersection of Spring Street. This was the point where on summer nights Harder's Military Band hauled its stand for the weekly concerts. A prime spot for any street exhibition, it was visible in each direction as far as one could see.

Besides his rigging, the aerialist brought his wife—at least he said she was and nobody thought to doubt it. Like her associate, she donned tights and leotard and patrolled the street while he strolled up above, passing the hat and rounding up volunteers to guard the guy ropes from small boys who liked to "make waves." A shapely leg and ready smile, plus a gift at easy repartee, helped her to increase the take.

When he made his sensational crossing of Niagara Falls long before, the Great Blondin set the pace for all these rope walkers to follow. Standing on the window ledge with his balancing pole, he would cross and return, make the journey blindfolded, walk it with a cheese box about his ankles, lie down, arise and run at full tilt back to the hall.

To insure a final rain of pennies from heaven, he would stand on the ledge, shouting that if the contributions warranted, he would carry a person back and forth on his back. No matter how little the fair collector realized, it was sufficient to warrant his making the trip while the betighted lady clung to his shoulders.

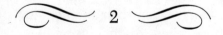 2

This was a time when organized baseball was in its swaddling clothes. Tennis was still a sissy game along with croquet and archery. Football was a practice of organized mayhem with the flying wedge moving eleven men in V formation to trample over the opposing team. Golf was some obscure practice which seemed to center about losing a small hard rubber ball and then spending the remainder of the day hunting for it.

But baseball was fast becoming the national pastime. There were the National League and the Western League, and great things were in the offing. But out in the middlewest these names were as indistinct as Midlothian or Ethiopia.

Baseball as we knew it was the domestic brand, originated on our own doorstep and nurtured by public subscription. Every town worth its salt had its own team and an umpire who went along to see to fair play when they met a rival nine. The two umpires alternated behind the bat and on the bases, and as each favored his own, the result was fairly even-steven in the long run.

Beaver Dam was the center of a hotbed of baseball. Over in Juneau, the county seat, some ten miles away, Pete Husting and Roxy Walters and Addie Joss were making names for themselves. Husting went on to pitch for Connie Mack in Milwaukee, Roxy was to become a big time outfielder and catcher, and Addie Joss was to gain lasting fame with Cleveland for his no-hit, no-run, no-man-reach-first, perfect game.

But they were to come later. Beaver Dam's baseball hero was Emerson (Pink) Hawley, "The Duke of Pittsburgh," who had his face on a cigar box cover and shared equal prominence with Robert Mantell in the cigars on sale at Lambeck's Barber Shop.

The Hawley family had a number of baseball players, but Emerson and Elmer were the stars. Had Elmer lived, baseball would have been given the battery unique of its history for Emerson and Elmer were identical twins. As babies their mother tied ribbons on their arms to identify them—pink for Emerson, blue for Elmer. And as Pink and Blue they became so thoroughly identified that their real names were forgotten. Not until his death—in his teens from pneumonia—did I know he was Elmer Hawley. Then my mother identified him by that name in explaining his death notice.

The Hawley twins started baseball from the cradle. They took to it as naturally as a duck to water. Wherever then went, a baseball went with them. They played at catch when their mother sent them erranding. They took part in every school game. As they grew older, they played with the town team.

There was a league of Dodge County towns, loosely hung together but sufficiently stable to assure a weekly game: Beaver Dam, Fox Lake, Columbus, Horicon, Cambria and Watertown. "Butch" Beaumont played with Waupun. Claude Elliott, who went to big time, pitched for Cambria. Hust-

Pink Hawley

No southern jaunts or pre-season training camps were the lot of the baseball player when Emerson (Pink) Hawley, The Duke of Pittsburgh, (*right*) was one of the National League's best pitchers. Handsome as they made them, he was a national as well as a hometown hero, and had his face and name on a cigar box to prove it. Off seasons he hung out at Charley Miller's Book Store, another attraction that brought the corseted belles of Beaver Dam to that rural emporium of culture, stationery and gossip. When training time rolled around, he enlisted the services of "Peanut Bill" (*left*). This local character quit his market fishing to serve as trainer and catcher. Concert Hall was used until the weather softened sufficiently for them to move on to the Dodge County Fair Grounds, a half mile up Front Street.

ing, Walters and Joss were the nucleus for Juneau's nine. And Beaver Dam had the Hawley twins.

As to form and ability, they were neck and neck. Playing as they did, with that understanding of identical twins, they alternated at pitching and catching. On the mound or behind the plate they never missed. After Blue's death, Pink Hawley concentrated on pitching and as a mound artist, he joined the Pittsburgh team. It wasn't long before reports came of his success and with it the title of "The Duke of Pittsburgh." Pink was something of a dandy in his attire and liked to sport the latest in fashion. But this in no way detracted from his pitching ability. He was tops.

It wasn't long before he attained the fame of a cigar box cover, along with "that eminent tragedian, Robert B. Mantell." Stuck somewhere away among my boyhood possessions I have a pair of those boxes, brimming over with tobacco tags of another day. *The Corsican Brothers* shows two white shirted figures duelling with swords, with the flowing Mantell signature across the bottom. The other displays Pink's genial countenance with the signature "Emerson (Pink) Hawley" beneath.

Big league pre-season training was yet to be adopted by club owners. Baseball was still a roughneck game and if a player was moderate in his boozing, could handle himself in field fights, and played his position as well as the next man, he could get by. He was supposed to show up in the spring sufficiently thin and agile to go to work.

Pink Hawley was given to plumpness, to put it mildly, and to get down to weight he set up a rigid training system for himself. Grandfather told him to use the hall as he saw fit and he moved in with baseballs and gloves and a portable steam bath. Until snow flew, he worked out at the Dodge County Fair Grounds. But with winter, he spent much spare time in the hall.

As an associate and general factotum, Pink engaged "Peanut Bill." A town character, Bill was so called because each fall he sold peanuts during County Fair week. He scraped out a living fishing in the lake, by boat in summer, through the ice in winter. But he was always ready to come when Pink called him. Bill caught Pink in his workouts, watched him jog about the hall, and supervised his sweatouts.

The steam bath was a crude contraption, a large box that closed with a hole for the head to protrude, a chair inside it and a lamp to heat it up. When he had sweat sufficiently, Pink would be released and given a rub-down. But in this matter, Bill was not always amenable. He possessed an inordinate thirst and the rubbing lotion was at hand. While Pink raged and ranted, unable to release himself, Bill would sit on the edge of the stage and tipple away. That the stuff was strong enough to kill a horse never entered his head and oddly enough, he seemed to thrive on it. To be sure it made him cockeyed, and more than once Uncle Bee had to come to Pink's rescue to prevent his ending up a pool of water. But as Uncle Bee was a keen observer and anticipated Bill's shortcoming, he always arrived in the nick of time.

Since Uncle Bee acted as substitute masseur when Peanut Bill toppled over, even fetching fresh rubbing lotion from Grandfather's office, he decided that the situation needed prompt action. So he solved the difficulty by concocting a homemade Mickey Finn. It probably was not the identical prescription handed out by bartenders to obfuscate vociferous patrons, but it worked just as well.

After a few treatments, Bill quit his shenanigans and became a good boy. He decided that his stomach was going back on him and he'd have to taper off on anything more potent than straight whiskey with a beer chaser. So Pink Hawley kept him in his employ as long as he remained in the big league.

 3

Of the casuals who drifted in and out during these winters was a trio known only to us as "Bill and the Boys." Since these birds of passage came and went with little ceremony, no record was made of their names, and more often than not they never told them since business was transacted on a cash basis and there was no reason for formalities.

The three were refugees from some circus. Bill, a man of middle years without a tooth in his head, was a sword swallower. The oldest boy was in his twenties, a fine acrobat and aerialist. The youngest of the trio was a lad of perhaps fifteen who donned clown makeup and played a junior size five string banjo.

Uncle Bee just then was making an excursion into handling the Franklin steel cored, copper-covered lightning rod, and his outfit included a nest of twenty-foot extension ladders. One of these was suspended between two of the iron pillars, swinging crosswise of the hall. From some place a parlor organ was brought in and Bernie Sabin volunteered to play it. With Bill's stand of swords and the miniature banjo, these were all the props for their performance.

In a dress suit somewhat the worse for wear, Bill introduced his young protégé as "the youngest banjo player in the world." After he had knocked out as many selections as the crowd would stand for, the older boy appeared, magnificent in pink fleshings. Bill started the ladder swinging and on it his performer went through a routine, somewhat limited but including most of the positions used on a stationary ladder under the bigtop. All this while Bernie Sabin ground out "I Love My Love in Springtime" and "If You Love Me, Darling, Tell Me With Your Eyes," waltz numbers well fitted to the tempo of the swing. Bill concluded the show with his sword swallowing exhibition and the audience filed out, well satisfied that it had received value in full for the dime each invested.

Perhaps this great satisfaction came because of Bill's final feat. From our house, Uncle Bee had brought a Civil War musket and a bayonet. Bill concluded his part of the show by swallowing the bayonet with the musket attached and then, by some hocus-pocus, he apparently disgorged it without touching the gun, the bayonet landing point first in the stage and the musket remaining upright, quivering from the impact.

I wondered in later years if this was a childish hallucination, grown greater with passing time. But Karl Germaine, one of the country's truly great magicians who quit the platform all too early, assured me that it really occurred. For he knew Bill.

The man, he said, was none other than a sword swallower billed as Chevalier Cliquot. He knew this must be the same individual since he was the only man ever to perform this feat.

Wrestling and boxing matches were staged occasionally to the delight of the young bloods who fancied themselves real sports and sometimes even bet a whole dollar on the outcome. Best remembered was an exhibition between Jack McAuliffe, lightweight champion of the world, and Billy Madden, lightweight champion of the United States. While it proved nothing, it created plenty of excitement and furnished saloon gossip for months to come.

These boxing and wrestling matches were hippodrome frameups usually staged during Dodge County Fair week when the participants were appearing at the grounds as added attractions or paid events. There were Rooney the Gripman, and Farmer Burns, and the Terrible Turk, who strutted the streets in native fez and trousers. These wrestlers grunted and groaned and kept the native sports in a fine state of excitement the three days that the matches veered back and forth until Rooney was declared the final winner.

McAuliffe and Madden had been before my time but with these later exhibitions I was called upon to help prepare the ring. The performers brought their own canvas and ring equipment and it was my job to take our light one-horse wagon and fetch a load of sawdust from the village icehouse. Crude padding though it was, it proved no more so than some of the palpable fakery employed.

The worst of it all was that I had to clean up the mess and dispose of it after the exhibition was over. It must have been a labor of love, for I can't recall ever having been paid for my work.

Chapter 18

WHEN THE CIRCUS TOOK TO THE STEAM CARS

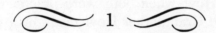

1

BESIDES managing Concert Hall, Grandfather and Uncle Bee handled the piece of ground where visiting circuses played for many years. The Babcock lot was a pasture of about six acres, properly fenced to restrain a horse and two cows, and some half mile from the center of town. It's accessibility and spread of even terrain made it an ideal spot for the first shows that pitched there until they outgrew their horse and wagon days and took to the railroad. Then they spread their canvas across town on the Dodge County Fair Grounds.

On this afternoon Grandfather was making out his bills. Twice a year he concluded that the family exchequer needed ready cash. Some of his patients paid on the nose, but much of his income was of the barter and trade school.

There was Pete Welsh, for instance. Belieing his name, Pete Welsh was
a redfaced Yorkshireman who owned a farm south of Beaver Dam where
he divided his time between raising crops and children. His increasing
family meant increased sickness, and he was one of Grandfather's regulars.
Each fall, come the harvest time, he would drive his loaded farm wagon
into our backyard.

"Well, Doc, I've come to pay my bill," was his greeting. "How much
do I owe?"

After much consultation, a fee would be hit upon and Pete would proffer
his payment: potatoes, half a hog, pumpkins, squash and a bushel or so of
apples. Appraised at current market valuation, a price was struck, delivery
was made, and the rest of the day was spent in storing the vegetables and
putting down the pork in the brine barrel.

But come midsummer when money was needed for current demands,
Grandfather would make out his bills. His bookkeeping was simplicity per-
sonified. A long brown-paper-covered, yellow-leafed book labeled "Bills"
was his only record, and his pencilled notations upon his return from a visit
oftentimes undecipherable, were weird to the extreme. It was Joe's task to
interpret them, make out the statements in untutored schoolboy scrawl, and
consign them to the mail.

Grandfather sat facing the window of his office in Concert Hall block.
His white hat was pulled low, his arms folded, as he gazed down at the
Old Corner Drugstore across the street. Once upon a time, he had owned
it with Grandfather Hoyt when both were practicing medicine. But the
drugstore burned, and Grandfather Hoyt made his pile as a forty-niner in
California, and business offered returns superior to the income of a country
doctor. So Grandfather Hoyt turned to cotton and woolen milling, and
Grandfather Babcock carried on the family tradition alone.

"Who's next on the list?" Grandfather asked.

"Old man down by the lower mill," Joe read with some hesitation.

"Let's see. That must be Old Man Haselmeyer. How much is it?"

"Three visits, three dollars. Dollar and a half for medicine. Total, four
dollars and a half."

"Scratch it off. He hasn't any money and he wouldn't pay it if he had.
Who's next?"

"Fat Polack woman up by the lake."

"Um—that's Mrs. Polczinski. She's the one those two young squirts
operated on for appendicitis. All she had was a bellyache. Only needed a
dose of blue mass. Sued the city they did and lost too. Served them right.
On the poor list. How much?"

WHEN THE CIRCUS TOOK TO THE STEAM CARS   263

"Five visits at a dollar a visit, five dollars. Medicine, two dollars. Total, seven dollars."

"That goes to the city. Send it to them." Grandfather was the city physician and as such treated the indigent and collected from the common treasury. "Or give it to me. I'll pick it up myself. Who's next?"

"Dutchman out by the gravel schoolhouse."

"Scratch it. He just came here this spring and he's hard up and in debt. Who's next?"

Joe's task was interrupted by a tall, well-built man with a flowing black mustache, derby hat and genial grin.

"Howdy, Doc," was his greeting. "Remember me?"

"Certainly I do," Grandfather replied. "You're one of the Ringling boys. Take a seat."

I remembered him from the year before—one of a family of brothers who started out with a musical show and now owned a one-ring circus with "Popcorn George" Hall trailing along as sideshow attraction. Popcorn George lived not far from us down state and his attractions consisted of an educated pig, a Circassian girl and a headless rooster. He was a regular at the Dodge County Fair each fall after he quit the circus and it was generally believed that he killed his porcine star when snow came, and trained another during the winter.

The Ringlings themselves were looked upon almost as a local institution. They came from Baraboo, Wisconsin, where Grandfather Hoyt had his buckwheat flour mill. Hoyt's Buckwheat Flour was a standby throughout the middlewest until the larger milling interests put it out of business.

"Well, I'm back again, Doc," the visitor continued with an ingratiating grin. "You know what I want, I suppose?"

"At least I can make a pretty good guess."

"We're playing here as usual and, as usual, we want your pasture lot again." Grandfather pulled his nose vigorously, indicating determination, and folded his arms again.

"Well—you can't have it."

"Can't have it?" his tone of injured innocence bespoke the latent actor in him. "Why, Doc. What do you mean—can't have it?"

"That's just what I mean and I'll tell you why. I let you have it last year—and the year before that. I took my live stock out and let you have it for ten dollars. You promised to clean up the mess and put back the dirt where you ploughed up your ring. Didn't you?"

"Yes, Doc, but—"

"Did you do it? You did not! You left the ring turned up. You left the

The Circus Kings of All Time

JOHN RINGLING   CHARLES RINGLING   ALF T. RINGLING   AL RINGLING   OTTO RINGLING

P. T. BARNUM   JAMES A. BAILEY

The Ringlings

When the five Ringling Brothers started their trouping, they ranged their heads in this fashion on all their advertising material until it became a trademark of the circus world. Later, they acquired the Barnum and Bailey Shows, and these were combined with the Ringling group. The addition was taken from the paper which Barnum and Bailey used during their active circus days.

All photos from the collection of Judge Donald C. Van Buren, Wauseon, Ohio

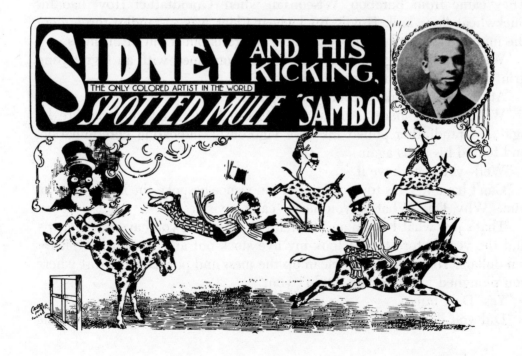

Sidney was a popular entertainer with Burr Robbins Shows

One of Barnum and Bailey Stars

whole pasture littered with papers and stuff. You left it full of holes and I had one hell of a time finding grass for my cows for the rest of the summer."

"Now, Doc, listen to me." The Ringling boy laid his derby on the table, presented Grandfather with a cigar and lit another for himself. "Now, Doc, listen. That was all a mistake. We ordered the ring turned back and the litter picked up and when we heard that it hadn't been, we fired the roustabouts we told to do the job. We'll take care of it this year. You'll have no occasion to complain—I give you my word you won't."

Grandfather eyed his cigar critically and took another puff.

"No, sir! No, sir! You told me that before."

"All right, Doc. Now listen. What did we pay you last year?"

"You paid me ten dollars—and you didn't put back the dirt or—"

"Very well. How about twelve-fifty this season? How about that?"

Grandfather shook his head stubbornly.

"And passes for your whole family."

Still no response.

"For both shows—afternoon and evening."

"Will you put back the ring dirt?"

"We certainly will."

"And clean up the trash?"

"Of course, of course, Doc. Why, I wouldn't think of anything else."

And so it was settled.

The night before circus day, Uncle Bee brought our horse and two cows down to the barn, boarded up the entrance to the cowshed and removed the big and little gates from the pasture's front fence. Experience taught him that in their pursuit of entertainment circus crowds are no respecters of property. The wagons rumbled in before daybreak the next morning, and in due time the entire family was occupying the best seats for the afternoon show.

The performance was probably about the same as those that came before and those that followed after. One show merges into another, and in the minds of Joe and myself one Ringling boy merges along with them. One thing is certain: all five were active in the show. Alf was the ringmaster with top hat and cracking whip. Charles led the band and the orchestra for the concert. Otto was in charge of the ticket wagon. And there was a wooden shoed clown in Dutch makeup who danced and tumbled on a slack rope close to the ground. We decided he was John. Alf T. was about, but we could not identify his particular duties.

There were the trapeze performers and acrobats, probably doubling; an elephant act, tight and slack rope walking, and Jules Tourneur, a whiteface clown of the old school, who was to remain with the boys throughout his circus career.

Tourneur was a singing clown. In the one-ring circus, the clown starred as a smart aleck, exchanging wise cracks with the ringmaster who retaliated by snapping his long lashed whip at him. Along about the middle of the performance, an overturned elephant tub was placed near the ring. Tourneur mounted it and sang a comic song to the accompaniment of the band.

These clown songs were quite apart from the regular comic numbers of the minstrel stage and the stage shows. We remembered some of them, but we never found a printed copy of them. One of Jules' numbers had the semi-serio-sadistic quality of many of those ditties.

> I went to Barnum's circus,
> I took my mother-in-law;
> She laughed at every silly thing,
> She almost broke her jaw.

> So when the big balloon went up,
> The Monarch of the Skies,
> I tied a guy rope to her
> And I gladly watched her rise.
> And she never came back—no, she never came back
> Though I waited an hour or more.
> And the last thing I said before she fled
> Was: "We'll meet on that beautiful shore."

The night performance ended and the Ringlings moved on. Bright and early the next morning Uncle Bee and I went expectantly to the pasture. As he had dourly anticipated, the ring had not been ploughed back and the lot was littered with odds and ends, trash and what not. Joe and I spent most of the day cleaning up the litter while Uncle Bee rehung the gates and replaced the dirt as best he could.

But with the next year, one of the Ringling boys came again and after the customary bickering, took over the pasture with the same promises and the same results. And when the Ringlings moved on to the Fair Grounds, the Gollmar boys succeeded them. Cousins of the Ringlings, the Gollmars followed in the family pattern, even to the billboard posters with the familiar five heads; and, I regret to say, in failing to pick up the litter and put back the dirt.

I'm inclined to believe that Grandfather would have let them have the pasture for nothing rather than let them go elsewhere; and I suspect that he was only holding out for those passes for the entire family, both afternoon and evening.

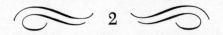

2

Ohio is known as a hotbed wherein was propagated many an early circus. Indiana, too, was long a stamping ground; and while Wisconsin produced the greatest of all, the Ringlings were only one of many groups that headed out from that state to hit the road with big top and menagerie.

P. A. Older of Janesville sold his sawmill for $5,000 in 1849 and invested in the Mabie Show. "Popcorn George" Hall left Horicon to join the Ringlings. W. C. Coup of Delavan, breeding live stock and farming, quit the plow for the steam calliope. "Doc" James L. Thayer was a Milwaukee tinsmith until he heard the call of the big top.

Somewhat out of the usual was Hiram Orton. Hiram sailed the great lakes, and laying off in Milwaukee one winter ran across "Doc Gilkinson" and Charley Tubbs. Doc was a clown and Tubbs a strong man and juggler of canon balls. Orton went to Portage where he launched a circus that continued for some time.

All of these would-be impresarios lived with a district bounded by a circle two hundred miles in diameter. Almost in the center was Beaver Dam, where our family pasture became the circus lot for these visitors. Ford Sterling, who was to become famous as Mack Sennett's chief of police of the Keystone Cops, was a frightened youngster who left his home upstate to be advertised as "The Boy Clown." It was there that I first saw Howard Thurston, working the sideshow bally for the Sells Bros. Circus. Harry Houdini came through one season from Appleton doing escape acts.

So Beaver Dam contributed its quota of circus people to these aggregations. Ollie Webb, long in charge of the Ringling cook tent, was one; and "Windy Jacobs," who could play any instrument from bass viol to harp, became a bandsman under Merle Evans. And the Miller boys, booking themselves as "Al and Otto, the funny clowns" took out a dog and pony show that came back, the poorer but wiser.

But what really places Beaver Dam in a top niche of circus history is the fact that from this little sleepy country town went the first circus to travel by train.

The story starts with George H. De Haven. Dan Costello had his own show. Dan was a clown who lived in Racine and Coup backed him in a boat show on the great lakes. Later they were to talk P. T. Barnum into lending them his name for the first great railroad circus of all time. At least, so they declared. But it was in truth the second, for a smaller railroad circus had preceded it.

De Haven joined these two as manager and they hit the Mississippi in 1861. The country was riven with war, but the show played on. There were frequent reports that Morgan and his guerrillas were after them but the dates were finished in safety and the crew got back into friendly territory the worse for the wear and tear of it all.

De Haven was a born manager. He knew what was what. Costello may have continued to improve the show, but De Haven gathered in the soft dollars. Not four months after he was on the show he owned it from backyard to ticket wagon. He toured through Texas when Texas really was tough, and came out of it with a whole hide and a bankroll to boot. Then he met Andrew Haight.

Of all the old timers in the circus field, practically forgotten today is Andrew Haight. He hailed from Dresden, New York, where he was born and bred. He spent his early years in the fashion of any other country lad, and by the simple means of least resistance, he found himself working for the local hotel keeper. Picking up a smattering of the business, he branched out for himself and headed westward.

Chance brought Haight to Beaver Dam. There was an opening for a hotel keeper and he took over the Clark House. The building was a spacious one and gained considerable reputation among the drummers of that period. It spread an excellent table, offered generous rooms and restful beds, and its bar was the equal of any in the middlewest. There was a poolroom and another quiet nook where the disputatious might place a small bet on the upturn of the faro deck or question an opponent as to his bluffing in tilting the pot.

The Chicago, Milwaukee & St. Paul railroad extended its line from Milwaukee to Portage, touching the outskirts of the village which numbered about a thousand inhabitants. Because of its accommodations, the Clark House became a mecca for traveling men dissatisfied with accommodations of country hotels and boarding houses. It attracted fly-by-night troupers who made it their headquarters for a week's stand in Concert Hall. Haight prospered and looked upon the world as his oyster. Well he might, too, since geniality overflowed there, and liquor and gaming were not under the ban of local and visiting sports who tried their luck.

Haight was about thirty-four years old when the circus fever struck him. He had listened to the stories of visiting salesmen. He had met the tank players who fired his imagination with adventures by field and flood. And George De Haven intruded himself into the scene.

De Haven was looking for a new partner. He sang a siren song and Haight listened entranced. He sold out the Clark House—lock, stock and barrel—and launched out as the backer of a circus. The two assembled their forces from the immediate vicinity. De Haven recruited his performers from those who had been with him. Haight devoted his attention to the commissary and those ends which naturally came under his experience. They reclaimed tent, seats and wagons, and opened their show on the old circus lot.

This was the first circus to be moved by train. Which of the two thought it up is moot. Between them, however, they decided that it would be simpler to travel by train than to pack across the country. As they figured it, they could time their jumps more accurately and with greater certainty,

The World's Greatest, Most Pleasing Wonders

The Seven Sutherland Sisters
CONCERT COMPANY.
H. BAILEY, Manager.
Hair 7 feet long, 4 inches Thick

Seven Sutherland Sisters

The Seven Sutherland Sisters were famous for their long hair and singing ability. They were featured in the sideshow of Barnum and Bailey's Greatest Show on Earth and much was made of their "hair 7 feet long and 4 inches thick."

Collection of Judge Don C. Van Buren, Wauseon, Ohio

there was less chance of breaking down with repairs and road upkeep, and it was something worthwhile for its advertising value.

So the newly formed organization made the first circus contract with a railroad, the Chicago, Milwaukee & St. Paul. It was to furnish them with engine and cars as needed. And one day in the summer of 1866 a special train hauled into the old depot on the edge of town and lay over until the night performance was ended.

Half of the adults and all of the small boys of the village were on hand when with flickering torches and much shouting the first loading was made. It was not so difficult then as it would be in years to come, for there was no menagerie, and the show itself in its infancy was little better than a dog and pony outfit.

So it drew out and away from Horicon, Hartford, Hustisford, Kenosha, Racine and the smaller stands. From the start, the experiment was a success. The train was as great an advertisement as the noonday parade.

Just how long the Haight-De Haven combination traveled by train is not on record. They played through Wisconsin, Indiana and Illinois, each doing his best to skin the other. De Haven was adept in annexing the soft dollar, but he figured without the Yankee shrewdness that marked the personality of his partner. Not for nothing had Haight dealt faro or looked the ambitious traveling man in the eye to call his bluff and rake in the pot. In four months he owned the show.

De Haven had played the south, but Haight was the first man to enter Texas after the end of the Civil War. Somewhere in this vicinity came changes. In 1867 he was owner of the *Coosa*, a steamboat headed up the Mississippi. He was out of the circus business after he lost a small fortune, only to recoup it as a hotel man and with the funds to return to two other ventures before he finally called it quits and sought his first love—an inviting hotel with a seductive faro layout and superfine whiskies.

When W. C. Coup took over the name of P. T. Barnum, he put his big show on wheels. But that was in 1873. Haight and De Haven had played our pasture lot and loaded their show at the old depot to start adventuring from Beaver Dam a good seven years before.

The Defender of Cameron Dam

The Defender of Cameron Dam, which I wrote in 1911, established the unenviable record of marking the start of the disintegration of popular priced melodrama and the small time rep shows. Of the two companies, one played Star and Havlin time, the other the small towns. They toured through Wisconsin, Minnesota and the Middle West as far as Ohio.

Up in northern Wisconsin, John Dietz had refused the lumber interests the right to float their logs across his property. The company refused to pay the fee demanded by Dietz and for years, the row dragged on. Dietz damed the river, and when the company secured an injunction, refused to accept it. The upshot of it all was a pitched battle, in which one posseman was killed, Dietz was wounded, and the family finally capitulated.

Upon this more or less true situation the play was based, as imaginative as were most of the "factual melodramas" of that time. For the big scene, a must for all these shows, Cameron Dam was blown to bits by a plotting agent—of whom, of course, the lumber company was ignorant so far as intent was concerned—and the soubrette, who had been knocked silly and left to perish, was rescued by the good Swedish sheriff in the nick of time.

Because of the interest in the Dietz case, the show established a record on the Star and Havlin circuit, breaking all house records in Milwaukee, St. Paul and Minneapolis. This illuminating criticism of the performance of the second company is typical of the country newspaper reports of that time.

"The play, *The Defender of Cameron Dam,* was given at the auditorium here Monday evening and attracted a large audience, many coming from the country. The play was interesting and the actors were all first class. It is said that there were more blank cartridges shot at this show than any other that ever visited our city."

BIJOU OPERA HOUSE

LITT and DINGWALL 999 Proprietors and Managers
JNO. R. PIERCE, Resident Manager

Week Beginning Sunday Mat., DEC. 11th

The Defender of Cameron Dam

A Comedy Drama in Four Acts
By Harlowe Randall Hoyt.

CAST OF CHARACTERS

(In the order of their first appearance.)

Teck-A-Mashee, known as Sore-Eye, a Chippewa Indian Lumberjack...Chief Eagle Horse
Gay-She-Gin-Nic, his pardner............................Chief Howling Wolf
Bom-y-Gay-Geezick, Teck-A-Mashee's squaw ....Starlight
Moo-Zoonts, Gay-She-Gin-Nic's squaw.............................Moonbeam
Yon Yonson, the sheriff who resigned....................Carl Boardman
Mrs. John Braun...Luella Montague
Katie Braun...Cecil Manners
Eric Shirley, the schoolmaster........................Cecil Kirke
Elsa Braun..Judith Raeburn
Karl Braun...Owen Girard
Joseph Mason, agent for the Standard Lumber Co......W. T. Hodges
John Braun, the Defender of Cameron Dam.....Charles T. Douglass
Burns Shirley, president of the Standard Lumber Co.....Emil Jerome
Jones. Shirley's butler...................................Harry Luening
William Parsons, sheriff of Clinton County..............Jack Raymond
A Deputy Sheriff ....Ralph Patton
Father O'Rourke, a Catholic priest ....Geo. Pratt

SYNOPSIS

ACT I.—The Braun Homestead on the Crabapple River. An October afternoon.
ACT II.—Library of Burns Shirley's Home. Ten days later.
ACT III.—At Cameron Dam. The next afternoon.
ACT IV.—The Defense of the Cabin. Three days later.
TIME—The Present. PLACE—Clinton County, Wis.

THE BIJOU THEATRE ORCHESTRA, UNDER THE LEADERSHIP OF WALTER CLAUDER, WILL RENDER THE FOLLOWING SELECTIONS

1. March—"The King of the Forest.................................A. Losch
2. Overture—"King of Diamonds"..............................C. Lavelle
3. Selection—"Popular Melodies"................................M. Shopiro
4. Waltzes—"The Serenade".....................................V. Herbert
5. Exit March--"Knock-Out Drops"..........................F. Klickmann

FOR THE MILWAUKEE AMUSEMENT CO. (Inc.)

Darrell H. Lyall..Manager
George Bates..Business Manager
Emil Jerome ....Stage Manager

Next Week -- THURSTON

The juvenile of this second company was a young actor named Walter Houston. In time he dropped the "o" from his name and became Walter Huston, one of our best known character actors of stage and screen.

The accompanying photograph has nothing to do with the play. All of the company wanted to get into the picture so they grouped themselves in this fashion, each to his own, as was the habit in those days.

AFTERMATH

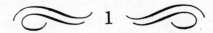

1

AMONG the last of small time entertainment to disappear before the inroads of the motion picture were the showboats of the Mississippi and adjoining rivers. On the day in 1817 when Noah Ludlow steered his unpretentious keelboat into Natchez-under-the-Hill, and ended a two-year pioneering trip, he broke the way for the famous showboats that were to follow. They lasted out the depression, when country theaters closed and movie houses took their place, and two of these boats still are doing a moderate business today.

They were large and small, these showboats, some seating as many as 3,400 people, some accommodating from 150 to 200 chairs. The average capacity was somewhere between these two figures. The *Floating Circus*

275

hit the high figure just before the Civil War until the Confederates expropriated her for a hospital. The *Golden Rod*, seating about 1,000, and the *Majestic*, seating 425, are doing business today on a reduced scale.

Showboats offered not only melodrama, but circus performances and minstrel shows, vaudeville, burlesque and motion pictures. Dan Rice, famous clown, carried his show in the *Allegheny* from 1851 to 1886, with a three years' lapse, but most of the time he played it under canvas.

Most of the companies were family affairs, and relatives and employees did everything from handling the boat, running the theater, selling candy, performing in the orchestra, and playing any part assigned them. Their performances may not have been particularly artistic, but they were good and loud; and since most of them dealt in the standard melodramas of the time, their success was certain.

They offered the run of the mill shows that rep companies played on land, and *Ten Nights in a Bar Room* and *East Lynne* were as familiar to the river dwellers as to the farmers of the mid-west. Many of these river towns were small settlements, isolated and almost inaccessible; so the showboat people found them rich pickings, and their reign continued there long after the country had turned to motion picture theaters and most of the small time companies had quit in disgust.

Gradually the melodramas petered out, and vaudeville was tried. At one time Harry Blackstone, the magician, played showboat; and with the passage of time quite a few professional actors looked on a summer season on the water as a vacation with at least enough pay to keep them afloat. They were short termers and rarely returned a second year.

Billy Bryant, whose family was famous on the river, started in 1900 and sold his showboat during World War II. It became a wharf boat at Huntington, West Virginia.

The *Golden Rod* was owned by Capt. J. W. Menke and for fifty years played the river towns. Edna Ferber telegraphed Menke for permission to visit the boat when she was writing *Show Boat*, but he did not reply to her request. In 1937 the *Golden Rod* tied up at the foot of Locust Street in St. Louis, Mo., laying up for repairs. The boat still is there. Performances are given by a regular company, and visitors to the city are often taken to the burlesque of *The Drunkard*. Old time melodrama is advertised with vaudeville between the acts, and special rates are offered organizations and theater parties. In view of the fact that Miss Ferber did not visit the *Golden Rod*, the following statement on the management's throwaway is somewhat enlightening.

"To derive full enjoyment from the evening's entertainment, turn back the pages of history to the days when show boats provided the only outside amusement that ever reached that vast area through which flows the mighty Mississippi, the Missouri and the Ohio, every river and bayou throughout the country.

"The *Golden Rod,* depicted in Edna Ferber's *Show Boat,* dates back to half a century. Capt. J. W. Menke, her owner and manager, has taken her up and down every navigable river of the West.

"Show Boat audiences are not ashamed of reaction. They laugh, they cry, they hiss, they cheer. Forget that you have ever seen a Jolson or a Barrymore. Give yourselves up to the enjoyment of the evening, as though these were indeed the Gay Nineties and that this was the one big night of your life. Fun by the Boatload."

Capt. T. J. Reynolds and his family played on the *Majestic,* built in 1923, and *The Girl and the Game* was given as late as 1948. Daughter Catherine was in the cast and Ernest Vevea, the "Toby," was a veteran of long association and a prime favorite with river audiences. A "Toby," incidentally, is a red-headed yokel who outsmarts the villain and rescues either the soubrette or the heroine as the situation demands.

As with Bryant, the depression hit the *Majestic* and during World War II, she tied up at Point Pleasant, West Virginia. After a final revival in 1948, following occasional performances aboard her by amateurs, drama students from Kent State University and Hiram College, Ohio, chartered her for summer tours along the Kanawha and Ohio rivers. Credit in dramatic work was given them for their participation in the presentation of *The Drunkard* and *John Loves Mary.* There are plans now for one or the other of these institutions to take another whirl at showboating.

So the era of the showboat passed, as did the country theater, and even these attempted revivals are bound to be short lived at the best.

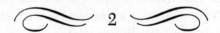

The passing of the provincial theater was due to a number of causes, each of which contributed its bit to end the reign of the rep companies of the eighties and nineties.

A new generation was replacing the old. Mandolin, guitar and banjo supplemented the piano and organ, and young folks preferred moonlight strolls for serenading and spooning to well-lighted parlors and watchful family spying. Occasionally they took a turn at amateur theatricals, but these became less frequent when the morning glory trumpet of the wax cylindered phonograph blossomed in the home and the first faint squeaks of wireless began to broadcast news and scanty programs.

And then Henry Ford put the automobile within the budget of every farmer and villager. In 1896, the horseless carriage was such a curiosity that Barnum and Bailey exhibited a Duryea Motor Wagon with its side-show freaks. But the Model T soon ended all this, wiping out the isolation of a little community circumscribed by its village limits.

During the nineties, too, road shows increased from two hundred to five hundred companies booked from New York. They covered the map like a blanket, and they grew even more numerous when Klaw and Erlanger organized the syndicate and booked the big time houses for forty-two weeks each year. Often these shows stopped at towns with adequate theaters, playing a week of one night stands to break the jumps between the larger cities. Rep companies found the sledding harder when their former patrons could visit a neighboring town and see a real New York production.

During the summer the brown chautauqua tents brought lecturers and entertainers of national reputation. The town women were invited to participate in a general social roundup, and a competent leader saw that the children were entertained with song, games and drills. And before the five days ended, all of them were paraded across the platform for their neighbors to see. Such audience participation is the backbone of many a high-ranking television program now.

All of these developments set a new standard in the entertainment world. The old melodramas were outdated. The small permanent stock companies were doing *The Aviator, Light Wines and Beer, The Sap,* and *The House of a Thousand Candles;* and some road companies latched on to them and played the old rep time. It was a losing battle, but the smaller villages hung on like grim death in this final struggle against the inevitable.

For by this time, Tom Edison's kinetoscope with its crank and fluttering prints had been developed into living pictures, and the first movies were drawing crowds to vacant stores that had been converted into nickelodeons with a sheet, some undertakers' chairs and a movie projector. Little by little they improved, and the surprised pioneers, when they found how the money rolled in, started to build motion picture houses.

First to suffer were the popular priced theaters of the cities who were purveying *Nellie the Beautiful Cloak Model* and *Bertha the Sewing Ma-*

chine Girl. Painted backdrops and mechanical effects couldn't equal the wild west backgrounds of Flatbush and Chicago Heights or a Rodman Law dynamiting a balloon or going over a waterfall in an open boat. And atop this, the Klaw and Erlanger houses produced such plays as *The Roundup,* with Macklyn Arbuckle as the star and a band of Indians who rode horseback down a runway from the flies for the most impressive Indian battle of its kind.

I experienced the last throes of both the melodramatic circuit and small time when in 1911 I wrote *The Defender of Cameron Dam.* It played the Stair and Havlin circuit and a second company visited the rep houses. The melodrama was based on attempts of the lumber interests of northern Wisconsin to dislodge a family from its cabin on disputed property. It had a timely appeal and made enough money to assure me three commitments for the following year. But when that season came, the circuit started to break up and producers sensed what lay ahead and that was the end of the commitments.

By the time *The Birth of a Nation* was produced in 1915, motion picture theaters had become accepted places of entertainment and started to roll out the red carpet for their patrons. The country manager saw a surer profit in a can of film than with a traveling company of uncertain antecedents. When his patrons walked into his theater from the street they lost all interest in climbing three flights of steep stairs. And the old halls were left to become storage space or at best a factory loft.

And there throughout the country they stand today, many of them, facing the world as bravely and proudly as they did years ago when they were the center of interest that brought their little world to the Town Hall Tonight.

INDEX